To
Matt and
Amy: who share
together
a dream to pr[eserve]
the beauty of
this country.
Fondly, Mo
10/94

FLEETING MOMENTS

FLEETING MOMENTS
Nature and Culture in American History

GUNTHER BARTH

New York Oxford
OXFORD UNIVERSITY PRESS
1990

Oxford University Press

Oxford New York Toronto
Delhi Bombay Calcutta Madras Karachi
Petaling Jaya Singapore Hong Kong Tokyo
Nairobi Dar es Salaam Cape Town
Melbourne Auckland

and associated companies in
Berlin Ibadan

Published by Oxford University Press, Inc.,
200 Madison Avenue, New York, New York 10016

Oxford is a registered trademark of Oxford University Press

Library of Congress Cataloging-in-Publication Data
Barth, Gunther Paul.
Fleeting moments : nature and culture in American history /
Gunther Barth.
p. cm. Includes bibliographical references.
ISBN 0-19-506296-5
1. United States—Civilization.
2. Man—Influence of environment—United States—History.
3. Man—Influence on nature—United States—History.
I. Title.
E169.1.B2315 1990 90-31526

2 4 6 8 9 7 5 3 1

Printed in the United States of America
on acid-free paper

TO

Marc Aurel Stommel

AND

Rawson Lyman Wood

Contents

Acknowledgments

I am grateful for the assistance my work has received from many quarters.

I benefited from the support of the Committee on Research, the Humanities Research Fellowship Program, and the Department of History at the University of California at Berkeley. The custodians of libraries and archives aided my research; specifically the librarians of the various collections on the Berkeley campus. I am much indebted to the Interlibrary Loan Department of the General Library. Jeffrey P. Katz of Reference Services taught me to use online databases.

I owe a special debt of gratitude to the librarians of the Bancroft Library. Its director, James D. Hart, introduced me to the William Hammond Hall Collection. Mary Ellen Jones guided me through that splendid record of the creator of San Francisco's Golden Gate Park. Anthony S. Bliss, Nicole Bouché, Walter Brem, Franz Enciso, Peter E. Hanff, Patricia Howard, Annegret S. Ogden, Richard Ogar, and William M. Roberts generously placed their knowledge at my disposal. As on many other occasions, Irene Moran, Head of Public Services, has graciously supported my work.

I am beholden to the various editors of the volumes of *The Frederick Law Olmsted Papers*; in particular, Charles E. Beveridge and David Schuyler. The editor in chief, Charles Capen McLaughlin, helped me find a way to end what at times seemed an endless task. For permission to use material from previously published articles in a new context, I should like to thank Norris Hundley, Jr., editor of the *Pacific Historical Review*; Solomon Wank and his co-editors of *The Mirror of History: Essays in Honor of Fritz Fellner*; and Susan S. Munshover and Craig Zabel, the editors of *American Public Architecture: European Roots and Native Expressions*. The Mountain View Cemetery Association made my research easier, and I gratefully acknowledge the support of its general manager, Jack Owen, and his secretary, Marsha Young.

My search for directions profited from conversations with colleagues, particularly Richard M. Abrams, Thomas G. Barnes, Woodrow Borah, Robert Brentano, Jan de Vries, Sheldon Rothblatt, Harry Scheiber, and William B. Slottman. Leon Litwack generously placed his volumes of the *New York Tribune* and the *New York Times* for the 1850s at my disposal. At the Institute of History of the University of Salzburg, Fritz Fellner, Georg Schmid, and Reinhold Wagnleitner discussed cities and gardens with me. At the Anglo-American Institute of the University of Cologne, Erich Angermann and Norbert Finzsch provided opportunities to talk about my work. My Berkeley students furnished insight and inspiration.

Dominic Barth adapted Jonathan Carver's map of 1778 to the purpose of the book. For assistance with the illustrations I am beholden to Samuel O. Alexander, Head of Technical Services, Geological Survey of Canada; Phyllis M. Knowles, Administrator, National Association of Olmsted Parks; Marilyn Wandrus, Chief, Branch of Graphics Research, National Park Service; and Merle Wells, Idaho Historical Society. In addition, the New-York Historical Society and the National Gallery of Art lent illustrations.

From several sides came special assistance. As in other endeavors, Sheldon Meyer of Oxford University Press freely gave aid and support. Werner Hundt helped in numerous ways over the years. In the final phase of the work Daniel J. Herman helped with the typing. My office neighbor, James H. Kettner, tolerated my interruptions and provided leads to words and materials. Robert L. Middlekauff read the manuscript, discussed it with me, and suggested evidence. James W. R. Leiby contributed literary skills and historical insights. George McMichael edited a draft of the manuscript and improved my grammar, my thinking, and my command of American literature. The understanding editorial work of Gail Cooper at Oxford University Press made the final stage of the project a pleasant experience.

As always, Ellen W. Barth has improved my ideas and prose, and I am especially grateful for her incisive mind. Her concern for ecology inspired my efforts and her forbearance enabled me to write the book.

I am dedicating the book to Marc Aurel Stommel and Rawson Lyman Wood. They taught me to respect nature and culture.

G. B.

Introduction

The magnificent view from the top of the French mountain stunned Petrarch. After an arduous ascent, the Italian poet saw directly below him the silvery band of the Rhone River and to his right the crest of the Cévennes Mountains. On his left, beyond Marseilles, the Mediterranean came into view, illuminated by the sinking sun that descended on a day Petrarch had longed for. His fascination with the scenery vanished when he looked at Augustine's *Confessions,* which he always carried with him. On the page of the book that Petrarch opened accidentally, Augustine chides the friends of nature for losing themselves in the admiration of mountains and valleys, disrupting in consequence the intensity of their devotion to God.

This April 26, 1336, Petrarch had climbed Mont Ventoux, the 6,237-foot-high peak about thirty miles northeast of Avignon in Provence, with no "other purpose than a desire to see what the great height was like."[1] In a letter written to his former confessor, at the end of a long day filled with physical strain and emotional turmoil, Petrarch explained the desire that drove him to the summit. The pangs of conscience brought on by the words of the early Christian philosopher had dispelled Petrarch's enjoyment of nature. His letter articulated the feeling of people who sensed that they had violated a sacred height by climbing a mountain and realized that they had almost forgotten God in their elation over the beauty of the natural world.

Following Petrarch's ascent of Mount Ventoux, the encounters of other people with nature from mountaintops have evoked a vast range of responses, depending on the temperament of the viewer and the appearance of the scene; however, the following centuries eroded the concern about a spectacular natural scene diminishing the intensity of religious feelings. The religious devotion that had curbed enjoyment of the splendid view from the summit gave way to an inquisitive spirit that steadily sought to extend the field of vision beyond the limits set by nature. In the seventeenth century, Simplicius Simplicissimus, the hero of a Baroque novel, hardly noticed the loss of his self, let alone the loss of his devotion to God, when he fell under the spell of nature in a phase of his lifelong journey of self-discovery.

The search for identity brought Simplicius to the height of the Black Forest in southern Germany. As a would-be hermit he not only lost himself in the beauty of the mountain panorama, but also turned against God and nature in a novel way. He resorted to the use of a telescope to overcome the natural limitations of his sight and to see better what he regarded as the heart of the visible world: the distant city of Strasbourg on the other side of the Rhine.[2] Gazing at the faraway city, brought closer through the lenses of his telescope, Simplicius forgot the longing for solitude that had drawn him into the forest.

The idea of nature as people's servant helping them to satisfy their concerns about themselves and the world provided a metaphor that justified using the environment to satisfy the lust for knowledge and power. Mastering and changing nature gained immense importance as part of the wide-reaching schemes of conquest during the exploration of the New World. Controlling the tops of hills and mountains, although they were still inhabited by the gods and spirits of the Indians, served very practical purposes in America. The summits provided vista points for the newcomers to discover what lay ahead. Before they could apply their organization and technology to serve the urge to possess the land, the conquerors stripped the country of its mystique with their own magic. They placed their names on the land in the course of following rivers, climbing hills, traversing plains, and crossing mountains.

In the opening months of 1632, the governor of the Massachusetts Bay Colony used the tall rocks along the Charles River and the Mystic River to learn the topography of his new commonwealth. John Winthrop and his companions, Winthrop's *Journal* related, behaved like many white people after them who sought to reduce the mysteries of the land between the Atlantic and the Pacific by giving familiar names to the strange sights they encountered.

One tall precipice the explorers named for the youngest member of the company, and another peak for the oldest, and when "they came to another high pointed rock" they gave it the name of a companion "who had married the governor's daughter-in-law." Another "very high rock" they called Cheese Rock. On its top they were forced to eat their cheese without the bread, which the "governor's man" had forgotten to bring along in his haste to get up there. The oversight had furnished them with yet another name for yet another hill, but they had already named several hills and exhausted the strength of their magic. The top of Cheese Rock yielded no new insights into the topography because it had started to rain, and they could not see much of the plains below.[3]

Countless newcomers after them marked their intrusion into North America in similar ways. They encountered nature in abundance and diminished the splendor of nature by defiling its treasures. From their Christian heritage they distilled their belief that the world was given to people, and they had no sense of obligation towards other forms of life. Only a few of the newcomers surrendered wholeheartedly to the spell of unspoiled nature.

At the end of the eighteenth century, the rise of Romanticism, softening the constraint on emotions maintained by the Enlightenment, encouraged Americans to look passionately at nature.

Transcendentalism sanctioned the new attitude with philosophical speculation. Communion with the natural world became religion for some people who surrendered to the new fellowship.

In Herman Melville's *Moby Dick*, which appeared in 1851, Ishmael in the masthead of the *Pequot* let his mind wander from the duties of the lookout in the crow's nest and reflected on the consequence of dreaming about being one with nature while carelessly moving foot or hand and slipping "with one half-throttled shriek . . . through that transparent air into the summer sea, no more to rise for ever. Heed it well, ye Pantheists!"[4] Melville's warning went untested by those nineteenth-century Americans who found in nature the spiritual support they no longer were able to find in the bonds of a Christian church. Although their search to regain their lost identity led them to nature, most would have shrunk from signing up on a whaler for a voyage of self-discovery.

With his trip on the Concord and Merrimack rivers and his life at Walden Pond behind him, Henry David Thoreau experienced his epiphany in the wilds of Maine in 1846, when he climbed Mt. Ktaadn and encountered the stern face of nature. "Within the skirts of the cloud which seemed forever drifting over the summit," he missed the peak of the mountain, but he felt acutely the presence of angry gods shielding the top. On his descent he "most fully realized that this was primeval, untamed, and forever untameable *Nature*. . . . This was that Earth of which we have heard, made out of Chaos and Old Night."[5]

Thoreau's encounter with nature beyond Concord alerted him to nature's brutal force and heightened his respect for nature. In the light of his experience, naming a rock was a rather perfunctory way of removing power from, and taking possession of, a part of nature. Placing names on the land amounted to a sleight-of-hand trick in the struggle between nature and culture and in the face of the fear that the elementary force of nature struck in human hearts.

These reactions represented a few of the manifold responses of Europeans and Americans to nature during the course of history. They were driven by an urge to master nature and restrained by the fear of setting free forces beyond their control. Nor did their drive to subdue nature come to rest there. The Protestant Reformation, although reinforcing people's dependence on God, left no lasting mark on their attitude towards nature in the New World.

Some invaders of America read God out of nature, and they felt free to alter nature according to their designs. In the course of making over the newly found land they were joined by others engaged in conquering nature according to what they considered to be God's command in Genesis 1:28–29: "Be fruitful, multiply, fill the earth and conquer it. Be masters of the fish of the sea, the birds of heaven and all living animals on earth." Few heeded Genesis 2:15–16, that God settled man in the Garden of Eden "to cultivate and take care of it." Most thought they had an absolute right to land, water, animals, lumber, and minerals, and backed their belief with popular sayings like, "The Bible says we have dominion over all things."

The tension between culture and nature has accompanied the rise of all large societies. In the case of the United States, the interaction is rather extensively documented when compared with the scant records of earlier ages. In the absence of details, the history of the attitudes of ancient empires towards nature has inspired general observations about the destructive aspects of ancient civilizations. They often left deserts behind, symbolically if not literally, if they developed unchecked by natural or man-made disasters. The records of the rise of the United States, however, preserved specific features of the tension between culture and nature because the encounter took place in an age of historical curiosity and recording techniques more attuned to complex circumstances.

Furthermore, Americans have adhered to a cultural mission that accentuated the potential for conflict in the encounter between culture and nature. They built a nation within the span of a century on the exploitation of gigantic resources. These activities frequently placed Americans in stark opposition to the nature of the continent they had set out to make over in the images of fields and gardens. "The Americans arrived but yesterday in the land where they live, and they have already turned the whole order of nature upside down to their profit," Alexis de Tocqueville, the French philosopher of government, observed in the 1830s.[6] Americans might have everywhere destroyed the nature and the Indians they encountered, had not belief or necessity checked them. Consequently, culture and nature often marked one another (in rather unequal proportions, to be sure) in many ways and in various settings during the course of American history.

The study of the interaction between nature and culture in American history is an awesome task. The documentation is extensive and complex. The subject pervades many areas of life. With the ongoing destruction of irreplaceable natural resources, an assessment of the relationship between nature and culture ultimately involves the issue of life itself.

These and many other problems in a study of the interaction between nature and culture in American history could be traced to the perennial wrath of Thoreau's Abenaki god Pomola who "is always angry with those who climb to the summit of Ktaadn."[7] Instead of misty mountain peaks hiding the true summit and confusing the climber, the god's wrath hides the goal of the study by steadily widening the range of the investigation.

Definitions of *nature* and *culture*, words used daily in connection with highly personal meanings, continue to present challenges that centuries of thought and shelves of books have sought to answer—so extensively as to leave them unanswered. And while that result could be viewed with regret, the lack of an answer reflects a kind of collective prudence, because any definition has to encompass the wide range of people's responses to nature and culture. "Like other symbols," an anthropologist argued while reviewing ways to narrow the meaning of "culture" as a concept, culture "does not have some true and sacred and eternal meaning . . . , but . . . it means whatever we use it to mean"[8]—the same assumption most of us will share about the meaning of "nature" as a concept.

With the meanings of the two concepts on equal footing as far as theory is concerned, an opportunity opens up to explore a segment of the relationship between nature and culture in American history. Destroying nature or surrendering to it mark the extremes of the contact, and somewhere between these extremes lie moments that could find nature and culture in harmony. Attaining that concord, or, more realistically, striving for it, ought to be recognized as a measure of civilization.

Such a perspective shows the significance of the brief interludes that find nature and culture in balance. They are part of a special group of ideals. Pursuing those ideals has for millennia disturbed mankind: insisting on the necessity to assert the common humanity of all people, to "love thy neighbor as thyself," to live the equality of races and sexes, to shield the balances of nature, or to heighten the city's potential as a source of civilization. These ideals are difficult to attain, and their elusiveness characterizes the fleeting moments of harmony between nature and culture. Furthermore, the effort it would take today to approach these moments of harmony gives them a significance beyond their role as mere facts of history.

American culture, making over the conquered land in the image derived from its Judeo-Christian roots, has only rarely approached that measure of harmony. The need to keep the elusive goal in sight and to recognize it as a mark of civilization has increased, however, not merely as a tribute to a rare accomplishment, but also to ensure the survival of civilization. In the face of increasing resignation to the belief that a balance cannot be reached, it is worthwhile to heighten the understanding of the necessity to pursue the harmony between nature and culture. At present, when many Americans are well aware of the limits of resources, the pursuit of happiness ought to be linked, not only to seeking access to the means of consumption, but also to the pursuit of harmony between nature and culture.

Although barely adequate to address this basic American problem, the determined pursuit of harmony between nature and culture could identify possible solutions within the democratic process that might ensure everyone's personal freedom and quality of life within the limits set by nature. In turn, these goals justify an exploration of the fleeting moments of harmony between nature and culture in American history and ensure the importance of those interludes in the national past and future.

The idea of searching for moments of harmony provided an opportunity to assess a wide range of sources for data attesting to the brief experience. Like all abstractions, the fleeting moments that found nature and culture in harmony have no life of their own. They merely guide the search of vast amounts of material for a statement, in manuscript or in print, that alludes to an incident that approximates that balance.

The following pages focus on a few of these transient moments. My concepts of nature and culture are based on a definition of *environment* as all the surroundings affecting human life. In that context, "culture" is the physical and mental constructs created by people to cope with their environment, while "nature" is that part of people's surroundings least touched by them. From these definitions, "wilderness" and "city" emerge as the extremes of the interaction between culture and nature in the American experience: the city signifying the triumph of culture, and the wilderness signifying the triumph of nature. At points of fusion, there appear moments of harmony created by nature and culture.

At other times words other than *nature* and *culture* might have been used to describe the basic divisions of life that provide the focus of my study. *God* and *Man*, the *natural* and the *artificial, nature* and *convention, nature* and *art* are a few of the words that come to mind readily. It would be presumptuous to deny that they are appropriate for a discussion of the subject. I avoided these words, however, because I assumed that their use might evoke connotations related to such a basic field of thought as theology or such a seminal thinker as Rousseau. Their use might also raise expectations for insights that I cannot fulfill. Consequently I have chosen to rely on the vague words "nature" and "culture," but I have used them consistently according to their relations to the environment. For analogous reasons I have used the words *harmony* or *concord* to describe a balance between nature and culture. The word *Eden* epitomizes fleeting moments of harmony between nature and culture, but I preferred to use "balance," "harmony," and "concord" to avoid religious connotations.

So much of human life has been shaped by nature, imagination, and urbanization that city and wilderness are the vital areas for a study of these moments. They provide a glimpse of the complex influences shaping an investigation of the relationship between culture and nature in American history. As a structure for my anomalous approach to the evidence, my investigation relies on the search for the Wilderness Passage, the work of the Lewis and Clark expedition, and the creation of the park cemetery and the big-city park.

These three parts of the book focus largely on people and events that have received (with the notable exception of Frederick Law Olmsted) relatively little attention in studies of the relationship between nature and culture in American history. The investigation bypasses the great minds of the nineteenth century—the thinkers, artists, and conservationists—who have received considerable attention. Their work extolled the role of nature in the lives of people preoccupied with building a nation by exploiting natural resources, and contributed to the creation of state and national parks to protect some of the remnants of nature for future generations. The attention given to the contributions of Ralph Waldo Emerson, Henry David Thoreau, James Fenimore Cooper, Thomas Cole, Margaret Fuller, George Perkins Marsh, and John Muir, to name just a few, suggested to me to look at the contact between nature and culture from another vantage point.

I have chosen to comment on the records of people who for a while lived on the edge of nature or on the edge of culture. Thus they experienced momentarily a balance between the two. Frequently, quite extraordinary circumstances in the course of ordinary events brought about these transient phases in their lives. As I envision it, in the early stage of the search for the Wilderness Passage through North America, explorers and adventurers were on the edge of nature. In the concluding stage of the search that solved the last riddle of the Wilderness Passage, the members of the Lewis and Clark expedition were on the edge of culture.

I have retained the language and spelling of my sources whenever I quoted them. This approach made it possible to retain the immediacy of expressions that distinguish the accounts. I have shunned heaping commentary on commentaries, although I can hardly claim that my analysis of the documents will speak directly about the feelings of all people. I am confident that a good portion of that enormous task will be taken up by my fellow workers in the Republic of Research and Speculation, while a small fraction of the task will be taken up by those reviewers who expect an author to write the book they have just not gotten around to doing themselves.

I regret that a great number of Americans—the Indians—merely move in and out of my lines. They show the dignity of human beings that a close contact with nature can produce, but I lacked the resources to treat that aspect of the topic fully. I resolved the dilemma in my mind by clinging to the hope that the book will also heighten the interest in the riches of a seemingly boundless subject. These and similar considerations also apply to the role of women and many other groups of people.

The section on the city treats the experience of a large segment of Americans. The creation of the park cemetery for the benefit of the dead and the living ensured the interaction of large numbers of people with nature. The making of the big-city park, discussed in the context of the creation of New York's Central Park and San Francisco's Golden Gate Park, gave many people a chance to encounter fleeting moments of balance between nature and culture.

In that urban perspective the brief interludes gain lasting significance because they reduced the confrontation between nature and culture. These moments indicate that large numbers of people can experience a balance between nature and culture if they seek to find a place for nature in their lives.

FLEETING MOMENTS

ONE

On Nature's Edge

"WHAT AM I TO SAY, my dear Hakluyt, when I see nothing but desolation," the Hungarian poet Stephen Parmenius asked his Oxford friend Richard Hakluyt in a letter sent from Newfoundland on August 6, 1583.[1] Six years later, Hakluyt translated Parmenius's "praeter solitudinem" as "very wildernesse" to make the Latin news from St. John's Harbour more intelligible to English readers of his collection of voyages to the New World. In 1972, the modern translator of the letter rendered the phrase as "desolation."[2] Hakluyt, the compiler of the *Principall navigations,* preferred "wildernesse." He knew that word described what his Hungarian friend had been seeing: a wild, dense, and trackless stretch of land.

Details of the experience of facing the wilderness dominated the reports from Sir Humphrey Gilbert's 1583 expedition to Newfoundland. To eyes that had discerned currents, winds, schools of fish, and flocks of birds over the watery waste of the Atlantic, the land seemed strangely empty. The Beothuk Indians, the native inhabitants of Newfoundland, stayed out of sight, long weary of French, Spanish, Portuguese, and English fishermen drying their catch on the shore of their island. They could not be seen, but at times fishing boats they cut loose testified to their presence. Gilbert's men could not see them or pursue them because trees and terrain blocked view and advance. To the Englishmen the seemingly impenetrable forest made Newfoundland a wilderness.[3]

The virgin forest was a tangle of growing and decaying trees, intertwined with fallen logs and thick underbrush. Its appearance heightened the feeling of an inhospitable shore and an uncultivated land. Frustrated, Parmenius and his companions asked Gilbert to set fire to the forest in order to gain an open space and a better view. Gilbert liked the idea of reducing the landscape to their need, of bringing light into the forest. Experienced Newfoundland fishermen spoke against the plan, however, and averted the folly. More familiar with the land than the newcomers, they warned that burning the forest would damage the rich fishing grounds. The fishermen talked Gilbert out of the idea by telling the story of a forest fire on another section of the coast. They believed that the resin oozing from burning fir and pine trees had polluted the water and kept the fish away for seven years.[4]

The plan to set fire to the Newfoundland forest indicated that Hakluyt's translation of Parmenius's phrase "very wildernesse" closely reflected a distinctly English mindset that could not account for the Hungarian poet's frustration. When Parmenius identified the wall of trees and brush as "desolation," the word he used indicated that he was not expecting to see anything. Parmenius, inclined to view the impenetrable forest as "desolation," could not benefit from the emotional charge that "wilderness" provided for Englishmen.

Parmenius was a conqueror who did not think of penetrating the wilderness. Ostensibly he had sailed to the New World to record the adventure in graceful Latin verse (the poetry he wrote in England had recommended him to Gilbert). Parmenius may also have hoped that the new sights would stimulate the flow of a new poetic imagination. Among his contemporaries, Luis Vaz de Camões became the poet of European expansion when he related his adventures as a Portuguese exile in Goa, Macao, and Mozambique in the 1550s and 1560s.[5]

Parmenius drowned in a shipwreck shortly after the departure of Gilbert's fleet from Newfoundland. As a candidate for poet laureate of the English expansion, the Hungarian scholar had already perished when he failed to recognize that the confrontation with the wilderness was the English destiny in the New World. Parmenius saw nothing but desolation, and his mind received no support from the thought processes of a culture that enabled Englishmen to cope with alien nature by projecting goals into the wilderness.

Sir Humphrey Gilbert did not live to write about the voyage either, but in his last hour he foreshadowed the English aptitude. He exhibited his countrymen's ability to find rapport with the wilds of land or water. On September 9, 1583, during the last Atlantic storm Gilbert faced, his frigate, the *Squirrel*, came alongside the only other remaining vessel of his fleet, the much larger *Golden Hind*. Its master spotted Gilbert below on the deck of the smaller vessel reading a book and heard his shout: "We are as neere to Heaven by sea as by land."[6] During the night, the *Squirrel* and Gilbert disappeared. He had met the turbulent Atlantic reflecting on Thomas More's *Utopia*: "The way to heaven out of all places is of like length and distance."[7]

Other Englishmen following Gilbert also regarded their movement into the wilderness as a passage to a new destiny. They eased their penetration of the New World by projecting seemingly unattainable goals into the wilderness. They followed a tradition set by the knights of medieval English romances who crossed vast, unknown wastes in search of the Holy Grail, a legendary, sacred vessel variously identified as the cup used by Christ at the Last Supper, the platter on which Joseph of Arimathea received drops of Christ's blood at the Crucifixion, or the dish of the Paschal lamb. The earliest version of these tales, which passed on ways of nature-worship as Christian mystery, came from Wales, where Druid rituals in remote areas had ensured the fertility of the soil until Christianity caught up with the practice. Such romances flowered in England and in parts of the Continent, but they withered at the turn of the twelfth century.[8]

The knightly search for the Holy Grail as source of physical and spiritual life sustained hope in decades of unrest and uncertainty. The mundane search for the meaning of life embraced other goals in subsequent centuries. Fighting the Crusades and traveling to Muscovy were as much attempts to enter into the spiritual and physical unknown as they were political and economic enterprises. A rationale emerged sustaining Englishmen's belief in searching the unknown by the time the New World presented them with the task of finding their way in North America.

Now secular visions inspired the penetration of the wilderness of the New World, luring and guiding the intruders by such far-flung, disparate causes as "empire" or "humanity." They conjured up a new faith that enabled Englishmen to come to terms with the vastness of America. Once, for the knights in search of the Grail, the wilderness had been one final obstacle to overcome before life's journey might be fulfilled. Now the wilderness itself promised to answer English hopes, providing a share of the riches other Europeans had taken from America.

The English shared many European experiences in their encounter with the New World. Although they had practiced conquest in Ireland, their first colonizing venture at Roanoke, an offshore island near Cape Hatteras, in what is now North Carolina, taxed their imagination as well as their political skills. They failed when they first faced North America's powerful nature. As for other European colonizers, gold and a waterway to the Pacific were the incentives for Walter Raleigh's colony, "Virginia," of 1585. Governor Ralph Lane, with the experience of warring in Ireland behind him, knew that nothing else would bring English settlers to Roanoke. Despite his determination to succeed, however, all efforts to find gold or a passage through the continent failed.

The cultural baggage of the Elizabethan adventurers proved inadequate for the complex responsibilities they faced in the New World. Their resources barely met the ordinary tasks of conquest and colonization, and they had no separate body of thought to deal with the unique character of American nature. The minds of the colonists remained shut to nature. The goals of the colony and European artistic convention, not the Roanoke scene, shaped the watercolors of John White, the official artist of Walter Raleigh's 1585 venture to Virginia. Colonial strategy conceived in England directed his brush and pen to geography, natural history, and ethnology. He enlisted art in an attempt to ensure the survival of the plantation in the context of Raleigh's scheme: as harbor for privateers preying on the Spanish silver fleet and as the source of products of a Mediterranean-type agriculture.

White's perception was sharpened by the thoughts of Thomas Harriot, the scientist of the expedition and the author of the first original description of North America in English published as a book. Among the artistic influences, the work of Jacques Le Moyne de Morgue, the Huguenot artist of a French colony in Florida from 1563 to 1565, ranked foremost. White followed the northern European Mannerist tradition and viewed strangers as savages, and these perspectives accounted for the Renaissance stance of his Algonquin Indians as well as his ferocious portraits of Eskimos, Indians, and Picts, or "Ancient Britons."[9]

In 1585, most of the 108 men at Roanoke knew nothing of the artistic conventions shielding White from reality. Reality forced itself on them directly as the awesome wilderness of the New World came to dominate their lives. A century later, the philosopher John Locke verbalized their discomfort when he told his countrymen that nature, not property, ruled America. Intuitively, he asked English adventurers seeking easy riches to leap backwards in time. In 1690, Locke's *Second Essay Concerning Civil Government* compressed his insight into one line: "In the beginning, all the world was America."[10]

In the century separating Roanoke from Locke's *dicta*, his countrymen entering North America found ways to accommodate their hopes to reality. They labelled as "wilderness" that part of American nature not producing landed property. This solution allowed them to follow their interests, unconcerned with philosophy, and come to grips with untamed nature. Applying the idea of wilderness to Locke's "wild Common of Nature," Englishmen employed an age-old notion that often had guided people facing strange places.[11]

The idea of wilderness served as a device to cope with the unknown continent. The practice provides a direction for an investigation of the transient moments of harmony between nature and culture in American history. In that context, "culture" surfaces as the intruders' mental and physical constructs that deal with their environment, while "nature" appears as those areas least touched by them. The interaction of culture with wilderness demonstrates the aggressive social and economic forces of a civilization contributing to the ceaseless destruction of nature. In turn, the interaction also highlights circumstances that find nature and culture in balance.

The English view of North American nature as wilderness conveniently divided the invaders from the inhabitants of the continent. In that perspective the Indians lived in the invaders' wilderness. It was their home in a real way, quite apart from any English cultural framework. When the English penetrated the nature of the New World with their culture by extending the idea of wilderness to North America, they placed yet another division between human beings, in addition to the distinction between Christian and heathen. Nature as well as religion now isolated the Indians, despite the fact that the people forming their culture groups differed markedly in their social organization from the solitary "wild men" of the European wilderness.

For several centuries, the European concept of wilderness reflected a cultural response to American nature. Generations of newcomers saw Indians only as integral to that pristine nature. The intruders' encounter with "nature's children" yielded mostly destruction and genocide. Rare moments of harmony between red and white people did occur, however. These instances of harmony allow us to bring into focus inferences about the interaction between European culture and American nature.

Europeans, Englishmen, and those who later called themselves Americans, achieved accords with Indians when unexpected experiences reduced prejudice. The starving colonists in Virginia and the starving Pilgrims at Plymouth, unequipped to meet the challenge of wresting a crop from the land, achieved accord with some Indians. These and other encounters stimulated a mutual respect between members of two deeply divided groups of people. The experience changed the life of the invaders living on nature's edge. Ultimately the experience enabled them to accept America as expansion of their identity, although that step very seldom included an identification with the Indians.

Experiences collected during the exploration of the wilderness in the seventeenth and eighteenth centuries bore fruit between 1804 and 1806. In these years, the Lewis and Clark expedition laid to rest the last remaining hopes for a Wilderness Passage between the Missouri River and the Columbia River. The explorers shattered a fading but a remarkably long-lasting vision. They proved that there was no feasible waterway through the continent. The prolonged exposure of an American expedition to the wilderness led to an additional discovery: the explorers' contact with the wilderness and its people brought them for a brief span of time in harmony with nature.

The accomplishments grew partly out of the expedition's sense of mission. Furthermore, it would have failed without a shrewd adaptation to the wilderness. In particular a harmonious relation with nature came easier because the Corps of Discovery, as the Lewis and Clark expedition was called at times, shared the previous wilderness experience of Europeans. They had probed North America for almost three centuries before the United States emerged in 1776. Then its citizens, by officially calling themselves Americans, claimed a special affinity with the continent, at least in name.

The young nation of English stock, with an amalgam of European, North American Indian, and African people, had been built by the political genius of the Founding Fathers. Similarly, the collective wilderness experience of various European groups contributed to the success of the Lewis and Clark expedition. Its work shows how Americans used their wilderness heritage and how they pursued independent ways. In the evidence, attesting to their inherited and original attitudes towards North America, there appear references to fleeting moments of harmony between culture and nature. These accounts put part of the experience of the new nation in the context of the European encounter with the nature of the New World.

Early Europeans in North America, while fiercely nationalistic in their ambitions, shared a goal that guided many of their explorations of the continent. For centuries after the continent had blocked Columbus's passage to the Indies, they searched for a navigable waterway from the Atlantic to the Pacific. The sought-for route received various names. Most often it was called the "Northwest Passage" and referred to the attempts to find a way around America by sea to the Far East. The term "Wilderness Passage" connoted a river route through the continent. It often included a search for the "Western Sea" or the "River of the West."

The vision of a short route to the Pacific was at times so powerful that it combined both versions of the passage. There were distinctions, however, between the search for the Northwest Passage and for the Wilderness Passage. The one remained a maritime affair, wedded to the Atlantic, the Pacific, and the Arctic oceans. The other took the landmass of North America as its field. Its explorers relied on inlets, bays, and estuaries as starting places, and then followed rivers, lakes, and Indian trails into the wilderness. Although the results of the individual searches affected both enterprises, the two different elements, water and land, demanded very different responses and kept the activities apart.

The distinct character of each venture was reinforced by compounded problems in communication. International and economic rivalries restricted the flow of information. Publishers tailored descriptions of distant scenes into travelogues suited to the whims of the reading public and its thirst for news of the Northwest Passage. All the explorers hoped to make the discovery themselves, and that attitude made many ventures solitary affairs. The costs of an expedition that promised no immediate financial rewards also kept the number of participants small. At times, discoveries became precious secrets.

Deep animosities fueled the hostilities of different groups and blocked the flow of information. Tars snubbed landlubbers and landlubbers snubbed tars; each group was inclined to doubt the information of the other. A learned explorer aboard a company ship showed, at best, condescension for the knowledge of an illiterate forest ranger. Officials rarely listened to their underlings in the wilderness, and disparaged their information when they brought disagreeable news. The jealousies and suspicions of men from various Old World countries compounded the barriers. Potential knowledge about the continent also remained untapped because most white people would only take the knowledge of Indians into account and view the wilderness with different eyes when profit or survival were at stake.

A basic difference distinguished the search for the Northwest Passage from the search for the Wilderness Passage. The distinction calls for a separate assessment of, and a separate name for, the latter to make the idea clear. As an illusion, the Wilderness Passage considerably surpassed the Northwest Passage, which had stimulated speculation about the existence of a waterway through North America. The Northwest Passage, after all, did exist as a reality of geography, like the Northeast Passage leading from Europe along the northern rim of Asia to the Far East. These maritime routes, people assumed, would be useful as soon as discovered. When they discovered that polar ice blocked navigation, the speculations of eighteenth-century armchair sailors turned to a new fantasy, that of an arctic sea free of ice.

An awareness of the distinction between the Wilderness Passage and the Northwest Passage allows us to make some moments of harmony between culture and nature visible. The search for the Wilderness Passage took Europeans into the heart of North America. On that trek they were slow to identify nature with scenery and continued to consider people as nature's dominating expression. They ignored painters, who at the turn of the fifteenth century began speaking of natural inland scenery as "landscape" to distinguish it from "portrait" or "seascape." Before the nineteenth century, most invaders of North America saw nature in the variety of people and life-styles found in the wilderness. In North America Indians as the children of nature took the place of scenery in the European encounter with the wilderness. Only the nineteenth century brought the triumph of landscape.

Before the change, during the search for the Wilderness Passage there appeared fleeting moments of harmony between culture and nature in brief encounters between Europeans and Indians. In these instances, Europeans recognized their common humanity with Indians. An examination of the pursuit of the Wilderness Passage provides an opportunity to detect instances when European ethnocentrism gave way to an appreciation of Indian life as a form of nature, and to analyze those moments in a distinct context.

The Wilderness Passage, like the wilderness as a cultural construct, was the product of a magnificent flight of the European imagination. The invaders used their creation to cope with the strange world they faced. Insights into the nature and the people of the continent gained by Europeans in the pursuit of the Wilderness Passage ultimately were inherited by Americans. With the territory gained from European empires in North America, they also acquired a share of the mirage that had driven Spaniards, Frenchmen, and Englishmen into the continent.

In 1782, the Great Seal of the United States proclaimed the *Novus Ordo Seclorum* in one of its Latin mottoes. Reinforced by the other symbols on the seal's reverse, the creed of The New Order of the Ages pointed into the vastness of the continent. Its message, apparent also on the back of today's one-dollar bill, outlined a task for the new nation beyond the cultivated land guarded by the pyramid on the seal.[12] Taking up the search for the Wilderness Passage, Americans consecrated a part of their European heritage.

The idea of the Wilderness Passage solved a dilemma of European culture facing the unknown. The search for the faraway destination reduced the mental distance between culture and its construct, wilderness. The invaders fastened their eyes on an unattainable goal, much as the knights of medieval legend did in their pursuit of the Grail. Like the knights, who believed salvation would reward their quest, the conquerors believed the Wilderness Passage would penetrate the unknown. They accepted the quest, despite the fact that reason and experience increasingly argued against its existence. Identifying a part of the wilderness with the supposed passage, they learned to know the unknown by filling it with their expectations. Familiarity shrank the gap.

Other cultural goals came to be linked with the Wilderness Passage. They also helped to diminish the distance between culture and nature. Religious zeal, stimulated by the chance to expand through the continent, fostered a yearning to understand the wilderness. And so did the awakening of a broad humanitarian concern, which fostered respect for the human dignity of the inhabitants of the wilderness. Enormous distances, in cultural terms, separated the search for an illusory waterway through the continent from the recognition of the common humanity of invaders and Indians.

At first glance, the waterway originally seemed just an adventurer's dream born of geographic ignorance and cultivated by geographers and propagandists of empire like Richard Hakluyt. The common humanity appeared to be nothing more than accepting and implementing enlightened views that had been ignored for centuries. In a deeper sense, both searches were voyages of cultural discovery. Bound together by related excursions, they marked the interaction of concepts with reality. In rare moments, the ventures produced an accommodation between culture and nature in the experience of the English invaders of North America.

The nature of the New World taxed the invaders differently. The Spaniards, in particular, faced different conditions than Gilbert's men at Newfoundland and Raleigh's men at Roanoke. They encountered nature in forms more accessible and easier to plunder. They found people living in cities, and instead of the dense Newfoundland forest that blocked the view of English adventurers, the Spaniards saw so many trees and flowers, birds and beasts, that their numbers alone defied description. Unlike the wonders of the East, which for centuries had only reached them through tales traveling the great caravan routes, the New World forced its realities directly on newcomers. After a long voyage, they felt so anxious to see the marvels and possess them that they rarely noted they lacked the words to describe them or the concepts to assimilate them.

After the conquest of the Aztecs, when the Spaniards had seen the flowering capital of Tenochtitlan, the imagined "Seven Cities of Cibola" appeared far more real than the Northwest Passage or the Wilderness Passage. When challenged to depict American nature, the few Spaniards who responded to the task described what they saw as Columbus had done. Like the Admiral, in his February 15, 1493, report on the first voyage to Ferdinand and Isabella, they would compare an object to something they had seen in Spain. They relied on superlatives or stressed unique features while they searched for terms to do justice to the sights. Together with Columbus, they followed a practice that remained characteristic of all explorers of the unknown before the invention of photography.

In exasperation, in the 1530s, one of the first historians of the New World, Gonzalo Fernández de Oviedo, wished for the help of the famous painters he knew in Italy. Since Leonardo da Vinci and Andrea Mantegna were not at his bidding, Oviedo himself made sketches to do justice to America when he lacked words to describe what he was seeing. Irrespective of his skills, his conviction that a sketch was a "very suitable way for the author to be better understood" provided an answer to the challenges of America's nature.[13] It would have worked, too, if the observed objects had guided the artist's hand, rather than the artistic conventions and the expectations of his culture.

There was rarely any objective portrayal of reality to acclimate the invaders to the nature of the New World. Cultural preconceptions shaped most stages of the encounter. The failure to render reality accurately was not something unique to those who portrayed the New World. It was, and is, the case with all art everywhere; however, in the case of the European contact with the New World the influence of culture became obvious because so many differences between Europe and America needed to be overcome.

After the Spanish hold on North America weakened and after the French withdrew from the continent, the exploration of North America, and with it the search for the Wilderness Passage, became increasingly an English affair. Somewhat later, Americans inherited the European quest for a waterway through the continent. Their solution of the final riddle of the Wilderness Passage was not only their own distinct contribution, but also the fruit of the experience and insight on the venture accumulated by their predecessors over centuries.

Early on, geography and history involved the English in the search. For Englishmen bordering the North Atlantic, the exploration amounted to a continuation of sailings that had become part of their maritime heritage. Tales of the voyages of St. Brendan, Irish monks, and Vikings had colored their thoughts about lands and passages in an ocean leading west. Their familiarity with mysterious fog banks, which promised many things sailors hoped to see, made the task an English affair when other Europeans shunned the mystery. The voyages of the Cabots marked the onset of the search, particularly John Cabot's explorations in 1497 and 1498. A hundred years later, Richard Hakluyt mentioned the voyage of Sebastian Cabot "for the discovery of a Northwest Passage" in the 1600 edition of Hakluyt's monumental compilation. His reference introduced the term *Northwest Passage* into English.[14]

The initial search for the northern or southern passage around America kept Europeans chained to their ships and out of the wilderness. Their attempts penetrated the wilds of another part of nature, the ocean. Ferdinand Magellan had discovered the strait around the southern point of South America in 1520.

Located more than a thousand miles south of the latitude of the Cape of Good Hope, the passage around Cape Horn offered no easy route to the Indies. The search for a convenient passage shifted quickly to the north. There, in the higher latitudes, the geographic theory of the day assumed, the Atlantic would somehow connect through an open channel with the Arctic Ocean and the Pacific Ocean.

When the alternatives for swift connections with the Far East dwindled the pursuit of the Northwest Passage entered the lofty realm of geopolitics. The makers of national policies usurped what initially seemed the wishful thinking of navigators for a speedy voyage. It appeared that the nation that found the shortcut would reap a twofold benefit. The discoverers would control the flow of commerce to China, Japan, and India. They also could exploit the sphere of influence along the channel through a continent, not yet stripped of its lures of fabulous treasure and docile people.

The belief in the existence of the Wilderness Passage lasted into the presidency of Thomas Jefferson. On January 18, 1803, three months before the Louisiana Purchase, he outlined the benefits of an expedition along the Missouri River to the Pacific Ocean in a confidential message to Congress. He emphasized that the nation discovering and controlling the route would be master of the continental trade. "While other civilized nations have encountered great expense to enlarge the boundaries of knowledge, by undertaking voyages of discovery," Jefferson stressed, "our nation seems to owe to the same object, as well as to its own interest, to explore . . . the only line of easy communication across the continent."[15] For centuries, fanciful variants of these thoughts had motivated European nations.

In the early sixteenth century, the two most powerful European nations took the lead. The Northwest Passage emerged as a concern of statecraft almost simultaneously in Spain and France in 1523. In June of that year, Charles I of Spain instructed Hernando Cortés in a letter about the importance of the search for a strait to connect Atlantic and Pacific. King Charles I thought the passage to be somewhere to the north of the recently conquered Aztec empire.[16] At the end of the year, Francis II of France sent Giovanni da Verrazzano to discover a westerly passage through North America.

Cortés did not come up with an answer, but Verrazzano's discoveries produced sufficient confusion to heighten the curiosity, due to his ideas about the extent of North America. Presumably Verrazzano based his estimate about the width of the continent on Vasco Núñez de Balboa's crossing of the Isthmus of Panama in 1513 and Cortés's penetration of the Aztec empire. The experience of Álvar Núñez Cabeza de Vaca had not yet corrected the assumption that the continent north of Mexico would be only as wide as south of it.

Álvar Núñez, two Spanish companions, and the Moorish slave of one of them were the first Europeans who crossed the continent north of Mexico between 1527 and 1536. Survivors of a Spanish expedition to conquer Florida, the four men rafted through the Gulf of Mexico from Florida to Texas. From there they walked to a Spanish outpost on the Pacific, roughly along the present boundary between the United States and Mexico. In 1524, however, when Verrazzano faced the question of the width of North America, the prevailing ideas about the narrow width of the continent still shaped the conclusions he drew from his discoveries.

Verrazzano's voyage along the Atlantic coast from Cape Fear to Newfoundland led to the discovery of Chesapeake Bay and New York Bay. By furnishing information about the Atlantic coast of North America, the discoveries joined Florida with Newfoundland in the European mind. They also stimulated the belief in an estuary or a lake at the coast. This so-called Verrazzano Sea would seem to connect with the Pacific because the idea of a narrow continent supported the supposition. As an upshot of the speculations stimulated by Verrazzano's discoveries, some people assumed that the Chesapeake Bay or the Verrazzano Sea linked with the St. Lawrence Valley. They believed that China could be reached on these waterways and on a Western Ocean.[17]

As a result of Verrazzano's work, the French developed ingenious ideas with which to probe the promises of North America. They soon held the most promising beachheads for exploration on the east coast of North America. Spurred on by the advantages of geography, Frenchmen ventured swiftly into the heart of the continent. They attained basic information about the rivers feeding the Mississippi from the East, building on knowledge about the lower reaches that, from 1539 on, Hernando de Soto and other Spaniards had collected. Their understanding of the continent made the French for almost two hundred years the European guides to the Wilderness Passage.

With the support of his king, the search for the Western Ocean carried Jacques Cartier (between 1534 and 1542) farther into North America than any other European navigator. On his second voyage, in 1535, he sailed his ship into the St. Lawrence River, changed to a pinnace, and finally, in a small boat, reached Hochelaga, the Huron town at the site of present-day Montreal. A portage brought him to the head of the great rapids. There Indians told him about Lake Champlain and other great lakes, which Cartier later came to regard as routes to China.[18]

Bold as well as pious, this daring man linked the vision of the Wilderness Passage to the reality of an empire in the continent of North America. Jacques Cartier's initials could stand for Julius Caesar. In that role the explorer occupied a hill on the St. Lawrence as the future center of the French realm in the New World and called it Mount Royal. The initials J. C. also evoked Jesus Christ and imbued Cartier with a sense of mission analogous to the missionary impulse Christopher Columbus derived from his name. In the name of Jesus Christ, Jacques Cartier helped spread the gospel. The mass marking the beginning of Cartier's missionary work had as its text, appropriately, John the Baptist's sermon in the wilderness.[19]

Cartier believed in the possibility of a continental empire built along providentially provided waterways. At the end of the eighteenth century, the idea became one of the motives for the Lewis and Clark expedition. English conquerors found themselves compensated with the promise of empire, which they substituted for the lack of treasures in their American territories rivalling the Spanish booty from the Aztec and Inca empires. From the dogged determination of Englishmen, who had lustily chased ever-illusive riches while stubbornly waiting for Dame Fortune to abandon the French, Americans derived a good part of their intrepid spirit. It guided Lewis and Clark in pursuit of America's continental destiny, from the headwaters of the Missouri over Indian trails across the continental divide, to tributaries of the Columbia and ultimately to the Pacific.

Cartier's actions had taken the search for the Wilderness Passage out of the hands of navigators and assigned the task to French, Spanish, and English explorers and adventurers. Some mariners refused to accept the icy barriers of the Arctic Ocean as end of their enterprises or to give up the hunt for easy treasures. They continued to fathom the continent directly. Henry Hudson exemplified this attitude, two years after the Virginia Company of London had asked Captain Christopher Newport to see if the James River linked Atlantic and Pacific.

In January of 1609, Hudson agreed with the Dutch East India Company to search for the Northeast Passage to the north of Novaya Zemly, a double island in the Arctic Ocean north of European Russia. When the ice pack blocked his way, the English navigator made for America to appease his mutinous crew and to look for the Northwest Passage. In September of 1609, Hudson sailed the *Half Moon* up the river that now bears his name to the present city of Albany, expecting to find the harbor of Canton around the next bend.

Most mariners who continued to pursue the elusive Northwest Passage combed the Atlantic, the Arctic, and the Pacific. Between 1903 and 1905, the Norwegian explorer Roald Amundsen became the first to make the Northwest Passage from the Atlantic to the Pacific.[20] He took a route presciently referred to as "The Suppos'd Eskimeaux Passage to the South Sea" on the blank space of the "New Map of North America, 1778," which accompanied Jonathan Carver's *Travels*. Amundsen and the mariners probing the High North tackled a wilderness, too, but one of water and ice.

The search for the Wilderness Passage really began with the change from sea to land, which came in the second half of the sixteenth century. For a while, merchant adventurers kept up the long-standing English exploration of the North Atlantic. Linking their interests with monarch and nation, they hoped through the discovery of the strait to share the trade with the Spice Islands, controlled by Portugal and Spain. In a letter from Seville in 1527, the English merchant Robert Thorne the younger had sought to impress his king, Henry VIII, with the significance of the search. In 1540, he and Roger Barlow published their *Declaration for the Indies,* which called for England to extend the probe for unknown countries into the South Pacific.

The search for the passage to Cathay was in his age "a matter . . . above all other," George Best, an Elizabethan mariner, remarked in his account of a North Atlantic venture.[21] Sir Humphrey Gilbert, while on leave from the war in Ireland in 1565, had sought Queen Elizabeth's permission for an exploration. From 1566 on he professed belief in the Northwest Passage. In the following years he attempted to prove its existence, by hook or by crook. The actual search he shrewdly left to others. His restraint indicated that he understood the motive behind the Elizabethan schemes for the New World. The lust for quick riches contributed to shifting the search for the Northwest Passage from water to land, to the search for the Wilderness Passage.

Gold loomed large in the Elizabethan mind. All pretense of seeking an ocean strait to the South Seas around the northern end of America vanished in 1576. In that year, the great navigator Martin Frobisher brought back to England a worthless black stone, said by some to contain gold, from the southern end of Baffin Island. His second and third voyages, in 1577 and 1578, amounted to a gold rush by the privileged. The Queen sent along a vessel, to be returned at once with gold ore. These incidents were "evidence of the insane passion of the age" according to George Bancroft, when he wrote the first multivolume history of the United States almost three centuries later.[22] George Best, who commanded a ship on the expeditions in 1577 and 1578, concluded that he found "in all the Countrie nothing." However, Best added an afterthought about the potential of the newly discovered land in words that presaged the hope guiding subsequent explorers of the continent: "Being well looked unto and thorowly discovered, it wyll make our Countrie both rich and happye."[23]

Gilbert based his actions on Frobisher's experience. After he had secured a charter for a part of the New World, he waited almost six years before he sailed. Then he went as directly to Newfoundland as the winds of the North Atlantic permitted, without searching for the ocean passage to China. In August of 1583, Gilbert gave up to chase after the Northwest Passage in what turned out to be the last year of his life. He switched from looking for a way around the continent to probing the coast for riches and a waterway through North America.

Gilbert's change of direction from the icy waters to the vast lands marked the start of the English search for a Wilderness Passage. In due course, Englishmen encountered the nature of the continent. By the turn of the eighteenth century, their two hundred years of experience had contributed to the start of American self-discovery, when the young nation formulated its responses to the continent.

Failure marked their early steps because the English beachheads did not favor grandiose exploits. Shortly after Gilbert's death, the men of his half-brother, Walter Raleigh, could neither find a water route to the West nor build a permanent plantation at Roanoke. Irrespective of the lessons of Raleigh's failure, the first successful attempt to establish an English colony in North America at Jamestown in Virginia immediately fell under the spell of the Wilderness Passage.

In November of 1606, the Virginia Company of London alerted its first settlers to the importance of navigable rivers. If they should encounter a stream with branches of equal size, the instructions urged following the one that "bendeth most towards the Northwest for that way shall You soonest find the Other Sea."[24] Captain Christopher Newport, who had been in charge of the voyage, sailed up the James River to the falls near the present city of Richmond, between May 21 and 27, 1607. He found the Indian chief Powhatan and a town that carried the same name, but the hills of the Piedmont blocked the water route to China.[25] Captain John Smith, who governed the colony from September 1608 to September 1609, assumed that beyond these mountains lay "a great salt water, which . . . is either some part of Canada, some great lake, or some inlet of some sea that falleth into the South sea."[26]

Some supporters of the Virginia venture had always considered the projected colony a way station to the Far East. The hope remained that the Pacific Ocean was just beyond the Appalachian Mountains, although Francis Drake had failed to find the exit of the Northwest Passage along the Pacific Northwest coast during his privateering voyage around the world. Shortly afterwards, in the summer of 1579, Drake had beached the *Golden Hind* for repairs some thirty days somewhere on the California coast north of San Francisco Bay, as related in 1628 in *The World Encompassed by Sir Francis Drake*. Neither of these facts shook those who believed in the Northwest Passage or in the narrow width of North America. In 1650, a manuscript map by John Farrer (or "Ferrar") placed the passage to the Pacific where imagination had located it—just north of Virginia.[27]

In New England, the faith in the religious mission was still strong enough to save most Pilgrims and Puritans from the worldly folly that excited the imagination of the Englishmen searching for the Wilderness Passage. Before the stalemate produced by the visions of faith and the realities of geography quieted the aspirations of most English settlers, one dauntless Englishman from a settlement on the Kennebec River in Maine startled the French at Quebec. In June of 1640, a group of Abenaki Indians from the southeast of the capital of New France brought the stranger to Quebec. He claimed to be searching "for some route through these countries to the sea of the North." Before the French governor shipped him back to England, Father Paul Le Jeune, a former superior of the Jesuit mission in New France, spoke with the Englishman. He learned that the man had checked the Atlantic coast from Virginia to Maine for "some great river or great lake" in the hope of finding people "who had knowledge of that sea which is to the north of Mexico."

With French geographic knowledge at his fingertips, the priest pitied the Englishman for the wrong direction his search had taken. However, Father Le Jeune thought it very likely that one could reach the Englishman's sea from Lake Michigan. "I have strong suspicions," he concluded his report about the conversation, "that this is the sea which answers to that North of new Mexico, and that from this sea there would be an outlet towards Japan and China."[28]

Father Le Jeune relied for his ideas about the location of the Wilderness Passage on information French explorers had accumulated during their swift movement into the continent. Soon after the establishment of the first permanent French settlement at Quebec in 1608, French explorers began developing what ultimately became the staging ground for the final English tangle with the riddle of the Wilderness Passage. What appears in one perspective as an extension of the Anglo–French rivalry into the New World, in another presents itself as a French answer to a shared anxiety about vast space. The French trails directed the English (or the "Americans" as some of them called themselves officially from 1776 on) to the true track of their search, a path close to nature and its people.

The strength of the French position rested on the geography of the St. Lawrence. The great river, its tributaries, and the Great Lakes supported the swift moves of Frenchmen into the heart of the continent. Their advance also depended on the ability of French officials to come up with resourceful responses to the wilderness. Their actions encouraged Frenchmen to develop a forest strategy by orienting French practices along the lines of Indian customs of forest craft and canoe travel.

Samuel de Champlain founded Quebec in 1608 and governed the colony until his death in 1635. He stands at the beginning of a line of French colonial leaders who managed to serve the interests of New France and Old France by bridging the gap between white and red people. For the pursuit of that goal, information about North America was essential, and Champlain made great efforts to gain a better understanding of the lay of the land. In 1634 he received news that his aide, Jean Nicolet, had discovered Lake Michigan and explored its western shore.

Backed by Champlain's skillful Indian diplomacy, Nicolet's mission was twofold. He sought to ensure the peaceful expansion of the French fur trade and empire and to gather information about the course of a water route to the Far East. He was to make contact particularly with the Winnebago, whom the French called "People of the Sea." He must have anticipated the encounter with high hopes, because he took along in his canoe a ceremonial gown as the garment appropriate for meeting the Chinese emperor. When the Winnebago welcomed Nicolet and his seven Huron guides, somewhere in the vicinity of the present city of Green Bay, Wisconsin, Nicolet "wore a grand robe of China damask, all strewn with flowers and birds of many colors."[29]

Nicolet concluded peace between the Huron, Winnebago, and French. That accomplishment may have helped him to overcome any disappointment that he did not reach China. At first glance, it is rather startling that in 1634 Nicolet thought he could get there conveniently by traveling on freshwater by way of Lake Huron, through the Straits of Mackinac, and along the western shores of Lake Michigan.

As a Norman from Cherbourg, Nicolet undoubtedly knew that it took salt water to reach the Far East, even if he had never laid eyes on *Gargantua and Pantagruel* and the novel's splendid tribute to French seamanship. From the mid–sixteenth century on, with the aid of François Rabelais's imagination, Pantagruel, Friar John, and Panurge made the fabulous voyage repeatedly with every new edition of the book. They sailed in one month from Saint-Malo on the Channel coast of Brittany to the Oracle of the Divine Bottle in Upper India, across the Frozen Sea north of Canada. These bold travelers gleefully compared their record time with the speed of the Portuguese, who in the view of Rabelais's characters took as much as three years on the conventional route around the Cape of Good Hope.

Before his great moment at Green Bay, Nicolet had lived for several years among Huron and Nipissin and learned their languages. The exposure must have heightened his understanding of their ways of talking. With that understanding went, presumably, the ability to assess Indian hearsay. Tall tales may have inspired some Frenchmen to place Cathay on the shores of Lake Michigan or to assume that China could be reached in a canoe crossing a large body of fresh water. With Nicolet's background it is unlikely that he shared these hopes.

The story of the Chinese robe was first related by Father Barthelemy Vimont, the superior of the Jesuit mission in New France. In 1643 he recounted the life and death of Nicolet, who had drowned the year before in an accident in the St. Lawrence River. The priest may have heard the story of the robe somehow, presumably not from the seven Hurons, but more likely from Nicolet himself. After his return from the West, the explorer had married and settled down as a fur trader and Indian agent at Three Rivers on the St. Lawrence, roughly halfway between Quebec and Montreal.

It is also conceivable that Father Vimont made the story up to fuel the Jesuits' continued interest in the search for a passage through the continent. Although a priest may be inclined to tell a tall tale as much as the next man, it does not seem likely in this case. The story of the Chinese robe has an authentic ring. Its colorful detail stands out in striking contrast to the measured language relating the other subjects of the report.

Most likely, Jean Nicolet's background accounted for the incident. Champlain had instructed him to find a way to China. The weight of the governor's authority allowed Nicolet to suppress his knowledge about oceans and salt water, at least enough so that doubts about the feasibility of his mission did not hamper his actions. As a faithful envoy, he brought along a Chinese robe, donned it at the right moment, and may have enjoyed the spoof. After all, it impressed the Winnebago, who called him "the wonderful man."[30] The sudden appearance of a magnificently decked European may also have helped the search for peace. Over the years the incident slowly gained magnitude. Telling it often, Nicolet came to ignore its contradictions. Ultimately he forgot those bits of his knowledge that could have made him look foolish.

There are other possible interpretations, and at least one more explanation ought to be mentioned. Born in 1598, the year of the Edict of Nantes, which temporarily ended the religious wars between Huguenots and Catholics in France, Nicolet spent his first twenty years in a country recovering from the strife. The assassination of the French king, Henry IV, by a religious fanatic in 1610 dramatized the heritage of the conflict. The long struggle may have convinced Nicolet that it was easier to reach China than to find peace.

In some ways, his experience in New France had shown him that the New World hardly differed from the strife-torn country of his youth. In New France, Nicolet faced the war between England and France in 1629. The conflict brought to the St. Lawrence the British buccaneers who captured Quebec in 1629. He also witnessed the age-old intertribal wars of the Indians of the Great Lakes region. Thus, when asked in 1634 to find the way to China and the road to peace, Nicolet may have prepared himself to seek the first and then been delighted when he found the second.

The Chinese robes Nicolet carried in his canoe spoke for his determination to be ready for all eventualities. That spirit characterized most men searching for the Wilderness Passage. Far from the trappings of his culture, the French explorer carried with him a gown that linked him to his society. The Lewis and Clark expedition also took along bits of a cultural support system. The explorers carried in their minds the knowledge of the wheel and in their boats strips of iron that they used as wheel rims when they needed wagons for their most difficult portage. With the help of these iron rims, six men built strong wheels and sturdy wagons within two days to trek supplies and equipment around the Great Falls of the Missouri.

The portage would have been "at all events too long to enable us to carry the boats on our shoulders," Meriwether Lewis explained in his journal.[31] Saving precious time, pieces of technology carried into the wilderness helped them master the portage around the Great Falls. The falls' existence had been unknown to the captains until the Mandan Indians mentioned the falls when the explorers wintered with them at the Great Bend of the Missouri River in 1804–05.

Nicolet put his Chinese robe on too soon, but his trip up the Fox River furnished the link in the route that would lead Frenchmen to the Mississippi. Although Louis Jolliet and Jacques Marquette concluded that the Mississippi reached neither Virginia nor California, when they traveled partly down the river in 1673, one dreamer of a French continental empire clung to the promises of the great water system as an answer to the quest for the Wilderness Passage.

In the late 1660s, Robert Cavelier, Sieur de La Salle, had heard from the Iroquois about the Mississippi and concluded that the river must flow into the Gulf of California and provide the passage to China. In 1669, La Salle had plunged into the wilderness from his seigneury near Montreal, appropriately or derisively called "La Chine," to find the road to the Far East and to make a fortune in the fur trade.

La Salle endured physical hardships and financial losses without losing sight of his goals. When he realized in 1682 that the Mississippi emptied into the Gulf of Mexico, he adjusted his geographical perspective and sought to open a Caribbean window for New France by bringing the mouth of the river under French control. Some of his men gave up earlier on his schemes. In 1680, on one of the journeys in pursuit of his dreams, La Salle saw again the Illinois fort he had established earlier, now abandoned by deserters. They had scrawled across the side of a ruined boat: "*Nous sommes tous sauvages.*"[32]

"We are all savages": with that message of La Salle's mutineers the search for the Wilderness Passage entered a new stage. The search now linked the use of wilderness as a cultural concept with the use of wilderness as a place to live. Life at the outpost had removed La Salle's men from their culture and obliterated the distinction between wilderness and the actual wilds. Adjusting to the new situation, in line with their old cultural concepts they were shedding quickly, they recognized themselves as savages when they joined Indians for whom the white man's wilderness was home.

From the onset of their contact with North America, the unknown world of the interior, its rivers, lakes, forests, and people, fascinated the French. Their culture embraced new lands and strange people easily and incorporated them into the nation. Some French governors and *intendants* used the lure of the wilderness in designing and executing their policy. Early on, Champlain had fashioned the approach. Jean Talon, the great *intendant,* had taken up the challenge of the unknown interior. "To that end," Talon "availed himself of Jesuits, officers, fur-traders, and enterprising schemers like La Salle," Francis Parkman, the nineteenth-century historian of New France, explained.[33]

The Canadian forest and its people affected in particular the rule of the boldest governor of New France, Louis de Buade, Count of Frontenac. The ambience of his autocratic regime allowed him to forge links to the Indians. As a descendent of the old French aristocracy, which had outlived its role in his homeland, he felt drawn to a doomed Indian world. He empathized with its great chiefs and fierce warriors. Together with them, he saw himself falling before the new men dominating the white man's world: administrators, bureaucrats, traders, technicians, and soldiers. Apart from New France and the European battlefields of Louis XIV, only a few places might have given Frontenac the opportunity to live the life of a *grand seigneur* in ancestral style. In France the vanishing breed had been relegated to Versailles, military service, or provincial figurehead.

During his first term of office, from 1672 to 1682, his vigorous expansionist policy led to his recall. His actions had brought him into conflict with church officials and the home government. Sent out again in 1689 to defend New France against the Iroquois and the British, Frontenac adroitly built his reputation as the defender of New France by his effective use of these two tasks for propagating his fame. He claimed that all his energies had been devoted to the defense of Canada against the British, to the defeat of the Iroquois, and to the strategy of a continental French empire. In reality, the furs of the western tribes and the profits from the trade were his only concern.

As representative of Louis XIV in Canada, Frontenac could nourish his infatuation with the old feudal ways. He did what he wanted and frequently got away with it. Versailles was far away. The apparent brilliance of his regime served him well. New France, however, suffered from the clashes between the old-time autocrat and the new system of bureaucrats and technicians.[34] Ultimately, only the Canadian forest, big enough to endure the likes of him, offered the freedom he craved.

Heart and purse drew the headstrong courtier into the wilderness. There he forged military and commercial alliances with venerated chiefs and mighty warriors. Their dignity and courage, their extraordinary individualism, evoked once more the glorious independence of his own caste, which now depended on the king. In the wilderness, Frontenac carried himself like a fashionable courtier reliving elegant summer nights in the forest parks surrounding the palaces of his homeland. He managed to hold on, however, to the fine line dividing dream and reality, because his heritage and instinct immediately alerted him when he had reached the point where aristocratic hauteur had to give way to fatherly love for the "red children" of France.

Addressing Iroquois or Hurons at their council fires, his speeches had the tone of a father speaking to his favorite son. The words bridged the gap separating the two worlds. After the oratory, the beating of the drums would overcome Frontenac, and the man of the world would cast off the memories of Paris, Versailles, and St. Germain. He joined the dances of chiefs and medicine men, moving in rhythms responding to messages of nature that knew no red or white race, but only members of a great nation.

With powdered whig and embroidered coat, laces glittering and decorations tinkling, the dancing governor's surrender to the Indian ceremonies also served royal policy. When he chanted the war song with his Huron allies, clutching a tomahawk and waving it over his head, every gesture of his body evoked the image of the feudal warrior of old and indicated that Comte Frontenac would lead the tribes in war as well as dance.[35]

"Any thing becomes a man who knows how to do everything with dignity, and in season." Thus, in 1743, Peter Francis Xavier de Charlevoix, author of the first consecutive history of New France, summed up Frontenac's performances.[36] Pride and diplomacy, pleasure and business, brought Frontenac to the Indian council fires. He never gained everything, but in the end his affinity to those kindred spirits and his culture's acceptance of the common humanity of Frenchmen and Indians frequently triumphed.

Among English colonial officials in North America dealing with the wilderness, Sir William Johnson matched Frontenac's fascination with Indians. As the nephew of a British admiral whose estate he managed in the lower Mohawk Valley, he prospered through trade, agriculture, and official favor. He had fought on battlefields, at conference tables and council fires, before he became a baronet in 1755. Subsequently he served as superintendent of Indian affairs for the northern colonies until his death in 1774.

Johnson combined a genuine affection for Indians with a remarkable hunger for their land. It was his policy, Johnson's first biographer related in 1865, "to cultivate an intimate acquaintance with the Indians." His second and third wives were Mohawk. Strong commercial ties reinforced the bond, "and no white man, perhaps, ever succeeded in more entirely winning their confidence." When it suited him, the English aristocrat fully embraced the way of the Indians: "He mingled with them freely; joined in their sports; and at pleasure assumed both their costumes and their manners, and cast them aside, as circumstance might require."[37]

Johnson commanded colonial militia and Iroquois allies during the French and Indian War, lending support to the Canadian notion that the conflict could be called the English and Indian War with equal justice. Afterwards, he kept divided the Iroquois and the other Indians, from the Great Lakes region to the southern frontier, to serve his interests and those of the British crown. Johnson and Frontenac shared attitudes towards the Indians that obscured the differences between the two men. Both exploited the Indians for personal gain, used them as pawns for their royal masters, and derived from the intimate contact deep emotional satisfaction. Frontenac addressed the Indians as "children," Johnson as "brethren."

The deep emotional satisfaction Frontenac and Johnson derived from their intimate contact with Indians distinguished them from other officials who also used Indian allies for their ends. For those officials the personal level of Indian relations remained a burden. Louis-Joseph Marquis de Montcalm, who commanded the French troops and Indian allies during the French and Indian War until his death in battle in 1759, referred in a report to his difficulties with the task. In July 1757, before one of his campaigns against the British, he wrote to the Ministry of War in Paris that in Montreal he had been obliged "to gratify the Indian Nations, who will not leave without me." He added that he had passed his "time with them in ceremonies as tiresome as they are necessary." For several days he "was to chant the war" and give feasts for several Indian groups to reunite for his campaign "these barbarians, so ferocious in war, so humane in their lodges."[38]

After 1783, American officials may have told themselves to deal with Indians like Johnson and Frontenac did, but they lacked heart. Their ethnocentrism and racial prejudice distanced them from Indians. Bound to an egalitarian and democratic creed, they were at a decisive disadvantage vis-à-vis Frontenac and Johnson of an earlier age. Both those aristocrats met people of a different race and station easily. They knew they were everyone's superior. That arrogance characterized other, less aristocratic intruders of the wilderness, too. They, however, lacked the certainty of mind and manners that would have allowed them to meet Indians as equals, without feeling they had lost something in the process. Although forest and Indian life captivated Meriwether Lewis and William Clark, both captains kept up their guard. As much as two Virginia gentlemen could, they allowed themselves to be drawn to Indian ways. After his initial encounter with the Shoshone on August 13, 1805, Lewis described their traditional affectionate embrace. The Indians rubbed his cheeks with their left cheeks, "and we wer all caressed and besmeared with their grease and paint till I was heartily tired of the national hug."[39]

Lewis and Clark neither daubed their faces with war paint nor joined dances at the council fires. However, some of their men and Clark's black servant, York, danced at the Mandan villages. "I ordered my black Servant to Dance," Clark recorded on January 1, 1805, "which amused the Crowd Verry Much." Clark also noted that York's dancing delighted Indians at one of the portages along the lower Columbia.[40]

York and his companions substituted for Lewis and Clark in the American quest for the common humanity of white and red people. The captains remained bound by their cultural bias. It had increased during the struggle with the practice of slavery, which invalidated one premise of the young republic. The servant York and the soldiers, weak leaven in the slowly rising dough of a democracy of all people, led the Corps of Discovery to a precious discovery. These servicemen, temporarily elevated to represent captains and country to Indians, related to people of a different race in ways reminiscent of aristocrats like Johnson and Frontenac.

Frontenac's attraction to Indian speech and ceremony showed a high-ranking French official's fascination with the ways of the forest. Other Frenchmen, ordinary ones measured by Frontenac's ancestry, carried his achievement farther. French culture showed less prejudice than English culture to Indians as a group, and some Frenchmen mixed their ways of life with the ways of nature. These *coureurs de bois,* or "forest runners," as the Frenchmen ranging the Canadian forest were called, preferred the free life of an Indian village to the restraint of a French community. With that preference firmly established, it did not take long before they began to act and think like Indians. Frequently through marriage or adoption the *coureurs de bois* became relatives of the Indians they lived with. Only their French, when the *coureurs de bois* chose to use it, gave them away to their countrymen.

Economic, demographic, and political influences also smoothed the transition of the *coureurs de bois* into the Indian world. Initially the fur trade had lured them into the forest. There Indians were their companions, and the exposure to Indian woodcraft taught them that living like Indians while gathering fur made sound economic sense. The nature of the trade kept the *coureurs de bois* on the move and dispersed them in many directions in search of new fur resources. They had no choice but to follow the beaver, which disappeared quickly from extensively hunted areas and seemed to be constantly retreating to more distant habitats.

As *coureurs de bois,* these French adventurers were bound to follow beaver and Indian. They avoided French officials, who found them irksome because they violated the monopoly of licensed merchants. New France's stability rested on fur, however, and officials cared more to have pelts in Montreal than to know how they got there. Parish priests in villages along the St. Lawrence and missionaries in the Indian country knew that Frenchmen living in the forest ignored their teachings. Although priests and missionaries warned their flocks of the dire consequences for their souls of such behavior, some parishioners always surrendered to the appeal of the freedom the *coureurs de bois* had found among the Indians. At times, missionaries on their travels to distant assignments used *coureurs de bois* as guides, but more often the Jesuits viewed them as the savages they hoped to baptize and civilize.

Regardless of the objections to the *coureurs de bois* from various quarters, French policy acknowledged their importance. Officials allowed some of them to winter as *hivernants* in Indian villages because they could acquire furs as soon as they became available.[41] Furthermore, it was advantageous to have these men in the Indian world because they provided links to the Indian nations. Finally, the official conduct of the French fur system depended on a good working knowledge of geography. Once the *coureurs de bois* had carried the fur trade into the Indian villages and eliminated the Indian middlemen, it became essential to engage in exploration so that the trade network could adjust easily to the location of new sources of fur. When administrators lacked funds to support expeditions, "forest runners" and "winterers," who depended on their knowledge of the land for survival, served as explorers.

English or American counterparts to the *coureurs de bois,* other than regular Indian traders, came to be called "backwoodsmen" in the eighteenth century. They were a less distinct group because they lacked the social cohesion of the *coureurs de bois*. Although backwoodsmen went beyond the settlements as hunters and trappers, they lacked many of the bonds linking the French *coureurs de bois,* in particular the outlook on life based on a mixture of two cultures. In the wilderness, the goals of the backwoodsmen continued to turn around the values of their society: profit, land, family, and religion.

Committed to chase and conquest, the backwoodsmen related only tenuously to Indians. Too many cultural impediments prevented an intimate relationship with Indians. When they took an Indian wife, they barely concealed their feeling of superiority in their dealings with Indian relatives. In times of war, if their interests coincided with the policy of the British government, they joined ranger companies to fight Indian enemies and European rivals.

The backwoodsmen were mostly solitary men, individualists like their prototype, Daniel Boone. As Leatherstocking he roamed through James Fenimore Cooper's novels, as Hawkeye and Straight-tongue, as the Deerslayer, the Pathfinder, and the Trapper. Collectively, his literary personality embodied various attributes of the American backwoodsman. Among these characteristics was a patronizing attitude to his Indian allies, Chingachgook and Uncas. Any such residue of white superiority the *coureur de bois* had exchanged for his share in the wilderness.

With the help of *coureurs de bois,* French explorers pursued the Wilderness Passage until the British took over New France after the French and Indian War. One of the French explorers, Louis Armand de Lom d'Arce, Baron de Lahontan, learned to appreciate Indians as human beings through his exposure to the world of the *coureurs de bois*. The experience added compassion for Indians to his writings about exploration. The emphasis on the common humanity of all people made up for his dubious role in the search for the Wilderness Passage.

Lahontan became fascinated with the people of the wilderness in 1684, when he encountered the earthy prodigality of the *coureurs de bois*. He saw them after one of their groups had just returned to Montreal with canoes full of beaver furs. They were feasting and playing until their earnings and almost everything else were gone and they were forced to set out again on another voyage. In his eyes, their reckless abundance rejected those accolades of French ways Lahontan professed to detest (after honors had bypassed him and disgrace threatened). Lahontan considered the *coureurs de bois* "well acquainted with the country and with the savages," and in his eyes these accomplishments elevated the *coureur de bois* close to the natural man.[42]

His contact with the *coureurs de bois* taught him to appreciate the forest. The experience enabled him to elevate his pursuit of the Wilderness Passage into a realm of speculation where he discovered the common humanity of all people. He found the answer to his search for a brotherhood of all people when he shifted his fascination from the *coureur de bois* as embodiment of nature to the Indian. His account of life in New France, published in Amsterdam in 1703, extolled the Indian as the ideal human being.

At first glance, Lahontan seems to embrace a literary tradition going back to antiquity. That tradition bestowed praise on barbarians in order to shame contemporaries and countrymen. His appreciation of Indian life showed, however, that he had shed his French ethnocentrism as well as the European fascination with the noble savage. His *Dialogues curieux* (1703) left the realm of philosophical speculation and recognized the Indian as his "dear brother and dear friend."[43]

In the first English translation of Lahontan's book, *New Travels*, the *Dialogues curieux* appeared with their complete title: "A Conference or Dialogue between the Author and Adario, A Noted Man among the Savages. Containing a Circumstantial View of the Customs and Humours of that People." In these conversations Lahontan offered insights into Indian life that he had gained as a French officer between 1683 and 1688. His outlook reflected his services at Fort St. Joseph, near the present Port Huron, Michigan, in 1687, and his participation in a Chippewa raid on the Iroquois in 1688 with a Huron chief, "The Rat." The Michigan command may have inspired him to invent a River Long west of the Mississippi as answer to the Wilderness Passage. The Huron chief may have been the model for Adario.

Lahontan's duties attracted him to French explorers who knew the lay of the land firsthand. He may have aspired to be one of them himself when he went into the field between September of 1688 and April of 1689. His work was discredited, however, after he claimed to have discovered the River Long as a possible link to the Western Ocean. The River Long proved to be Lahontan's undoing as a conventional explorer when attempts to check his statements and to locate the river in Minnesota failed to corroborate his account.

Lahontan's contribution as an explorer took place on a plane that offered other insights than those one expects to derive from the observation of the topography. Under ordinary circumstances, when Lahontan was writing about what one might call everyday affairs, he provided meticulous records of events and careful descriptions of people, artifacts, and topography. When he discovered the common humanity of all people, his accurate portrayal of reality gave way to his impressions and illusions dealing with the world of the River Long. The changed language indicated his entry into a unique realm. Lahontan's ascension of the mysterious river and his reports about the encounters with Eokoros, Essanapes, Mozeemleks, and other imaginary Indian nations living along its banks set the stage for his departure from the familiar.

During that illusory winter, Lahontan indeed gained a familiarity with the northwest shores of Lake Michigan; however, he neither accounted for forest and prairie nor compared them with such ideals of seventeenth-century French culture as Poussin's heroic landscapes. Lahontan's discovery of nature pursued a trail into the wilderness that bypassed geography, art, and time. His search led him into the Indian world where he found evidence for the humanity of all people.

Lahontan obscured the trail leading to his precious discovery. The frontispiece of his *Nouveaux voyages* showed a naked man who looked like a mythical hero of antiquity in stance and build, and the curly beard and hairstyle reinforced the impression. The arrow in his raised left hand and the bow in his lowered right did not bring him any closer to being an actual Indian. The figure stood with his left foot on a legal tome while his right foot was poised to crush crown and scepter. The Latin legend, *Et leges et sceptra terit,* spelled out the message of the symbols: "He crushes law and crown."

Etching and legend hardly prepared readers for an account of Indian life and a discussion of the nature of human nature. Undoubtedly, both were added by a publisher to ensure the success of the book. They appealed to the interest of European readers brooding over the blemishes of civilization and hoping to find in an exotic society a cure for its ailments. The 1705 edition of the *Dialogues curieux* would carry the publisher's intentions one step further.

While the 1703 version of the *Dialogues* mirrored genuine Indian conditions, the next edition interspersed veiled references to political conditions in France and England. Ethnographic materials discussing the health of the Indian or the advantages of a non-patriarchal society, gave way to topics that the publisher thought would intrigue or agitate the European reader: law and lawsuits, authority and taxation, capital and labor. Both speakers, Lahontan and Adario, now freely used abstractions: Society, State, Justice, and Nature.

The distance of the 1705 version from the reality of a utopian Indian tribal society was increased by several references to the king of France. In the first edition, neither he nor anyone else was held accountable for the European dilemma. A society built on property rights was alone responsible. The new edition was marked by tirades against Louis XIV, who was called a tyrant, Croesus, and a parasite.[44]

The text of the book may have been altered either by Lahontan or by an editor. Whoever made the changes had turned the description of a utopian Indian society into a familiar device to castigate the shortcomings of French and European society. Lahontan's initial message about the brotherhood of all people was lost. The shift in the perspective raised no objections because Europeans were distant from the interplay between culture and nature in the wilderness of North America. They could not recognize the potential for the discovery of a common humanity in the course of the search for the Wilderness Passage.

Lahontan moved the quest for the Western Ocean into the realm of fantasy. His chimera seemed to make the brotherhood of all people directly attainable. As a preparatory step he portrayed a utopian Indian commonwealth, superior in its political and social structure to European states. His account of the Indian bucolia on the banks of the River Long revealed the avidity of regular explorers and the credulity of ordinary readers. They assumed that a passage through North America would offer a way to Tartary. Both groups failed to recognize a destination more alluring than Cathay, which Lahontan had located firmly in the neighborhood of the Wilderness Passage: Utopia.

Since the first printing of *Utopia* in Louvain, either late in 1516 or early in 1517, Thomas More's "Nowhere" has been repeatedly located somewhere. At times, as is suitable to a masterpiece of imaginary literature, "Nowhere" was outside the known world, placed close to the Elysian Fields or among the Fortunate Isles.[45] These precedents may have inspired Lahontan to locate his Indian utopia near the end of the Wilderness Passage. He imagined the illusive Wilderness Passage as a safe place to demonstrate the elusive harmony of nature and culture.

Somewhere in the same area, Jonathan Swift placed the Brobdingnagians of *Gulliver's Travels* in 1726. He specified the location on a map that showed their country near the Strait of Anián. That was the name the geographer Giacomo Gastaldi had used for the passage in the earliest printed reference to the presumed channel between Arctic Ocean and Pacific Ocean in 1562. The magnetism of the Strait of Anián as the location of Utopia lasted for centuries. In 1879, Jules Verne placed there a utopian city in *The 500 Millions of the Begum.*

Not all utopias in the North American wilderness were mere literary creations. Much depended on the explorers' perspective. Lewis and Clark found no utopia in the vastness of the continent, because the singlemindedness of purpose that distinguished their command of the expedition kept their minds on distinct goals. In the 1730s, however, one European seeker of the brotherhood of all people looked differently at the wilderness while passing as refugee through the English colony of South Carolina. He found a utopia in the Cherokee country. Christian Priber quickly adopted Cherokee dress and customs, learned the language, and established a town dedicated to the liberty and equality of all people. In the "Kingdom of Paradise," he urged, the "law of nature should be established for the sole law."[46]

His intention to realize his ideas had not been well received in Europe, as might have been expected, and it was said that he had to leave Saxony (which some considered his native country) on account of his views. In North America, however, at mid-eighteenth century, many components of his utopia still served as Cherokee tribal customs in the Blue Ridge Mountains. Priber, a brilliant mind who went into the American wilderness to find the European "noble savage," found himself richly rewarded. He was fortunate as a utopian because he did not have to belabor reluctant people with his ideas. The blueprints of the perfect society, which the intellectual descendant of Plato, More, and Campanella carried with him, jibed with Cherokee practices. As a result, the interaction between European theory and Cherokee custom in the wilderness led to a moment of harmony between culture and nature.

Priber's account of his utopia does not seem to have survived his experiment. Some of its outlines have been preserved in Antoine Bonnefoy's journal and James Adair's *History of the American Indians,* and a few references to Priber can be found scattered here and there. Bonnefoy, a French voyageur (a boatman), lived as a captive among the Cherokee and feigned enthusiasm for Priber's project of a utopian society to find opportunities for planning his escape. Adair, in 1775, published the best eighteenth-century history of the southern Indians. Both writers praised Priber's intellect and character. Others called him a rogue and a lunatic, a Jesuit and a French agent; but all detractors stood in awe of his humanity. Priber "was learned, and possessed of a very sagacious penetrating judgment," Adair summed up his view, "and had every qualification that was requisite for his bold and difficult enterprise."[47]

The social order of the Kingdom of Paradise rested on natural rights. Commonly understood and practiced by the members of the utopia, Priber's use of natural rights philosophy limited the need for a legal system. Each "individual was to have as his only property a chest of books and paper and ink," Priber elaborated.[48] Men and women were equal, as among the Cherokee, or were to be equal as soon as they joined the utopia. Society raised and educated children. Everyone shared labor and its fruits. The establishment of a City of Refuge incorporated other elements of Cherokee society into Priber's utopia. Following time-honored Cherokee tradition, the sanctuary provided a haven for all people—red, black, and white—who felt threatened by others.

Some of the political features of Priber's utopia went beyond an emerging Cherokee nationalism. They aimed at supporting the creation of an empire of southeastern Indians. Priber served merely as an advisor, however, taking "the superintendence of it only for the honor of establishing it."[49] He filled the offices with Indians and crowned a Cherokee peace chief as emperor. "An old favourite religious man," in the words of Adair, the chief may have been the inspiration for Joshua Reynold's portrait "Cherokee Emperor."[50]

Parallels between the Kingdom of Paradise and ancient and Renaissance utopias in European culture abound. In particular the relationship of Priber's Kingdom of Paradise to Thomas More's *Utopia* stands out, exemplified by Priber's affinity to Raphael Hythloday, More's narrator.[51] Unlike the great European models, which Priber's experiment seemed to evoke in the Blue Ridge, the wilderness utopia actually worked from 1736 to 1743. And compared with some of the utopias radical reformers built during the Reformation, the Kingdom of Paradise showed far fewer excesses.

The growing English–French rivalry for the Southwest crushed the Kingdom of Paradise. Traders also eagerly helped end it. They looked askance at an Indian society asserting its independence, sharing property, and eliminating profit. Indian traders captured Priber when they found him on Creek territory without his Cherokee supporters. Turned over to British authorities, he died soon afterwards as a prisoner in a Georgia fort.

Priber's excursions into the ideal sphere of human relationships intimately linked culture and nature in the South Carolina backcountry. His utopia also approximated the ideas of Lahontan and other eighteenth-century socialists; however, Priber did not have to search for the course of an illusive passage as locale of his utopia. Priber's ideas found their way into people's minds when his Kingdom of Paradise ensured the common humanity of all. On the other hand, Lahontan's ideas created no utopia, but they did inspire the continued pursuit of the Wilderness Passage.

Lahontan's general map of Canada, which accompanied the French edition of his *Nouveaux voyages* of 1703, nourished much optimism about the Wilderness Passage. Near the left-hand edge, somebody glancing at the map could spot the River Ouaricon, the origin of the word "Oregon." The name acquired a magic of its own and gave the search for the Wilderness Passage new impetus when the British read Lahontan. They imagined a river that would provide the Wilderness Passage and called it the Oregon.

The aura of mystery surrounding the River Oregon grew in the final stage of the French search for the Wilderness Passage. French explorers produced the commercial rationale of a continental empire along major lines of communication. They anticipated by two generations Alexander Mackenzie's geopolitical and economic vision, which the British explorer and fur trader derived from his intimate knowledge of western North America. Speculations about the course of western rivers in relation to the Wilderness Passage motivated his great exploring expeditions. Ultimately, Thomas Jefferson inherited the French and British visions. He instructed the Lewis and Clark expedition to search for a possible connection, in the form of a short portage, between the Missouri and the Columbia rivers.

Roughly at the time of Jefferson's birth, in 1743, the actual search for a western river that could serve as Wilderness Passage, began with Pierre Gaultier de Varennes, Sieur de la Vérendrye. An explorer at heart, he became a fur trader to draw support from a small trade monopoly granted by the governor of New France. His reports about the upper Missouri and the Saskatchewan regularly mentioned the significance of the Wilderness Passage for trade, to satisfy officials in Quebec and business partners in Montreal. In essence, La Vérendrye's efforts were the last major French attempts to unravel one riddle of the continent.

In 1738 and 1743, La Vérendrye and his sons searched for the Wilderness Passage to the southwest and the northwest of the French outposts west of Lake Superior. They also hoped to find a way to the high-quality fur of the Canadian Northwest. Finally, these moves were intended to block the inroads of English fur traders who were descending from Hudson Bay into the French fur-trading empire. The motives of the La Vérendryes also dovetailed with the political and scientific rationale that guided the French penetration of the continent. At the time of the La Vérendryes, however, the fur trade had become the mainstay of New France, and exploration for the sake of discovery had become unprofitable.

In the French imperial context, the activities of the La Vérendryes coincided with the efforts of French colonists from New Orleans to explore the upper Missouri. In 1738, coming from Lake Superior, La Vérendrye reached the Mandan villages at the Great Bend of the Missouri in present-day North Dakota. About that time, Frenchmen from Louisiana came up the Missouri and its tributaries as far north as the present-day South Dakota.[52] The La Vérendryes pushed on over the western plains. They may have reached the Bighorn Mountains, but they made their contribution to the search for the Wilderness Passage along a more northern route.

In an attempt to avoid the Sioux country, they discovered the advantages of the Saskatchewan River as a gateway to the Far West over the Missouri route. In a 1749 memorandum about the discovery of the Saskatchewan, one of the brothers stated that one La Vérendrye had ascended the river to the confluence of the forks that form the main stream. At the spring rendezvous of the Cree, the La Vérendrye brother had "enquired minutely, according to his father's orders," about the source of the river. "They all replied with one voice," the report continued, "that it came from very far, from a height of land where there were very lofty mountains; that they knew of a great lake on the other side of the mountains, the water of which was undrinkable."[53]

The continuation of the La Vérendryes' strenuous search for

the Western Ocean fell into the hands of a group of New Englanders after the conquest of New France by Great Britain. These New Englanders had served during the French and Indian War, some of them as rangers. When peace came, they somehow remained attached to the most famous colonial ranger, Major Robert Rogers. After the war Rogers had failed to get a commission for a three-year expedition to discover the Wilderness Passage. Instead he obtained command of the fort at Michilimackinac, guarding the strait between Lake Huron and Lake Michigan.

Always ready to enhance his fame or gain a fortune, Rogers used the post, not only for trading illicitly with Indians, but also for staging exploring expeditions. The idea of using the fort as a base for trade and exploration came naturally to a man who as hunter and Indian trader invariably had his eye on big game and large profits. He also thought himself to be in an advantageous position for making important discoveries in the unknown West and finding, if lucky, the Wilderness Passage. During his service in South Carolina as captain in the Cherokee War in 1761, he had encountered the ideas of Arthur Dobbs, then governor of North Carolina, who had conjectured earlier that the Northwest Passage ran somehow from Hudson Bay to the Pacific Ocean.

When no proof was found for Dobbs's speculation, Rogers may have felt doubly sure that from Fort Michilimackinac he could be onto something, perhaps by staging an expedition and somehow intercepting the Wilderness Passage. He made the most of his hunch. In 1765 in London, in his petition for the western expedition, Rogers first used the word *Ouragon* as the name for the great River of the West that now figured so large in talks about the Wilderness Passage. He may have come across "Ouragon" accidentally because during his stay in the British capital, Rogers was quite a busy man. He published, not only his journals, but also a survey of North America and a drama about Pontiac, the Ottowa chief who between 1763 and 1765 had campaigned against the British. As aspiring litterateur, Rogers may have heard

English men of letters speak about the "River Ouariconsint" (a variant of *Ouisconsink*, the French name for the Wisconsin River) when they discussed Lahontan's writings.

In preparation for the publication of Lahontan's *Nouveaux voyages*, the engraver of the book's general map of Canada had been forced to hyphenate "Ouariconsint" because he lacked space. The artist had placed the final syllable a line below, providing the casual viewer of the map with a brand-new waterway, the "River Ouaricon."[54] Fascinated by the promise inherent in the mysterious name, Rogers used variations of it, "Ouragon" and "Ourigan," when he launched his scheme to reach the Wilderness Passage.

For this ambitious project, Rogers chose his men carefully. He intended to rely primarily on James Tute, a former captain of Rogers's Rangers. In a subordinate position he saw a role for Jonathan Carver, who had served with Tute's brother in the French and Indian War. Not much came of Rogers's project; it fell short of its great design. However, at just the right moment, the levelheaded Carver mustered sufficient imagination and editorial help to make Rogers's scheme immortal. Carver published a book about his share in the scheme in London. His success as an author upstaged Rogers, whose chance for carrying out the journey evaporated because his schemes interfered with the interests of men in power.

Carver came from Connecticut, and from his service in the French and Indian War he knew something about geography. He became a draftsman, and in the journal of his 1766–67 journey in Rogers's service he reported carefully what he saw of the country and its people. His *Travels,* which he published in 1778, added enough color to his journal to meet the requirements of the London book market for exciting reading and to keep alive speculations about the location of the Wilderness Passage. As a result, his book actually contributed more to exploration than his journey did.

In 1766, Carver went west from Fort Michilimackinac to the Falls of St. Anthony, within present-day Minneapolis. Major

Rogers had instructed him to map his route and to return in the spring, unless sent on in search of a waterway to the Pacific . If that expedition in search of the Wilderness Passage got under way, Carver was to travel under the command of Captain James Tute, whom Rogers instructed to look for the "great Reriver Ourigan that fall into the Passifick Occian about the Latitude fifty."[55]

Carver traveled west by the Green Bay–Fox River–Wisconsin route. He ascended the Mississippi and entered the Minnesota River, where he wintered with the Sioux. When he heard nothing more about a Wilderness Passage expedition, he came back by way of Lake Superior to Michilimackinac, which he reached in the fall of 1767. The following spring he went to Boston. No publisher wanted his travel account, and in 1769 he sailed for London, where subsequently he eked out a living as a writer.

During his brief expedition, Carver hardly had time to explore anything, let alone look for the Wilderness Passage. He had thought, however, about the implications of what he was looking for, and so his imagination saw more than all the La Vérendryes who actually did a lot of looking. One of them, in 1750, had explained to a minister of Louis XV that his father arduously searched for the passage to the Western Ocean, "and made myself and my brothers travel with such a vigour that we should have reached our goal, whatever it was, if we had only had a little more help."[56] Carver also lacked support, but instead of La Vérendrye's determination to reach a vague goal, he had the ability to write so imaginatively about the Wilderness Passage that it looked real.

His talents as a writer emerged as soon as he returned from the journey. One of Carver's letters showed the requisite for any travel writer—the ability to embellish a story. The occasion of the letter also showed Carver's ability to grasp any opportunity and turn it to his advantage. After his return to Fort Michilimackinac in September, 1767, he appealed in a letter to his wife's compassion. He then left her behind in Massachusetts, deserting her to marry another woman in London without having obtained a divorce.

Carver explained in his letter that it "would require a volume to relate all the hardships and dangers" he had suffered. He depicted himself as a lonely man: there was no one to speak his native tongue, he wrote, because his companions, a *coureur de bois* and an Iroquois handling the canoe, knew no English.[57] His loneliness must have been imagined, or, at best, rather temporary: in his journal, Carver recorded that he traveled to the Mississippi in the company of William Bruce, a Montreal trader, the first Briton to enter the Northwest. Later on, Carver met with Captain James Tute and James Stanley Goddard and returned with them to Michilimackinac.[58]

Without his companions who might have checked up on him, Carver wrote at length about the geography of North America. He had the good sense to put his account in the hands of a gifted editor. Regardless of what some critics had to say about Carver's originality, the results pleased his readers. They learned much about the speculations surrounding the Wilderness Passage. In the first edition of his *Travels through the Interior Parts of America*, published in 1778, Carver, his collaborator, or both, drew freely on earlier books by Father Louis Hennepin, Pierre François Xavier de Charlevoix, and Baron Lahontan. With their help, Carver turned the journal of his voyage into a book that would command attention in London. That was no mean accomplishment. He and his editor faced a reading public spoiled by travelogues from many parts of the world. Moreover, Captain James Cook, the great British maritime discoverer, had just earned the admiration of English readers with accounts of his two circumnavigations of the globe between 1768 and 1775.

Such literary competition accounted for the need to give Carver's journey loftier purposes than his journal warranted. The editor focused the book on the search for the Wilderness Passage and toned down the original concern for the fur trade west of Fort Michilimackinac, which dominated Carver's actual record of his journey. The plain language of the journal gave way to the polished prose of the capital, and Carver emerged as the leader of the expedition, with the proper credentials to explain the riddle of the Wilderness Passage.

Carver invented an extensive plateau, framed by the Shining Mountains, in the heart of the continent. Four rivers originated there, which ran towards the four directions of the globe. Among them was the Oregon, the River of the West, which emptied into the Pacific at forty-five degrees northern latitude and brought Carver and his speculations close to the Pacific exit of the Wilderness Passage.

The "River Oregon, or the River of the West," Carver explained, flowed "upwards of two thousand miles" west from the Shining Mountains. It emptied into "the bay of the Straights of Annian," which, "having been first discovered by Sir Francis Drake, of course belong to the English." [59] Carver's imagination, abetted by his editor, located the mouth of the River Oregon just south of the legendary Spanish admiral De Fonte's Pacific entrance of the Northwest Passage, which stretched from the Strait of Anián to Hudson Bay. For additional support of his view, Carver linked the mouth of the River Oregon with the discoveries of other Spanish explorers, Juan de Fuca and Martín de Aguilar.

Carver packaged the scraps of geographic knowledge nicely. The Shining Mountains, part of the Rocky Mountains, gave the watershed the pyramidal symmetry cherished by the French strategists of continental conquest. If Carver had paid less attention to his French authorities on the geography of North America, he might have come up with a pyramid of three sides instead of one with four. Then he would have anticipated the triple divide of the Canadian Rockies, where rivers from the glaciers of the Columbia Icefield begin courses that lead to three oceans, the Pacific, Arctic, and Atlantic. Carver's idea of the watershed dated back to Sir Humphrey Gilbert's concept of a continental divide. The Oregon River itself had first appeared in Major Rogers's 1765 petition for an expedition from the headwaters of the Mississippi to the Pacific Ocean.

Spanish lore about the mysteries of the continent contributed De Fonte's entrance and the Strait of Anián to Carver's geography. De Fonte, a mysterious Spanish admiral, occasionally received credit for first sighting a Pacific exit of the Northwest Passage. The Strait of Anián supposedly cut through the continent, connecting the Pacific with the Atlantic. Others thought that both oceans linked up in the north. There were also people who believed that the Arctic Ocean or another water system facilitated the connection.

The centerpiece of Carver's geography was the River of the West: the Oregon. By 1778, it tied together the complex speculations of the seekers of the Wilderness Passage. More than two thousand miles long, the Oregon River conveniently cut through the mountains of the vast wilderness separating the English outposts west of the Great Lakes from the Pacific. Its general direction gave status to the Northwest Coast in the eyes of explorers and geographers as a possible location for the exit of the Wilderness Passage.

The number of people involved in the search steadily increased and distracted attention from individual explorers. Details of discoveries shared by several explorers were quickly absorbed if the findings promised to expand either the geographic knowledge of a newly opened area or the irrepressible optimism of new flights of fancy. As a result, far-flung discoveries by solitary explorers had little impact. Their contributions to knowledge were rarely circulated or, often, reached only a few people who viewed them skeptically.

One important answer to the riddles about the Wilderness Passage had come six years before the publication of Carver's *Travels*. Word of mouth informed anyone who cared to listen that in 1771 Samuel Hearne had reached the mouth of the Coppermine River. The employee of the Hudson's Bay Company followed the river to the Arctic Ocean, where he saw a strip of clear water with the ice beyond. His accomplishment put an end to the long-standing dispute about a Northwest Passage from Hudson Bay to the Pacific Ocean. If such a waterway had existed, Hearne would have crossed it.

Although the report of the journey eliminated the Canadian North as possible site for a Wilderness Passage, some people discredited the story. They assumed that an employee of the Hudson's Bay Company would act like Frenchmen of old. Englishmen had routinely suspected them of keeping their geographic knowledge secret or of distorting it to baffle their rivals. Furthermore, Hearne was a Company man, and the directors of the Hudson's Bay Company regarded all employee reports as Company matters; their information was reserved for internal use. Some of them might have thought it the best thing to do with the report because Hearne had found little that had bearing on the conduct of company business.

Consequently, few people actually concerned themselves with the geographic implications of Hearne's report. Somehow the report was passed on to the Admiralty, and so Captain James Cook had a chance to read it before his second voyage because of his interest in a possible Pacific Ocean exit of the Northwest Passage. Hearne's account of his exploration did not appear as a book until twenty-four years after his journey.

Hearne himself assessed the economic value of his discoveries realistically. A modest conclusion ends his *Journey from Prince of Wales's Fort, in Hudson's Bay, to the Northern Ocean,* published in London in 1795, three years after his death. His discoveries, he suspected, were "not likely to prove of any material advantage to the Nation at large." He merely felt pleased to have silenced the detractors of the Hudson's Bay Company. For many years they had clamored that the company lacked initiative to explore the continent or expand the trade.[60]

In the 1740s one of those detractors, Arthur Dobbs, who later served as colonial governor of North Carolina from 1754 to 1764, had badgered the British public about the Northwest Passage. In

1745, in order to silence him, Parliament passed a bill offering a reward of £20,000 for its discovery. The members must have felt pretty confident that no one would succeed quickly with the Northwest Passage after all these years of searching. They offered the large sum despite the war with France and rumors of an impending invasion of Scotland by the Young Pretender.[61]

No trace of the agitation about the Northwest Passage appears in Hearne's travel account. Its conclusions reflected the independent mind of a remarkable man whose journal depicted him in harmony with nature on the so-called Barren Grounds of the Canadian North. Without a white companion, he traveled for nineteen months in the company of Indians.

Under the leadership of Matonabbee, a Chipewyan chief, Hearne left the Prince of Wales's Fort at Hudson Bay, near the mouth of the Churchill River, in December of 1770. He reached the Coppermine River in July of 1771, and returned by way of the Great Slave Lake and the Slave River. Traveling with strangers through a strange world, he came to understand both better. He learned to measure his success, not by his disappointments in what he had hoped to find, but by discovering the geographic realities. He reached the Coppermine River, but he found that it emptied into the Arctic Ocean. He actually saw the current of the mysterious river, envisioned by other traders as waterway to transport fur from the interior, but in reality scarcely navigable by canoe. During an extensive search he found only one piece of copper, despite glowing reports about a vast mine at the mouth of the river. That piece found its way to the London headquarters of the Hudson's Bay Company and thence into the British Museum.

Hearne's real discovery was of a different order. He managed to bridge the gulf between nature and culture when he recognized humanity as his bond with Matonabbee. The intrepid Indian chief impressed him by his brutal prudence and discerning kindness. Hearne had failed twice to reach the Coppermine River without Matonabbee. The experience made him realize that he brought little more than his endurance and courage as a traveler to the venture. He lacked most qualities essential for the success of an expedition.

Without an indomitable will and a knowledge of the wilderness, Hearne could not succeed as leader of such an enterprise. He was also neither a mineralogist nor a geographer. His watch stopped because he forgot to wind it; his quadrant got lost; and these mishaps muddled the journal entries about his whereabouts. Earlier, in his career as a trader, he had failed miserably to get along with Indians. Now the experience of traveling beside a man equally eager to reach the Coppermine River forged a bond that sustained him so that he could compile a remarkable record of Chipewyan life as lived by Matonabbee.

The timid man of quiet courage developed enduring qualities. They enabled him to give a sympathetic and accurate portrait of Indian ways. A genuine diffidence about himself and a respect for his surroundings distanced him from his native culture. He took with equanimity almost everything he encountered. He saw Matonabbee kill one of his wives: she had doubted the chief's ability to attend properly to more than seven of them. Hearne watched the steadily increasing number of Indians joining the party for no other purpose than to kill any Eskimo they might encounter. During a massacre of Eskimos, with "the poor expiring wretches" skrieking and groaning, Indians killed a young Eskimo woman so close to his feet that Hearne could barely disengage himself "from her dying grasps."[62]

Hearne witnessed the butchery and the mutilation of the bodies. He observed other startling incidents and encountered revolting beliefs during his journey. Yet he viewed the events not from his cultural perspective but from a position that bound Indians and him to a common humanity. "Notwithstanding his aversion from religion," Hearne characterized Matonabbee, "I have met with few Christians who possessed more good moral qualities, or fewer bad ones."[63] The language of passages like these indicated that the book's editor, Dr. John Douglas, Bishop of Salisbury, respected Hearne's discerning mind and published the manuscript almost exactly as written.

Hearne recognized the limits of his own culture when he observed Matonabbee's remarkable survival skills. The arduous trek and the elusive goal heightened his awareness. Hearne "stood neuter in the rear" during the massacre of the Eskimos, after Matonabbee's assessment of the possible consequence of the chance encounter with the Eskimos had clashed with Hearne's inclination to leave the Eskimos alone. In other instances Hearne's culture also surrendered to the values of a culture shaped by the command of nature in the High North. Appalled by the Indians' abuse of women as beasts of burden, Hearne accepted Matonabbee's explanation that men had to be free for the hunt at all times to provide sustenance for all.[64]

A perceptive observer of people and country, Hearne regarded Matonabbee's selection of the route a masterstroke. On his two earlier expeditions in search of the mysterious river, Hearne had left the Prince of Wales's Fort in a northwesterly direction, roughly on a straight course to the mouth of the Coppermine. He and his companions promptly starved trying to cross the Barren Lands because they found no game. Instead of going directly north, Matonabbee avoided starvation by moving west in the winter, along the northern edge of the forest with the herds it sheltered. He turned north only in the spring, when deer and caribou, the major targets for the hunters, were also trekking north. His prudence ensured Hearne's success.[65]

With his tribute to the resourceful and cruel Matonabbee, Hearne placed nature on the same level as the tenets of his own culture in the High North. The awesome journey to the Coppermine River strengthened his objectivity. After his return, as a regular employee of the Hudson's Bay Company, he quite naturally again felt superior to everyone, including other Britons in the field. In 1774, when he built Cumberland House to check the advance of British traders from Montreal into the Saskatchewan Basin, he dismissed these "pedlars" as wily competitors in the Indian trade. Grudgingly he respected their success, which only heightened his arrogance as a Hudson's Bay Company man.

When Hearne encountered Matonabbee, he did not assume his own cultural superiority. He gained a high degree of impartiality by surrendering to the Indian as the embodiment of nature. Undisturbed by white traveling companions or competitors in search for the Coppermine River, the vast void and the snowy waste of the High North environment did not divert Hearne's path towards a common humanity. There was no grandiose scenery, which might have distracted an eighteenth-century Englishman touched by his countrymen's love of landscape. A drawing made by Hearne in 1777, "A North-West View of Prince of Wales's Fort in Hudson Bay, North America," showed the walls and bastions of the fort and a few vessels offshore.[66]

An aesthetic appreciation for the sublime High North could hardly have been cultivated in the twenty-four-year-old Englishman, who had gone to sea at the age of eleven. From his service as mate on one of the sloops of the Hudson's Bay Company, he had made his way back to land. There he led, in his fashion, three expeditions through the High North. On the last of them, guided by Matonabbee, Hearne embraced as nature, not the principles of aesthetics, but the world of the Chipewyan Indians.

Hearne's acceptance of Matonabbee's wisdom has no parallel in the annals of the exploration of the continent, except for one Spanish example. Almost three centuries earlier, Álvar Nùñez Cabeza de Vaca, when stripped of all trappings of his culture, underwent an analogous experience. Reduced to the level of bare survival, he found a common humanity with his Indian hosts. For several years, group after group of Indians guided him and his companions through the arid Southwest to the northernmost outpost of the Spanish world on the west coast of New Spain. "We passed from one strange tongue to another," Núñez reported to the King of Spain, "but God our Lord always enabled each new people to understand us and we them. You would have thought . . . that they spoke our language and we theirs," he exulted.

When the last Indian nation turned over their guests to slave-hunting Spaniards at Culiacan in 1536, his host-Indians refused to believe that Álvar Núñez and his companions belonged to the same people as the Spanish slave hunters. The Indians insisted that "we came from the sunrise," Núñez recorded their anguished reply to the Spanish captain commanding the slave hunters. They came "from the sunset," the Indians explained; "we healed the sick; they killed the sound; we coveted nothing but gave whatever we were given, while they robbed whomever they found and bestowed nothing on anyone."[67]

Records attesting to the experience of discerning a common humanity between white and red people are rare before the nineteenth century. Some white people overcame obstacles in the path of a mutual understanding; however, few Christians could bring themselves to extend their faith in religious brotherhood to non-Christians.

Outstanding friends of the Indians, like Roger Williams in the seventeenth century and John Heckewelder in the eighteenth century, considered Indians inferior unless the Indians embraced Christianity. Williams and Heckewelder cared for Indians and protected Indian life, but the Puritan clergyman and the Moravian missionary felt that only acceptance of Christianity could dispel Indian inferiority. When they brought the Christian religion into the Indian world, their action inadvertently hastened the destruction of Indian culture and the people it sheltered. Christianity remained ensnared in the ethnocentrism of European culture, while most white captives who elected to remain in the Indian world had nothing left but their lives and took on their captors' culture.

At the beginning of the nineteenth century, the belief in progress began to supplant Christianity as the epitome of white culture. Indications of progress became the test of other cultures. The members of the Lewis and Clark expedition felt inspired by the stamina and resilience of Sacajawea, the Shoshone wife of their French-Canadian interpreter. On other occasions they marveled at the wisdom, virtue, and bravery of chiefs and warriors.

Captains and men never grasped that any Indian could match their abilities and intelligence, however. Neither did it ever occur to them that the Indian cultures could equal the accomplishments and promises of their republic.

In the 1770s, Hearne's accommodation to nature marks a stage in the search for the Wilderness Passage, evidence of an advance in the British way of coping with the vast North American continent. His findings did not, however, lay to rest the speculation about the existence of a passage in the Canadian North. Hearne's discovery stimulated a scramble in the Far North, which involved, in particular, the Canadian rivals of the Hudson's Bay Company for the fur of the North. While the traders of the Montreal companies in the Athabaska district hunted for the waterway, the British navy probed the Pacific coast of the continent for its exits.

All groups looked for a specific waterway. Their ventures no longer penetrated the unknown, when explorers had searched almost at random for the Wilderness Passage. The impetuous approach had for decades disguised the agonies of failure and mitigated the hardships accompanying success. The definite sense of direction now attached to the search also deprived the wilderness of its mysteries. The Indians who called it home now faced the thinking of intruders shaped by new knowledge and motives. They sought other resources, which slowly began to rival the appeal of the fur trade.

In one sense, the adjustments to the growing knowledge about the continent marked the final stage of the search for the Wilderness Passage. In another sense, the adjustments characterized the American involvement in the search, which foreshadowed nature's calamitous fate in nineteenth-century America. The sprouting knowledge of geography encouraged far-flung enterprises. Americans interacted with the wilderness, propelled by calculated risk and guarded imagination. Their identification with the national interest reduced nature to an instrument of national growth.

The possibility of a water route for the Wilderness Passage in the High North was ruled out when Captain James Cook proved that the continent lacked room for it. On his third exploring expedition, his vessels hugging the coastline of the Pacific Northwest, Captain Cook discovered that the land stretched much farther west than had been expected. In May of 1778, the expedition sighted a large break in the coastline, roughly where the sixtieth-parallel northern latitude intersects the 153rd meridian. A six-day sail up an ever narrowing bay (now called Cook Inlet) convinced the navigator that it was not the mouth of a major river. Now he felt certain that not enough unknown space was left in the Far North for the Wilderness Passage. Pushing farther north, the expedition continued along the Alaskan peninsula and passed through the world of the Russian fur trade on the Aleutian Islands. Cook sailed into Bering Strait until a wall of ice turned the ships back on August 18, 1778. He had found that only the Bering Strait led from the Pacific to the Arctic.

When Cook's maps appeared, the inlet now carrying his name showed a few insignificant streams the expedition had found. This information pushed some members of the Canadian Northwest Company into action. Stationed at Lake Athabaska, almost seventeen hundred miles due east of Cook Inlet, they assumed that Cook Inlet was the mouth of the big river that would carry fur to the Pacific. One of them, Alexander Mackenzie, tested the speculation. In two awe-inspiring ventures, in 1789 and 1793, he demolished the last hope. No river ran from Lake Athabaska into Cook Inlet or into any other strait connecting with the Pacific.

In 1789, Mackenzie's voyage established that the river leaving the Great Slave Lake, north of Lake Athabaska, in a northwesterly direction soon turned almost due north. It skirted a massive mountain range to the west, a section of the Rocky Mountains, and emptied into the Arctic. In one hundred and two days, "accompanied by five Canadians & three Indians," Mackenzie covered the 3,000-mile-journey to the Beaufort Sea of the Arctic Ocean and back to Lake Athabaska. "This expedition," he laconically summed up after his return, "proved without a doubt that there is not a North West Passage" north of the sixtieth-parallel northern latitude.[68]

Still, there was the vast expanse of land south of Lake Athabaska, which now received Mackenzie's attention. In 1792, Mackenzie followed the Peace River from Lake Athabaska in westerly direction to the vast range he had seen on his earlier expedition. In the next year, with three fur traders, four voyageurs, and two Indians, he traversed the rugged mountains. In canoes or on foot, the group followed streams or trails on a course generally responding to Mackenzie's sense of direction.

Finally, the Bella Coola River brought them to the Pacific Ocean, some distance north of Vancouver Island. "I . . . mixed up some vermilion in melted grease, and inscribed, in large characters, on the South-East face of the rock on which we had slept last night, this brief memorial—'Alexander Mackenzie, from Canada, by land, the twenty-second of July, one thousand seven hundred and ninety-three.' "[69]

The great accomplishment made Mackenzie the leader of the second group of white men to cross North America with the help of Indians. A reserved man, he kept most people at a distance, including Indians, but he regularly captured the good will of Indian parents by giving sugar to their children. Mackenzie succeeded about two hundred and fifty years after Álvar Núñez Cabeza de Vaca made the first crossing in the south. He also proved that there was no continuous waterway in the north that could qualify as the Wilderness Passage.

The mystique of the passage lingered on, despite Mackenzie's toil and insights. The European mind had difficulty coming to terms with the gigantic range of mountains stretching through western North America. Spanish officials suddenly felt the lure of the Wilderness Passage again. The explorations in the Far North and the activities of Russian, English, and Canadian explorers and traders alarmed them. Once, the major threats to the Spanish possessions had come from French Canada and Louisiana. Now intruders seemed to gather in the mystic North. The changed source of the assault reawakened the concern about the control of the Northwest Passage that Charles I had voiced to Cortés in the spring of the Spanish empire. Now, in the autumn of the empire, all the legendary passages in the North gained new importance. There were plenty of them: the straits of Anián, De Fuca, De Fonte, and the so-called Englishman's Strait. Francis Drake had supposedly taken the last in 1580, when he got his booty from the privateering cruise along the Pacific coast quickly back to England.

Without Spanish control of the waterway, the Spanish officials assumed that the recent extension of the viceroyalty of New Spain into Alta California would not be safe. The Russians, who had been trading in Alaska since Vitus Bering's voyage of 1741, had no use for a Northwest Passage. The Spaniards suspected, however, that the Russians would move down the Pacific coast towards New Spain, come across one of the passages, and assume control of it.

The renewed Spanish interest in the Northwest also thrived on attempts to improve communications between the Spanish possessions in America and the Far East. Ships sailing between Acapulco and Manila on their return voyages from the Philippines were driven towards the coast. Their crews had added to the tales of the North. In 1588, the imagination of Ferrer Maldonado had placed the Strait of Anián somewhere near sixty degrees northern latitude, leading into the Northwest Passage. Below that latitude, Martín de Aguilar had discovered a river in 1602 that no one had found again.

For nearly two centuries the Spanish tried to reach the north. They succeeded in July of 1774, when Juan Perez from San Blas, by way of San Diego and Monterey, sighted what we call the Queen Charlotte or Haida islands. In the following week, he anchored at Vancouver Island. There he traded to the Indians (among other things) two silver spoons, which Captain Cook saw four years later. They became part of the Spanish claim of the northern coast against the British rival—in the absence of a formal act by Perez that would have established possession.

In 1775, during a second Spanish attempt to secure a foothold in the Northwest, Bruno de Hezeta found "the mouth of some great river, or some passage to another sea."[70] He imagined that it corresponded with the strait discovered by Juan de Fuca in 1592. A strong current, a dangerous bar, a sick crew, and approaching darkness kept him from entering the estuary. At dawn his ship had been blown far to the southwest. Seventeen years later, a Boston sea captain, Robert Gray, sighted the mouth of the river, crossed the bar, and named the river Columbia, after his ship.

Gray's action supported an American claim to the area, which increased Americans' interest in the location of the Wilderness Passage. The concern of the young nation, determined to share the sphere of influence on the West Coast, gave the long search a new direction. The knowledge of the mouth of the Columbia fitted into a variety of speculations. First of all, it was located in a little-known part of the Northwest Coast. To the north, Spaniards, Englishmen, Canadians, and Russians had some knowledge of the coastline. One explorer, Alexander Mackenzie, had actually traversed the continent there roughly along the line of the fifty-fifth parallel, but no white man had ever traced the course of the Columbia. To the south, the Spaniards knew much of the coast below the forty-second parallel. In the interior, in 1776, the Escalante expedition from Santa Fe had reached the vicinity of the Great Salt Lake, the northernmost point of the Spanish penetration of North America.

Between the routes of Mackenzie and Escalante, however, there remained a vast unknown territory. With the Columbia River as major attraction, that wilderness was big enough to revive an age-old dream. Anyone primed for adventure and inspired to flights of fancy by Carver's River of the West could fill the void of unknown territory with a scaled-down version of the Wilderness Passage.

Carver's River of the West, the mythical two-thousand-mile-long River Oregon, pointed west from mid-America. It also provided Carver's contemporaries with an estimate for the intervening distance to the Pacific. After other explorers had shown that no passage existed in the North, the national purpose of the United States appropriated Carver's speculation. It became a distinct part in Thomas Jefferson's vision. He and his countrymen relied on Carver's River of the West when they entered the final search for the Wilderness Passage.

An expedition through the wilderness sent out by the President of the United States led to the young nation's first decisive encounter with the pristine nature of the unknown part of the continent. It brought thirty-three men, one woman, and a baby in touch with unknown parts and people of North America. The experience put the travelers' culture on an even footing with churning rivers and deep canyons, with powerful Indian nations and straggling bands.

The experience of the Lewis and Clark expedition presaged the encounter of nineteenth-century American culture with the nature of the continent. It outlined the interaction of a purposeful imagination, defining and guiding the national interest, with the wilderness. For moments, the Corps of Discovery found culture and nature in accord. Its discoveries also revealed a nature that could be exploited for a vast range of purposes, stretching from building a nation with boundaries reaching from the Atlantic to the Pacific, to satisfying the urge of an individual to pursue his happiness. The discoveries of the Lewis and Clark expedition enabled the forces of nationalism, democracy, industrialism, and urbanism to mold nineteenth-century America into a nation built on the destruction of nature.

»» TWO ««

On Culture's Edge

"THE REFLECTION OF THE SUN on the . . . mist . . . from these falls" made a rainbow, which enhanced "the beauty of this majestically grand scenery," Captain Meriwether Lewis noted in his journal on June 13, 1805. Almost immediately the description bothered Lewis, one of the leaders of the first major exploring expedition sponsored by the United States government. "I . . . was so much disgusted with the imperfect idea which it conveyed of the scene that I determined to . . . begin agin."[1]

On second thought, Lewis let the sentence stand as his first impression of the Great Falls of the Missouri River. As if to cover up his audacity, he quickly fell back on the conventional words of an educated man of his time to cope with scenery. He even jotted down his wish for the pencil of Salvator Rosa or the pen of James Thomson to evoke in his reader's mind the sweeping majesty of nature as portrayed by the seventeenth-century Italian painter and by the eighteenth-century British nature poet.

Despite their credentials, neither artist could have solved Lewis's specific problems with the scene. The painter had made a reputation with flamboyant canvases, and the poet had found fame casting tempests in the frame of everyday scenes. Salvator Rosa "imparted to his canvas a character of wildness and extravagance," a Philadelphia art critic commented a few years after Lewis's struggle for words at the Great Falls, and made "Nature . . . merely ancillary to such impressions."[2] Similarly, Thomson and the Romantic poets after him took feelings derived from familiar sights for expressions of the relationship between man and nature.

In contrast to them, Lewis faced unknown scenes, and he shunned excessive imagination. In his journal he aimed at observing accurately a setting that no white person had ever seen. Overwhelmed by the enormous task, Lewis resorted to literary conventions. He felt that only with their help might he "be able to give to the enlightened world some just idea of this truly magnifficent and sublimely grand object, which has from the commencement of time been concealed from the view of civilized man."[3]

Lewis's quandary also reflected the general dilemma of finding adequate ways to describe the unknown nature of a new nation. Gonzalo Fernandez de Oviedo faced the same predicament in the 1530s. One of the first historians of the New World, he longed for the skills of a Leonardo da Vinci and an Andrea Mantegna when he lacked words to depict the flora and fauna. Lewis's difficulty reflected the state of the arts in his country, whose artistic currents still ran in only a few channels. Few people had painted an American landscape or celebrated it in poetry or prose. In general, portraits dominated American painting, except for the scenes in the large pictures of artists like Benjamin West. Poetry elaborated the patriotic themes struck by Philip Freneau, and prose emulated the Gothic novels of Charles Brockden Brown.

The continent Lewis was about to cross had not yet been domesticated by the clichés of landscape writers. Lewis's pen seeking to do justice to the unknown scenery between 1804 and 1806 could rely on only a few models. The *Travels* of William Bartram, naturalist and the son of the botanist John Bartram, had been published in Philadelphia in 1791. The first volume of *American Ornithology,* by Alexander Wilson, was to appear in Philadelphia in 1808. With words and illustrations both books inspired other naturalists and introduced the American imagination to strange scenes, but the messages did not affect Lewis.

Although deficient by his own standards, Lewis's words radiated his excitement when he saw the pristine scene. They reflected the thrill of adventure as well as the struggle for a language to do justice to them. The expedition, which marked the culmination of political, economic, and social forces officially launched in 1776, was actually the last of a long line of adventures in the search for the Wilderness Passage. And yet, although it took place after the North American journeys of Álvar Núñez and Alexander Mackenzie, this crossing of the continent by citizens of the United States was a "first" in the context of American self-discovery.

The explorers' endeavor to find the right words for the new sights benefited from the advancements of the age of "first" books written and published in the United States. Among the reference works the expedition took along, Lewis had the first American textbook of botany, Benjamin Smith Barton's *Elements of Botany*, published in Philadelphia in 1803. Other areas, however, lacked the coverage to satisfy Lewis's needs. Neither draftsman nor painter accompanied the "*corps of volunteers for North Western Discovery*," as Lewis called the expedition on August 26, 1804, in the Orderly Book, a record kept of all written orders.[4] Nor did the captain ever comment on their absence. Instead of wishing for a painter among the members of the expedition, he wished for a camera obscura, a device used by artists in the seventeenth and eighteenth centuries to obtain the correct projection of a scene or object. At times Lewis's mind took splendid flights of fancy, but he strove to make them appear useful. Despite his lack of words and art, he hoped eventually "to give to the world some faint idea of an object which at this moment fills me with such pleasure and astonishment."[5]

Lewis struggled to fuse the scene at the Great Falls of the Missouri with the idea of landscape he had formed when at the falls of the Potomac and the Schuylkill in the East. His search reflected the growing influence of landscape painting and of romantic ideas of scenery, which encouraged his generation not merely to view American nature but also to envision it. When Lewis jotted down his first impression of the Great Falls, he noted dejectedly that an "imperfect idea" of the scene had produced what he considered a poor description. He never explained the meaning of the "imperfect idea"; however, the conventions of his day about landscape presumably had given birth to it, and he had tried using the idea to incorporate the details of the scene into a "perfect description" of a landscape. If he had committed the rudiments of the "imperfect idea" to paper, the elements of imagination he rejected in favor of measurements might have become clear. When he turned again to assessing the scene, he merely concluded that the greater size of the Missouri falls made them "a more noble, interesting object" than their counterparts in the East.[6]

After his initial amazement at the dimensions of the stunning view, words came more readily to the captain's mind. On the following day, June 14, a tremendous roar drew Lewis to the next falls. "Here the river pitches over a shelving rock, with an edge as regular and as streight as if formed by art," he reported. "The water descends in one even . . . sheet to the bottom," his words described the fall of the water to the new level of the river, where it "rises into foaming billows of great hight and rappidly glides away, hising, flashing, and sparkling as it departs."[7]

Lewis's attempt to compare the beauty of the two falls disrupted his splendid description of the view. Groping again for expressions, he came up with phrases to gauge landscape that the eighteenth century had superimposed on nature: "At length I determined," he wrote underlining his verdicts emphatically, that this one "was *pleasingly beautifull*, while the other was *sublimely grand*."[8]

When Captain William Clark, the other leader of the expedition, described the second cataract on June 18, he concluded: "This is also a handsom Scenery, a fall in an open leavel plain."[9] His observation went beyond the intellectual framework of Edmund Burke's essay of 1757 on the sublime and the beautiful and supported Immanuel Kant's elaboration of the phenomena: in 1790, Kant had suggested that boundlessness characterized the sublime; while the beautiful, depending on form, derived its appeal from boundaries. The captain's statement related only accidentally to the philosopher's speculations, however, because Clark put into his journal what he saw, without getting distracted by reflections in his observations.

During the portage around the Great Falls of the Missouri in June and July of 1805 Lewis and Clark faced some of the problems involved in the discovery of North America as landscape. As gentlemen and officers they responded to the challenge by fortifying their views with references to the fashionable sublime. Beyond the scenery they actually described, other spectacular sights—the vast plain, the awesome mountains, and the great ocean—affected the captains on their expedition. Only on a few occasions, though, did their words turn the scenes into landscapes and the views into visions.

In general, the expedition's diarists rarely surrendered to the urge to evoke something fashionable in their description of the scenery. David McKeehan, a western Virginia schoolmaster who in 1807 edited and published the first account of the expedition, Sergeant Patrick Gass's journal, explained the choice of language in his preface to the book: "Mr. Gass having declared that the beauties and deformities of the grandest scenes are equally beyond the power of description, no attempt has been made either by him or the publisher to give adequate representations of them."[10]

Although some of the diarists of the Lewis and Clark expedition might have found time for literary vignettes to satisfy convention, they rendered useful views of scenes. Their words stood the test of practicality well because the attention the writers paid to details created verbal counterparts to topographical sketches.

The explorers saw many previously unimagined sights and people on their journey. They wanted to adapt their extraordinary experiences to the harmony of scene and taste American culture aspired to at the turn of the eighteenth century; however, hardship and fatigue drove the explorers to the edge of their culture. They shed layers of cultural accretion governing the regular discipline of an army unit for vital forms of communication sustaining people exposed to the force of nature. Their concern fastened on matters more mundane than ordinary tasks or aesthetic niceties: their mission and survival.

For fleeting moments, that experience brought the Lewis and Clark expedition into concord with nature. It moved the explorers to an outlook and a language that recognized the beauty and value of the new American scenery in its own right and on its own terms. The magnitude of their encounter with the unknown stunned the diarists and at times taxed their resources to the limit.

The course of their long, long journey presented so many obstacles that the explorers sometimes ignored the wonders of nature and recorded instead features that seemed to encourage their advance—or presage their doom. Hazards and crises occupied their minds. Although the vogue of the sublime and the beautiful demanded attention, judgment about the beauty of any scene—particularly a new one—was and is a highly subjective affair. Preconceived ideas about the sublimity or the loveliness of a sight proved to be a roadblock in the path to an adequate language for a pristine landscape.

The explorers rarely enjoyed the degree of security that would have enabled them to view a mountain ridge or an Indian nation as a majestic scene or a beautiful spectacle. "There appears to have been very little romance or sentiment about any of the party," the biographer of the last survivor of the expedition emphasized in his book about Patrick Gass in 1859; "all such insubstantial ideas having been starved out by hard, practical experience."[11] Exhausted and anxious, at the end of a long day, nine explorers entered their experiences into the journals they kept (with various degrees of regularity), inspiring one Lewis and Clark scholar to declare that they "were to become the writingest explorers of their time."[12]

The journals had little immediate effect on their countrymen. Six journals were eventually published, but a century went by before the captains' journals appeared in print verbatim. Published in 1904, "upon the Hundredth Anniversary of the Departure of the Trans-Mississippi Expedition of Lewis and Clark, this first publication of the Original Records of their 'Winning of the West' " was dedicated to Theodore Roosevelt. The dedication of the eight-volume edition to the twenty-sixth president of the United States alluded to the title of his multi-volume history of the settlement of Ohio and Kentucky. At the turn of the nineteenth century, Roosevelt's message-laden writings helped to shape the popular image of the West far more than did the words of Lewis and Clark, but his concern for language was still to leave its mark on professional historians.

Theodore Roosevelt considered "the quiet absence of boastfulness" characteristic of the explorers' prose.[13] Their reticence may have been not only modesty but also fatigue in facing a final chore as a strenuous day came to an end. Tired, the writers reviewed their encounters with nature in utilitarian terms. They jotted down the obstacles, resources, and curiosities they had come across. Their restraint inadvertently gave power to many features of nature which the explorers encountered. Despite the resources of their culture that they carried into the wilderness, they felt at times helpless in the face of natural forces.

The interaction of these forces and attitudes ensured the balance between nature and culture the expedition experienced. The awareness of a harmonious relationship between the expedition and the environment vanished when the insights of the explorers disappeared with the journals into attics and archives. Subsequent generations of Americans, without the benefits of the words of Lewis and Clark, saw the discovered assets of the Far West as guarantees for their pursuit of happiness. The nineteenth century perverted the expedition's dedication to utility, preserved in the sparse prose of the explorers, into a craze of exploitation. The swift advances of technology and the rapid increase of people intent on sharing the resources of the continent made the abuse and the destruction of nature an unexpected result of democracy.

The continental trek of the explorers, bound together by the discipline of an army unit, did not tax the regenerative powers of nature beyond recovery. Small in present-day terms, the party was large for its time, but the captains' military authority prevented the worst abuses of nature. Twenty-nine men formed the core of the expedition, the special Army unit under the command of "Capt. Lewis and Capt. Clark, who are appointed by the President of the United States to go on an expedition through the interior parts of North America," Sergeant John Ordway explained in his farewell letter to his parents on April 8, 1804.[14] At the Mandan villages, a French-Canadian interpreter, his Shoshone wife Sacajawea, and their baby came to be added to the two captains, the interpreter, two French-Canadian rivermen, Clark's black servant York, nine young men from Kentucky, and fourteen army regulars.

The hardships the explorers shared and endured established utility as denominator for their behavior and united the disparate people. They felt concerned about their safety as well as the usefulness of their actions for the welfare and success of the expedition. Their commitment to the expedition shaped their thoughts and accounted for the egalitarian attitude of the intrepid group. Frequently reinforced by necessity, the democratic spirit of the command surfaced in various ways.

A degree of freedom unknown to enlisted men at the time affected the army routine and the journal writing of the expedition. Inherited as routine from the Revolutionary army, courts-martial were considered quite ordinary affairs. Enlisted men sat on the court, with the exception of the trial of crimes punishable by death, when both captains served. Lewis and Clark broadened that egalitarian approach to discipline on several occasions. Two days after the death of Sergeant Charles Floyd, on August 20, 1804, the soldiers elected Private Patrick Gass as his successor, and he was promoted sergeant.

Gass did not mention the election in his book at all. Perhaps the procedure struck him as unusual; perhaps he preferred to think of himself as a "regular" sergeant, who had reached the rank on merit rather than the vote of his comrades. Furthermore, his publisher, who edited his account before it appeared in print, might have resented the creeping egalitarianism implicit in the election and omitted the reference. On November 24, 1805, all members of the expedition, including York and Sacajawea, voted on the location of the winter quarters on the Pacific. Gass merely said in his account of the voting that "the party were consulted by the Commanding Officers as to the place most proper for winter quarters." In contrast, Clark recorded each vote in his account of the election.[15]

When it came to the actual task of writing journals, the differences in rank, education, and temperament evident in the explorers' spelling were obscured by the underlying uniformity of the style used to record the daily events. In an age when consistency did not yet govern orthography, the similarity of form minimized the impact of the many variations of spelling. For their model the writers, officers as well as enlisted men, relied on Army prose.

The style had been shaped by the Army's need to relate events and assess topography with their significance for the marches and countermarches of the campaigns foremost in mind. Army prose focused on chronology, the orderly sequence of events, and then turned to topography and weather; in particular, the requirements of the terrain for issuing orders and the effect of a day's weather on the soldiers' morale. These observations produced a prose that at times inserted extraneous descriptions, stimulated by observing natural sights, in the linear narrative of daily events. In his assessment of Clark's style, one literary historian stressed that it suppressed personality in order to bring the writing "as close as possible to the face of the country."[16]

The requirements of military prose colored the depiction of many scenes. About two months after the start of the expedition, Clark described the plain surrounding a hill, "which afforded one of the most pleasing prospects I ever beheld." Below him he saw a beautiful river "about 80 yards wide Meandering thro: a leavel and extensive meadow, as far as I could See." The prospect was "much enlivened by the fiew Trees & Srubs which is bordering the bank of the river, and the Creeks & runs falling into it."

Bypassing any impulse of his imagination to pull the careful observations together as landscape panorama, Clark's commitment to accurate description directed him more and more to details. The low land "is covered with Grass of about 4 1/2 feet high," he continued; "the upper land is also covered with Grass and rich weeds & flours." On the rise of the land, "small groves of trees are seen, with a numbers of Grapes and a Wild Cherry resembling the common Wild Cherry."[17] Clark's military service had taught him his style of writing.

With its commitment to utility and accuracy, the language of the Lewis and Clark expedition brought distant sights instantly near. Relating the expedition's new experiences with natural forces, the immediacy their words conveyed went beyond the wisdom developed in the safety of a study, the images created in the isolation of a studio, or the speculations spun amid the chatter of a drawing room. The explorers' background and training had begun separating them from the literary and artistic practices of the day. Their adventures in the unknown parts of the Far West, hardening the expedition for the vicissitudes of the trail, completed the break with the seductive influences of convention. Exposed for twenty-nine months to instances of harmony between nature and culture, the explorers collected firsthand observations that reflected the original character of their venture. Their insights would have been lost had they followed any descriptive model.

Before the turn of the eighteenth century, few North American explorers had shown a concern for presenting verbal portrayals of an entire landscape as a way of arranging its details according to their beauty. When moved to describe aspects of nature, they described the course of rivers and the lay of the land or depicted Indians and their customs. The French and Indian War, at mid–

eighteenth century, induced officers and topographical engineers to draw views of North American scenery that supported troop movements and combat needs. A little later, the seemingly age-old natural wonders of the young republic came to be regarded as its antiquity and directly challenged the vocabulary and the imagination of Americans. They reacted in words and images, which quickly accepted the sublime and the beautiful as frames of reference. As a result, fresh responses came to be buried under formalities.

For Thomas Jefferson, the spectacular features of the American landscape evoked the fashionable European ideas of the sublime and the beautiful. "So beautiful an arch, so light and springing as it were up to heaven," Jefferson described the Natural Bridge on his property in Rockbridge County in the 1787 edition of his *Notes on the State of Virginia.* "It is impossible," he stressed, "for the emotions arising from the sublime to be felt beyond what they are here."

Edmund Burke had associated the sublime with pain, and Jefferson regarded the view from the top "painful and intolerable," but the one from below "delightful in an equal extreme."[18] Kant identified that dynamic state of mind as characteristic of the sublime while regarding the beautiful as its restful counterpart. His view of the vibrant character of the sublime suited the American scene well.

Americans had become attuned to change as result of their encounter with the New World. Their movement into the continent exposed them to stunning sights, which also drew them to the doctrine of the sublime. Water, as restless and driven as the invaders themselves, fascinated Americans from the beginning of colonization. They viewed ocean, river, stream, and lake as the parts of the American scenery that exceeded the corresponding features of all other lands, but the smart words of artistic theory often sapped the strength of their convictions.

Niagara Falls, the most imposing form of water in the English colonies of North America, was an early example of this. The largest waterfall in the East (from the 1760s on) helped Americans expand a scenic view into a landscape vision. The sheer magnitude of the spectacle, the constantly falling mass of water, expanded their perspective. Responding eagerly with pen, pencil, and brush, Americans added to their description of the scene the modish ideas that turned a setting into a suitable landscape.

The Niagara landscape was identified early on as "Nature's Grandest Scene." It derived its position as an American icon from the "sublime" as one of the dominant ideas of the Romantic Age. The sublime gave meaning to the masses of water plunging violently over a perpendicular barrier of rocks to the bottom far below. In the eighteenth century, the word *sublime* generally meant "high" or "elevated" and "ideal" or "heavenly." It frequently referred to God or Godlike attributes. Applied to nature, the sublime stood for the blend of terror and delight that Burke had described in his seminal essay. The emotional and aesthetic qualities attached to these ideas enabled observers to see God in any striking scenery.[19] The visions stimulated by the contemplation of forest, mountain, or waterfall, modulated by aesthetic theory, turned the descriptions of segments of nature into literary landscapes.

The 2,219 lines of a poem by Alexander Wilson, a pioneer of ornithology and American nature literature, testified to his ability accurately to describe scenery and people, flora and fauna, but his penchant for accurate observation could not protect him from the attraction of the sublime. In 1809 and 1810, his poem ran through nine numbers of the Philadelphia *Port Folio,* the first periodical designed to create an awareness of a distinctly American literature. That he published the poem anonymously ("By the Author of American Ornithology") showed Wilson was a levelheaded man who knew the limits of his poetry.

At first, the lengthy title, "The Foresters; a Poem: Descriptive of a Pedestrian Journey to the Falls of Niagara, In the Autumn of 1803," gave the wrong year for the journey, but later installments corrected the mistake. The poem depicts the two-month, twelve-hundred-mile hike of the thirty-eight-year-old Wilson and his two companions from Philadelphia to Niagara in the fall of 1804. Many stanzas, fluctuating in length between six and twenty-four lines in heroic couplets, were an excellent guide to the Pennsylvania and New York backcountry, with Wilson's careful delineation of many birds he saw or shot thrown in for good measure.

When the hikers finally heard the roaring of the falls, ideas began to inundate the description. Cascading from line to line, the rhetoric of the sublime now ran through the lines like the water of Niagara over the cataracts.

> This great, o'erwhelming work of awful Time,
> In all its dread magnificence sublime,
> Rose on our view, amid a crashing roar
> That bade us kneel, Time's great God adore.[20]

The force of nature, enlarged through the reflections on the sublime, shattered the poet's neat narrative. "Great God of nature," he expostulated,

> Where shall my tongue fit force of language find
> To speak the dread sensations of the mind.[21]

In his letters referring to Niagara Falls, Wilson resolved his predicament about the right words by using the phrase "stupendous cataract."[22] His anguish over finding words commensurate with his experience reflected not only the limits of his language but also the extent to which nature dominated his generation's culture. At the beginning of the nineteenth century, Wilson's difficulties identified him as a participant in the discovery of American nature as landscape. He and his generation started their exploration with an intriguing assumption: the possibility of a concord between nature and culture.

The intimate relationship between the opposites, so much on the mind of Wilson's generation, spoke clearly from a portrait painted by the twenty-three-year-old Rembrandt Peale in 1801. The painting, "Rubens Peale with a Geranium," gives culture

served as frontispiece of Jonathan Carver's *Travels*, published in London in 1778. This adaptation illustrates Carver's contribution to the search for the Wilderness Passage by linking the rivers of eastern North America with his River of the West. He speculated that four major rivers flowed toward the four directions of the globe from a tableland in the heart of North America: the Bourbon River, the St. Lawrence River, the Mississippi River, and the River of the West, which emptied into the Straits of Anian. That blithe assertion linked Atlantic and Pacific by way of the Western Sea and the Northwest Passage. The bold geographic vision was buttressed by references to the discoveries on the West Coast. In the Far North, Carver conceded that "These Parts are unknown," but on the top of the map he placed the Northwest Passage as "The Suppos'd Eskimeaux Passage to the South Sea."

Most invaders of North America cut their paths through the wilderness and destroyed t Indians it sheltered. Economic instinct and cultural mission called for farms and light the forest. In a weekly London journal of 1847, an illustration, "The Emigrant," anc poem, "The Emigrant's Complaint," convey the cultural loss accompanying the conqu of the forest. The emigrant is facing the sun rising "aslant the endless woods," as the fi verse describes his stance, welcoming the Sunday truce when his axe "shall mar no tre and he can lose himself in painful memories of faraway places and people. Irrespective all reflections, the dismantling of the forest continued, sustained by an advancing mocracy's organization and technology and the growing number of people seeking th share in the riches of the continent. *Howitt's Journal of Literature and Popular Progres* (June 12, 1847), p. 323.

ıe picture of three fur traders straining to move their canoe against the current shows e hardships of travel Frenchmen and Englishmen endured while they sought to traverse e forest of North America in search of the Wilderness Passage. The memory of that ic still speaks from the caption of the illustration, "In a Stiff Current." Based on a ıwing by Frederic Remington, the outstanding artist of frontier adventures, the picture companied an article by Julian Ralph, a brilliant reporter commissioned by *Harper's agazine* to write about his travels through Canada and the United States between 1891 d 1893. The illustration faces page 337 of Julian Ralph's "Talking Musquash" in *Harper's w Monthly Magazine* LXXXIV (March, 1892), pp. 492–510. The title means "talking ıskrat," or talking business, in the language of the fur traders of the Hudson's Bay ompany.

The photograph of the lower Coppermine River shows one of the rivers of Cana Northwest Territories as Samuel Hearne may have seen it during the brief subarctic sum of 1771. The Coppermine rises in the Barrens and flows north for five hundred mile Coronation Gulf of the Arctic Ocean. Dr. Denis A. St.-Onge of the Geological Sur of Canada took the photograph in the 1980s from a hill south of Bloody Fall Gorge the center of the photograph) looking north sixteen miles to the Arctic Ocean. In right background, Coronation Gulf forms the horizon. The Gorge, actually a serie rapids, was named by Hearne after he witnessed a massacre of Eskimos on July 17, 17 on the beach to the left, north of the Gorge. For most of the year the area is a w expanse of frozen earth and water. *(Courtesy of the Geological Survey of Canada [G 204961])*

From September 11 to September 22, 1805, the strenuous crossing of the Bitterroot Mountains in North Idaho on the Montana border taxed the members of the Lewis and Clark Expedition to the utmost. The eleven days of their harrowing journey on the Lolo Trail, an Indian trail across the mountains, were the ultimate ordeal of their journey. Confronting the Bitterroots ended three centuries of speculation about the existence of a Wilderness Passage through North America. The members of the expedition had hoped to find a short portage between the headwaters of the Missouri and the Columbia. Instead they struggled for 220 miles of gruelling mountain travel until they reached the Clearwater River, a tributary of the Snake River, which in turn empties into the Columbia. *(Courtesy of the National Park Service, United States Department of the Interior)*

Rembrandt Peale's 1801 painting of his brother, *Rubens Peale with a Geranium*, reflects the harmony of scene and taste, the harmony between nature and culture, which some Americans aspired to at the turn of the eighteenth century. A close look at the picture produces an awareness of the elementary division of the painting and a sense of its essential unity. The artist allotted equal space on the canvas to man and plant. His shy and reserved brother carefully holding the plant and the vigorous and brilliant geranium slightly reaching out to the man suggest the effect of restraint and cultivation that fostered the fleeting moments of harmony between nature and culture. *(The painting is reproduced with the permission of the National Gallery of Art, Washington; Patrons' Permanent Fund.)*

Almost thirty years after the Lewis and Clark expedition encountered its first grizzly in 1805, Karl Bodmer sketched a grizzly bear hunt when he accompanied a German scholar, Maximilian Prince zu Wied, to the Upper Missouri in 1833–1834. *Hunting of the Grizzly Bear* is one of the colored engravings the Swiss artist contributed in 1839 to the so-called *Atlas* of the various editions of Maximilian's *Travels*. Bodmer's drawings are praised for heir authenticity. His picture of the grizzly hunt, however, with the carcass of a buffalo n full view, was probably influenced by tales about the grizzly adventures of the Lewis and Clark expedition. The tales often spoke about a ferocious monster, without acknowledging that attacking a peaceful giant did indeed produce ferocity. The picture shown here is a black-and-white reproduction from the original *Atlas*. *(Courtesy of The Bancroft Library)*

The Bitterroot Mountains, the major obstacle in the path of the Lewis and Clark exp dition, are part of the almost four-hundred-mile-long Bitterroot Range, which forms mo of the border between Montana and Idaho. They stretch from Lolo Pass due south eighty-five miles to Nez Perce Pass. Their height and terrain, and their dissected easte face, discouraged many westbound travelers in the nineteenth century. The passing almost two centuries since the crossing of the Lewis and Clark expedition has chang the details of the scene, but the view of the Lolo Trail section of the Bitterroot Mounta still shows the difficulties of the terrain that tested stamina and spirit of the explore *(Courtesy of Dr. Merle Wells, Boise, Idaho)*

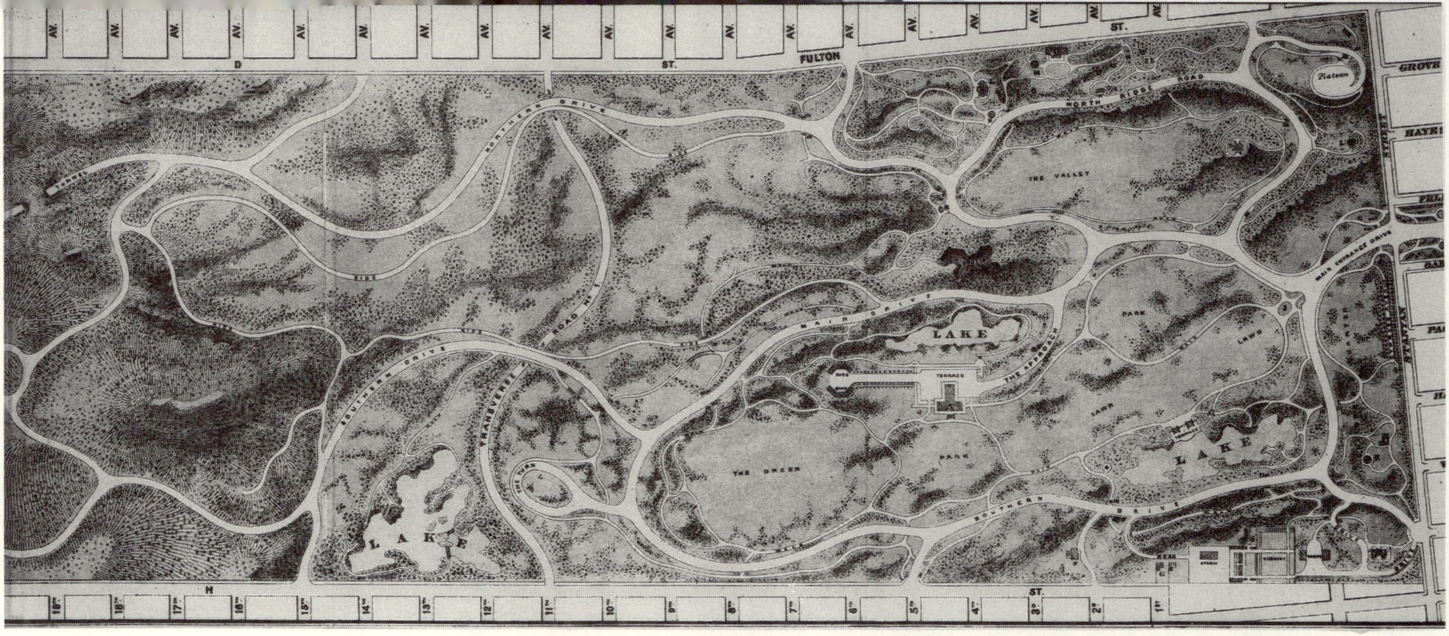

The map of the eastern section of San Francisco's Golden Gate Park, which accompanied the 1873–1874 Park Commissioners' Report, shows a variety of architectural additions to William Hammond Hall's design of a "Woodland Park." Hall and Frederick Law Olmsted, the creator of New York's Central Park, learned to make concessions to special-interest groups who hoped to shape the big-city park to their needs. In turn, both men drew steadily growing numbers of urbanites into the parks and educated them to the benefits of an encounter with nature in the big city. Hall attracted San Franciscans to the Children's Quarters with the Play-house, the Café with the Dairy, and Cypress Avenue close to the main entrance drive before the city engulfed the park and San Franciscans better understood its intangible benefits. San Francisco *Municipal Reports* (San Francisco, 1874), pp. 478–479. *(Courtesy of The Bancroft Library)*

Auburn-Cemetry in Boston is the title of the engraving in Joseph Meyer's *Universum* o 1853. Published since the 1830s in Hildburghausen in Thuringia, the popular annual o news had suffered after the Revolution of 1848. Meyer's son Hermann Julius came as refugee to the United States, founded a branch of his father's publishing house in Ne York, and kept the spirit of 1848 alive in the *Universum* article on Mount Auburn Cem etery. Its natural setting is praised; the despotic character of the narrow German graveyard condemned. The symbolic message of trees and water extolling freedom captivated th writer, who ended his paean quoting poetry about nature as the bond of humanity an the forest as a temple where "the Christian, the Heathen, the Turk, and the Jew ma rest." *Meyer's Universum* (Hildburghausen/New York, 1853), vol. XV, pp. 220–22 *(Courtesy of Dr. Marc Aurel Stommel)*

he appearance of a part of New York's Central Park in the summer of 1863 has been corded by a stereograph, a picture prepared for the stereoscope. The visitor is looking om the west over the Lake to the Bow Bridge. The picturesque scene, the size of the ishes, and the height of the trees testify to Frederick Law Olmsted's successful engineering nature in the metropolis of the United States. In the summer of 1857 he took charge Superintendent and built the park. The introduction of park sites into the collection pictures viewed by a stereoscope attested to the spreading fame of Central Park. *(Courtesy the New-York Historical Society, New York City)*

In 1865, when the photograph from the Cliff House was taken, the site of San Francis future Golden Gate Park was a vast area of shifting sand dunes. The Ocean Beach R led from the Cliff House to two other popular resorts of the 1860s, the Seal Rock Hc below and from there about two miles along the Pacific Ocean to the Ocean Side Ho Here and there, the shacks of squatters punctuated the desolate scene. After the Gol Gate Park had been established in 1870, William Hammond Hall stabilized the s dunes. During his tenure as Superintendent from 1871 to 1876 he designed the park through his vision of the Woodland Park brought the forest to San Francisco. *(Cour of The Bancroft Library)*

and nature equal weight. Rembrandt's younger brother, who had poor eyes, is wearing spectacles, holding another pair in his left hand, and reaching with his right to the potted plant on the left side of the table before him.

Rembrandt Peale balanced the endearingly frank portrayal of his brother's weakness with a painstakingly tender portrayal of the geranium. Each subject, man and plant, fills one half of the canvas. On the viewer's left is Rubens, reserved and shy, and on the right the geranium, brilliant and luxuriant, reaching towards the brother's head with lush leaves and vigorous sprouts. The consummate rendering of the geranium matches the sympathetic likeness of the young man.[23]

The equal attention man and plant received in Rembrandt Peale's portrait in 1801 indicated the advance of civilization in the United States within a generation. The balance of the painting mirrored a distinct measure of civilized people: the search for harmony between nature and culture. Roughly thirty years earlier, in 1765, the twenty-seven-year-old John Singleton Copley had painted a similar subject; however, the share of the canvas he allotted to the two poles of life indicated that his generation regarded nature differently.

"Boy with a Squirrel," a brilliant exhibition piece, won the painter his election as a Fellow of the Society of Artists of Great Britain. It shows an elegant youngster in profile behind a mahogany table, brought into strong relief by the rich tones of the velvet drape in the background. The colorfully dressed youth seems to be gazing through a window, entirely ignoring the squirrel, which his whim has placed on the immaculately polished table top. A glass of water and a few nuts on the table keep the squirrel in place, while a choker, with its expensive gold chain casually handled by the boy, doubly ensures that the pet does not stray.[24] The power of cultural conventions, trying to mold the urban life of the colonies in the ways of British cities, put nature in a subordinate role.

Within a generation, several influences contributed to bringing American culture closer to nature. The breaking of ties with

Great Britain played a major role. The American Revolution created not merely a new nation but also one with a new scale of nature. Independence cast the way Americans viewed nature under a nationalistic spell. In 1786, after a visit to several country seats in England, John Adams, one of the Founding Fathers much occupied with probing the dimensions of the new order of things, pronounced that "nature has done greater things and furnished nobler materials" in the New World than in the Old.[25]

Americans who accepted the premise felt much encouraged by the Romantic movement's emphasis on nature. The fame of the pristine forest spread abroad and attracted distinguished literary figures to the United States. François Auguste Chateaubriand, the celebrated French author and statesman, traveled in America in 1791 and 1792. One of the first and leading writers of the Romantic movement, he was fascinated by the aura of mystery surrounding the search for the Wilderness Passage, and he surrendered quickly to the lure of the West.

Chateaubriand joined a scheme for the discovery of the elusive channel and claimed to have descended the Ohio and Mississippi in 1791. Actually Chateaubriand may have traveled no farther west than Niagara. On the Canadian shore of Lake Erie, it is said, his ecstasy about pristine scenery swept him away. He jumped out of the boat, ran into the forest and began hugging trees. A loud roar rudely interrupted his impetuous communion with American nature and chased him back to the boat, where he realized that the waves pounding the beach had made the noise.[26]

Instead of dramatizing the concord between nature and culture, Lewis and Clark lived it. Experience gave an authenticity to their language that enabled them to deal with the strange world they traversed. Their description, which rarely surrendered to the sublime or the romantic imagination, relied on ordinary words to account for an original scene. When the explorers did follow convention, they not only acknowledged the help immediately, but also its degree.

On May 31, 1805, the expedition passed through the most

spectacular section of the "White Rocks" of the Missouri River, roughly between the Judith River and the Marias River. Water, wind, and sand had sculpted the light sandstone of the region into castles, cathedrals, and citadels. Karl Bodmer, the Swiss artist who accompanied Prince Maximilian zu Wied to the Upper Missouri in 1833, drew the pyramids, pillars, and pedestals, and by gracing them with statuary, made the sandstone formation a fertile playground for the imagination.

The sandstone formations "exhibit a most romantic appearance," Lewis recorded. Clark used identical language, adding a "k" to the adjective *romantic* as if to give its relatively rare use added emphasis. If the diarists had not often used each other's language, one might assume that the phrase "exhibit a most romantic appearance" had been prescribed by the Orderly Book. Sergeant John Ordway started his description of the "White Cliffs" with it, using Clark's spelling.[27]

Lewis's impressions of the "White Cliffs" have been frequently quoted because the poetic language he used is so scarce in the journals. "A thousand grotesque figures," he marveled, "with the help of a little imagination . . . are made to represent elegant ranges of lofty freestone buildings." With "the help of less imagination we see the . . . ruins of elegant buildings." He felt as if those scenes of "visionary inchantment" would never end because "so perfect indeed are those walls that I should have thought that nature had attempted here to rival the human art of masonry."[28]

Instead of a fertile imagination, thoughts of a different kind swayed the members of the Lewis and Clark expedition in their encounter with the mysteries of the wilderness. Their thoughts agreed well with the idea of usefulness that motivated them. An alliance of science and art, characteristic of American culture at the turn of the eighteenth century, shaped their relations to nature. They searched assiduously for rational explanations of the natural phenomena they encountered. Their commitment to the task of the expedition further tempered the romantic sentiments of the explorers.

During his service as Jefferson's private secretary, Lewis had been gradually inculcated with the idea of an expedition committed to scientific investigation. In that office, he looked into the affairs of the Army and performed other presidential assignments for more than two years—from April 1801 until July 1803. From the summer of 1802 on, he increasingly shared the president's political and economic objectives for a western expedition as well as his concern for scientific discoveries. During those years, Lewis made the rudiments of a scholarly investigation in Jefferson's great library.

Before leaving the East Coast for his journey through the continent, the captain read in the sciences, at times with the president's friends among the members of the American Philosophical Society. His efforts at studying astronomy, natural history, geography, meteorology, ethnology, medicine, and the practical arts showed his commitment to a scientific expedition. The extensive descriptions of plants, animals, and birds that Lewis contributed to the journals of the expedition attested to his seriousness of purpose. Furthermore, he instilled that devotion to scientific investigation into the Corps of Discovery, at least within the range of his mentor's interests. Jefferson was drawn more to botany and zoology than to geology, and Lewis and Clark consequently paid less attention to geology and mineralogy.[29]

Their exploration of a conical mound on the South Dakota plains showed their strengths and weaknesses. On August 25, 1804, a stifling, hot day, the captains probed the mystery of the Hill of Little Devils, as Lewis's map of 1806 called it. The neighboring Indian nations considered it the home of small monsters in human form, always on guard with sharp arrows to kill anyone entering their world. The story piqued the curiosity of the explorers. They went part of the way to the mound by water, and after they had left their boat at a river, Lewis and Clark and nine of their men trudged for four hours, tired and thirsty, over the level plains to the isolated hill.

After his inspection of the mound Clark noted that the wind, driving "with unusial force over the naked Plains and against this hill," propelled insects into the leeward shelter. There the explorers saw a vast number of small brown martins, members of the swallow family, catching the insects. The Indians had told them that the large assembly of birds attested to the special nature of the hill. "This is in my opinion a Sufficient proof," Clark concluded, "to produce in the Savage Mind a Confident belief of all the properties which they ascribe to it."[30] Rationality and science, in Clark's case the accurate description of careful observations, corrected for him the Indian belief about the collection of birds.

The devotion of Lewis and Clark to careful investigation thrived on a lofty sense of mission, which guided the captains' thoughts and actions. Wedded to that obligation, they labored to instill into their companions the constant devotion to the progress and the success of the expedition as part of their duty. For the captains it was an inspiring task that required unfailing attention. During crucial stages of the journey, their exhortations enabled the men to rise above drudgery and to rally to the awesome responsibility. On other occasions, the men may have taken the sense of mission as an unavoidable burden that went with the extraordinary assignment of a special Army unit.

The soldiers' complaints were rarely recorded, but they could well be inferred from the captains' praise for their devotion. Portaging around the Great Fall of the Missouri, "at every halt these poor fellows tumble down and . . . many . . . are asleep in an instant," Lewis recorded on June 23, 1805. "Some are limping from the soreness of their feet," he went on, "others faint and unable to stand for a few minutes, . . . yet no one complains, all go with cheerfulness."[31]

In light of their obligations, the captains' encounter with nature went beyond finding the right words for a landscape or creating verbal panoramas to do justice to a scene. Lewis and Clark believed that understanding new aspects of nature was the most efficient way to cope with seemingly infinite varieties of plant, trees, and animals. While ideas of the sublime and the beautiful, as well as romantic sentiments, inspired later travelers encountering the wonders of the continent, the explorers sharply curbed their emotions with a distinct dedication to utility, a mark of their enterprise.

The leaders of the expedition felt themselves pledged to an undertaking for the benefit of mankind. Their interaction with nature went beyond sentiments that might have added ideas and feelings to viewing and describing a scene. On the Missouri River, setting off from Fort Mandan on April 7, 1805, they compared their six small canoes and two pirogues to the fleets of Columbus or Captain Cook. Their boats did not seem quite so respectable, Lewis reflected, but were "still viewed by us with as much pleasure as those deservedly famed adventurers ever beheld theirs."[32]

The explorers, like their role models, yearned for their destiny to lead them to discover inexhaustible treasures for their countrymen. The magnitude of their task justified the comparison. They were "now about to penetrate a country at least two thousand miles in width," Lewis said, "on which the foot of civilized man had never trodden." The euphoria of the moment swept him away. "Entertaining as I do, the most confident hope of succeeding in a voyage which had formed a darling project of mine for the last ten years" (Lewis evidently dated his emotional involvement in the enterprise back to the year he joined the Army), "I could but esteem this moment of my departure as among the most happy of my life."[33]

Lewis and Clark found their companions equal to the promise of the momentous day. Unyielding necessity and military discipline had unified the unruly lot of men they had gathered during the winter of 1803 to 1804 in an encampment on the eastern shore of the Mississippi, opposite the mouth of the Missouri, variously called the Wood River cantonment or Camp Dubois. With stern discipline, reinforced by six courts-martial, the captains had made a mixed collection of soldiers, backwoodsmen, and guides into an extraordinary unit, pledged to the success of the mission.

The men measured up to the captains' expectations. The party was "in excellent health and sperits, zealously attached to the enterprise, and anxious to proceed." Lewis, who earlier in the same entry chided himself for possible distortions "when the imagination is suffered to wander," concluded his eulogy of the men: "Not a whisper of murmur or discontent to be heard among them, but all act in unison, and with the most perfect harmony."[34]

The spirit of mission lightened Clark's awareness of the ordeal facing the expedition when he saw the Rocky Mountains "for the first time with certainty" on May 26, 1805. "I felt a secret pleasure in finding myself so near the head of the heretofore conceived boundless Missouri," but he immediately qualified the reference to his emotions. "When I reflected on the difficulties which this snowey barrier would most probably throw in my way to the Pacific Ocean, and the sufferings and hardships of my self and party in them, it in some measure counterbalanced the joy I had felt in the first moments in which I gazed on them." The goal of the expedition saved him from losing himself in reflection. "As I always held it little Short of criminality to anticipate evils," he resolved; "I will allow it to be a good comfortable road until I am compelled to believe otherwise."[35] Tersely responding to a command of his culture, Clark set out to overcome the natural obstacles in the path of the expedition.

The unexpected hardships of the journey heightened Lewis's sense of mission. His thirty-first birthday, on August 18, 1804, found the expedition between the Platte and the Vermilion rivers, making its way up the Missouri to the Mandan villages. Lewis made no reference to his birthday. "Cap L. Birth Day," Clark noted laconically in his journal; "the evening was closed with an extra gill of whiskey and a Dance untill 11 o'Clock."[36] Lewis's thirty-second birthday came after the expedition had mastered the sub-zero winter of the Mandan villages, portaged the Great Falls of the Missouri, and made the crucial contact with the Shoshone Indians. The occasion provoked Lewis to an eloquent statement about the spirit of mission that guided him.

"I reflected that I had done but little, very little, indeed, to further the happiness of the human race, or to advance the information of the succeeding generation," Lewis stated on August 18, 1805. "I viewed with regret the many hours I have spent in indolence," he added dejectedly, "and now soarly feel the want of that information which those hours would have given me had they been judiciously expanded." Overcoming the gloom, he rallied his spirits by reminding himself that the past cannot be recalled, and "resolved in future to redouble my exertions and . . . to live *for mankind,* as I have heretofore lived *for myself.*"[37]

The events preceding this journal entry spurred Lewis to his bold resolution. Vital to the success of the expedition, they were of a different order from his encounter with the striking scene of the Great Falls, which he could write off by evoking the sublime. Two days before his birthday, Lewis had initiated negotiations for horses with Chief Cameawhait and his group of Shoshone Indians. The task had fallen to him because he chanced on the Indians when he went ahead with three men to scout the way. At that moment Clark, better versed in Indian diplomacy, was acting as river expert, guiding the canoes up the Missouri.

If Lewis could obtain horses now, he felt, they would enable the expedition to move their baggage from the head of canoe navigation on the Missouri across the continental divide to the drainage system of the Columbia. Horses were now essential for the success of his mission. The captain was as anxious about the outcome of the parley as the Indians, who seemed concerned during the negotiations that they were being lured into a death trap by strangers.

Lewis had asked the Indians to follow him to the Missouri, where he expected to meet Clark and the expedition with the canoes. Communicating mostly by signs, he hoped he had impressed them with his peaceful intentions, the promise of presents, and the pledge of trade goods. He feared that the Indians might leave him if they felt betrayed, disperse and hide in the mountains, and deprive the expedition of any chance to get horses. Such an outcome, he speculated, "might so discourage the men as to defeat the expedition altogether." At night he hardly slept, "my mind dwelling on the state of the expedition which I have ever held in equal estimation with my own existence."[38]

At the same time, at the Missouri, Clark struggled to maintain the esprit de corps. He faced tired people, exhausted from the daily drudgery of pulling the canoes against the rapid current of the shallow river or carrying craft and cargo over shoals and ledges. The complaints about the hardships and the desire to beach the canoes and go by land only increased their fatigue. "Capt. C. encouraged them and passifyed them," Lewis recorded, cryptically.[39] The taciturn Clark must have used a kind of persuasion that went beyond the threat of court-martial, which the captains no longer considered appropriate after the exposure to the long winter with the Mandan had tightened their bonds with their men. Undoubtedly he bolstered the men's stamina by reminding them of the significance of the current ordeal for the success of the expedition.

One of the expedition's tasks was finding the headwaters of the Missouri River. That goal also furnished the explorers with their own variant of the romance that other intruders in the wilderness found when they hugged a tall tree or contemplated a mountain ridge. The name "3000 mile Island," which, on August 11, 1805, William Clark gave to a large island in the Missouri that at that moment seemed to him three thousand miles from the river's mouth, indicated that the magic of numbers helped the expedition reach its destination. By naming the island, the explorers took possession of a part of the continent, as many intruders had done before them. They also used the name to combat one of nature's primary defenses against interlopers: distance.

Clark had attempted to guess the distances beyond the Mandan villages to the continental divide and the Pacific during the winter of 1803 to 1804, when the expedition stayed five months at Camp Dubois on the Mississippi. He underestimated the length of travel considerably. He estimated nine hundred miles for the trip from the Mandan to the continental divide, while the expedition actually covered fifteen hundred miles. For the trip from the divide to the Pacific, he put down 650 miles. It actually took 834 miles. He was short about one thousand miles for the stretch between the Mississippi and the Pacific; the explorers covered 3,958 miles. Furthermore, the actual travel time Clark calculated was off, because he did not take rest periods or Indian councils into account.[40] Approaching the source of the Missouri, however, the men sensed very directly where they were. They spent a large part of every day in the shallow water dragging the canoes behind them over obstacles in the river, which increased with each day they came closer to the headwaters of the Missouri.

While Clark directed the slow advance of the canoes, Lewis, with three men, pushed ahead on a well-traveled Indian road to the source of the river. He kept the daily progress report of his journal entries remarkably free of the excitement that urged him and his men higher up the trail. "The road took us to the most distant fountain of the waters of the Mighty Missouri," he calmly noted on August 12, 1805, "in surch of which we have spent so many toilsome days and wristless nights."

Once he had taken care of the routine entries, Lewis unburdened himself. "Thus far I had accomplished one of those great objects on which my mind has been unalterably fixed for many years," he exulted (with an understandable disregard for the actual length of time he had been concerned with the Missouri). Undoubtedly the momentous occasion warranted some exaggeration. "Judge then of the pleasure," he rejoiced, "in allaying my thirst with this pure and ice-cold water." Two miles below the spring, one of the men had celebrated in his own way. Hugh McNeal "exultingly stood with a foot on each side of this little rivulet and thanked his god that he had lived to bestride the mighty & heretofore deemed endless Missouri."[41]

Emotionally and logistically, the moment was long overdue, because the expedition had fallen behind its timetable. The pressure to live up to the exalted expectations surrounding the assignment interfered with the explorers' assessment of reality. They expected the source of the river to be in the path of the expedition, but the "most distant fountain" the explorers came across was not the source of the Missouri. On August 10, when the four men had reached a point where the river divided into two equal branches, Lewis chose the one leading generally in the western direction the party intended to go. To reach the source, a naturalist and historian of the expedition explained, a traveler must climb the other branch (Red Rock Creek, today) "to Upper Red Rock Lake in southern Montana just west of Yellowstone Park."[42] The explorers' cultural heritage had strengthened their belief that they might find an easy portage between the two water systems by following the Missouri to its source. That hope explained the significance they attached to the fountain.

The summit of the pass, a short distance from the spring, tested the strength of the four men's zeal. Lewis "discovered immense ranges of high mountains still to the West of us with their tops partially covered with snow." His disappointment must have been immense, too, but the captain quickly overcame his frustration by rushing into action. He hurried down a steep slope to a "handsome bold runing Creek of cold Clear water." Here, Lewis exulted, "I first tasted the water of the great Columbia river."[43]

When Private Joseph Whitehouse, who had been with the canoe party, caught up with the advance, he momentarily forgot the frigid water and the freezing mornings on the river. Captain Lewis and his men, he wrote in his journal, "drank at the head waters or Spring of the Missourie and went only about a mile and drank out of the head Spring of the Columbian River which ran west." Faithful to the mission, he repeated the captain's words; the version of reality preferred by the explorers.[44]

Lewis and his men actually drank water from a tributary of the Lemhi River, which, by way of the Salmon River and the Snake River, ultimately finds its way to the Columbia River. The magic of water, powerful enough to forge a convenient continental link, sustained Lewis's illusion. When the entire Corps of Discovery, now mounted on horses they had obtained in the meantime from the Shoshone, "arrived at the extreme source of the Missouri" on August 26, 1805, Lewis stopped a few minutes. The men drank and rejoiced at "having at length arrived at this long wished for point." By now, taking the waters on both sides of the continental divide had become a ritual, and when they reached "the fine spring on the other side of the mountain," Lewis "halted to dine and graize our horses."[45]

The sense of mission enabled the explorers to balance nature and culture. Their duty fortified them against the disappointment and drudgery inflicted by a terrain that did not always oblige their expectations. With a few exceptions, their commitment also ensured peaceful encounters with Indians. The explorers' need, desire, and ability to move westward without defying nature placed the contact between the members of the two races on the basis of a common humanity. Although Hearne and Mackenzie had set the outstanding examples, the accomplishment of Lewis and Clark stood out in light of the history of conflict that marked the paths of the Anglo-American intruders in North America.

The friendly relations of the expedition with Indians were based to a considerable extent on the explorers' awareness that the success of their mission depended on the good will of Indians. That realization frequently checked the cultural bias of captains and men. On July 26, 1806, on their return trip, while tracing the course of the Marias River in present-day Montana, Lewis and three companions camped with a group of Blackfoot Indians, whom they had met along Two Medicine River. Next morning one of the men stabbed and killed an Indian who was trying to run away with two guns he had stolen. While the main party of Indians used the confusion to drive off some of the explorers' horses, Lewis killed a Blackfoot when he attempted to get his horse back. During the struggle, two men drew their guns to shoot another Indian. Lewis interfered because that Indian "did not appear to be about to make any resistance or commit any offensive act." The third man, who by now had joined them, also asked the captain "if he might not kill the fellow," which Lewis "also forbid as the indian did not appear to wish to kill us."[46]

It was a confused morning, but despite his fear of the Blackfoot Indians, Lewis kept himself and his men from shedding more blood or from risking their lives. His restraint formed a striking contrast with the behavior of white men before and after him. It was indeed remarkable because in general the explorers considered the Indians inferior people. In Lewis's time, almost a century before ideas of cultural relativism would gain some credence, the explorers regarded the Indians as savages.

The label *savages* automatically put the Indians in an inferior position, characterized by squalor and cruelty. Hand in hand with the stereotype went a belief in the essential irrationality of Indian behavior. At times the Indian attitude, defying the logic so much cherished by white people, seemed to threaten the Corps of Discovery. The explorers' concern about their timetable created other impasses. Several Shoshone warriors wanted to air their views about selling horses to the explorers, and the Indian custom of hearing everyone on an important matter prolonged the negotiations. The fate of the expedition "appeared at this moment to depend in a great measure upon the caprice of a few savages who are ever as fickle as the wind," Lewis summed up his impressions about the negotiations with the Shoshone on August 16, 1805.[47]

Despite their bias, the explorers showed compassion for the plight of Indians. A few starving Shoshone shocked Lewis when he saw them devouring the raw guts of a deer. "I really did not untill now think that human nature ever presented itself in a shape so nearly allyed to the brute creation," he wrote in his journal on August 16, 1805. "I viewed these poor starved devils with pity and compassion."[48] However, neither gratitude to the Shoshone, who were instrumental in getting the explorers across the mountain barrier, nor empathy with the plight of hungry people modified the stereotype.

The Indians' concept of time fit Lewis's preconception. The

Shoshone seemed to go back and forth endlessly before the explorers could obtain horses from them. The etiquette of the council needed to be observed, and gifts had to reach chiefs and warriors in the right order. The Indians' intransigent individualism and concern for everyone's dignity gave everyone a voice in deliberations. The time consumed by the formalities of the parleys irked an Army captain used to issuing orders that he expected to be obeyed promptly. "Determined to keep the indians in a good humour if possible, and to loose no time in obtaining the necessary number of horses," Lewis "directed the fiddle to be played." Although all went well on August 26, 1805, Lewis remained troubled. The soldiers danced cheerfully, "much to the amusement and gratification of the natives, though I must confess that the state of my own mind at this moment did not accord well with the prevailing mirth as I somewhat feared that the caprice of the indians might suddenly induce them to withold their horses from us."[49]

Some of the prejudices stemmed from a bent of the white mind that denied the Indian some basic human traits. At the end of a trading session with Indians at Fort Clatsop, on December 12, 1805, Clark wrote that they "never close a bargin except they think they have the advantage."[50] That tendency to put Indians into a category of creatures different from human beings marked the entire history of the contact between the two races, despite the many observations that Indians shared many of the white men's traits. "They are . . . so malicious," Captain John Smith observed about "the natural inhabitants" of Virginia roughly two hundred years before Clark, "that they seldom forget an injury."[51]

In addition to the designation of "savages," the intruders of North America had embedded in the collective subconscious and the common speech of white people another popular phrase. They referred to the Indians, and addressed them, as "our children." In common parlance, it was not an endearing term. Instead of conveying affection for people succumbing to the pernicious onslaught of disease, trade, and force, the use of the epithet revealed the conquerors' condescension.

Lewis and Clark employed the phrase as a matter of course. In councils and during meetings they addressed Indians as "our children," without any thought beyond the assumption that the words expressed the proper relationship between the various Indian nations they encountered and the Great White Father in Washington they represented. At times, the circumstances of the captains' use of the term indicated that they relied on it to assert the limits of a formal relationship that actually seemed to give way to human contact.

At the junction of the Snake River and the Columbia River, which the expedition reached in October, 1805, a Nez Perce chief arrived in camp with two hundred men soon after the fires had been started. Beating drums and dancing, the Indians formed a half circle around the explorers and sang. All smoked together, and the captains assured the chief of "our friendly disposition to all nations and our joy in Seeing those of our Children around us." After presents had been exchanged, the Indians returned to their camp, "but Several returned and delayed with us untill bedtime," Clark reported.[52]

The Indian welcome at the Columbia meshed with the traveler's relief at having finally reached the river that would take the Corps of Discovery to the Pacific. The incident increased the explorers' affections for the Nez Perce, who had greeted them amicably after they straggled into their settlement, exhausted and disheartened from the difficult crossing of the continental divide. The phrase "our children," however, kept intact the distance between savages and civilized people the captains thought necessary to observe.

The reception indicated that the Nez Perce had not often been exposed to a large group of white men. The Nez Perce's decorum formed a striking contrast with other Indian nations the expedition met farther down the Columbia River. At the camp of the Kreluit, who served as middlemen in the trade between coastal Indians and those higher up the Columbia, the expedition met several canoes of men dressed for meeting white people. "They had scarlet & blue blankets Salor Jackets, overalls, Shirts and hats independant of their usial dress," Clark described their appearance. He noted other attributes of white civilization the Kreluit had acquired: "Most of them had either . . . Muskets or pistols and tin flasks to hold their powder." The changed appearance of the Indians bothered him. "Those fellows we found assumeing and disagreeable," Clark concluded. He was also put off by the Indian attitude, which the trade goods of his culture had affected; "however, we Smoked with them and treated them with every attention & friendship."[53]

The impulse to care for the Indians, which the spirit of mission demanded, found frequent expression in the medical help provided by the explorers. Early on, the major share of this task fell into Clark's hands. Among the ailments of his many patients, he invariably faced forms of rheumatism, strained muscles, abrasions, and sore eyes. For treatments he relied on sympathy and common-sense cures, bleeding and sweating, ointment and eyewash. In order to dull pain, he resorted at times to laudanum (a tincture of opium) from the medicine chest of the expedition.

The captains realized that the cures, or for that matter, any medical treatment, increased the good will of the Indians. The progress of the expedition depended on the Indians' attitude towards the explorers. That held true for the westward voyage as much as for the return journey. When the snow of the Bitterroots blocked their return trek through "those dreaded mountains," the expedition spent almost a month with the Nez Perce at the north bank of the Clearwater River, near present-day Kamiah, Idaho. At this location, generally referred to as Camp Chopunnish (after the captains' name for the Nez Perce), Clark practiced his medicine extensively because the expedition remained longer there than at any other place, except at Fort Mandan at the Great Bend of the Missouri and Fort Clatsop near the Pacific coast.

Clark, whose reputation as physician among the Nez Perce dated back to his cures during the westbound voyage, treated a constant stream of Indians who sought his help. "After brackfast," Clark reported on May 12, 1806, "I began to administer eye water and in a fiew minits had near 40 applicants with sore eyes, and maney others with other complaints."[54] He drained abscesses, relieved depressions, and tackled cases "intirely out of the power of Medison." The explorers relied on Clark's healing power to its limits in their diplomatic and trade relations, but they watched to see that their medicines and treatments did not harm the patients.

Clark's most famous cure at Camp Chopunnish involved an unnamed chief. The case provided, not only insight into the captain's medical repertoire, but also into other effects that a prolonged contact with one patient in Indian society could have. Although quite healthy in general, the chief had been unable to move his limbs for some time. The captains considered the symptoms in detail and speculated about their origin. Baffled by the patient's ailment, they turned from diagnosis to therapy in the hope that a cure would not only help a sick man but also maintain and strengthen their good relations with the Nez Perce during the long stay.

Clark applied a range of remedies, but they produced no result. He kept trying without success, and then realized that he had a sick chief in his care whom the man's relatives now considered to be his exclusive problem. Clark finally turned to sweating, although he had initially favored "cooling medicines." The first attempt to sweat the patient failed, but after a larger sweat pit had been dug, the limbs gradually responded to repeated heat treatment. "The sick Chief is fast on the recovery," Clark diagnosed on June 8, 1806; "he can bear his weight on his legs, and has acquired a considerable portion of strength."[55]

Concern about humanity, trade, and diplomacy contributed to the chief's care. During a month while the snow of the Bitterroot Ranges blocked the return trail of the expedition, treating a leading man of the host nation ensured the guests' continued welcome. In general, the welfare of the expedition must have often decided who received care. On the return trip up the Columbia, when the expedition tried to obtain horses on April 18, 1806, Clark "dressed the sores of the principal Chief . . . and promised . . . some Medicine for to cure his sores." He also treated the chief's wife for her pain in the back, although he considered her "a sulky Bitch," because he thought helping her would provide a "good oppertunity to get her on my side." The woman soon felt much better after Clark had rubbed camphor on her temples and back and applied warm flannel to her spine. "This I thought a favourable time to trade with the chief who had more horses than all the nation besides." His calculation proved correct when the grateful husband accepted Clark's offer for two horses.[56]

The medical aid offered by the expedition to Indians was a human contact the captains readily incorporated into their daily duties. They found that it was much more taxing to deal with a more intimate relationship than doctoring the sick. In general, they tolerated sexual relations between their men and Indian women as a matter of course. Lewis told himself that it was impossible "to prevent this mutual exchange of good officies altogether, particularly on the part of our young men whom some months abstanence have made very polite to those tawney damsels."[57]

The subject of sex, extending for the captains from disease to chastity, stimulated calls for medicine and opportunity for reflection. Venereal disease had to be treated in particular during the stay in the winter quarters at Fort Mandan and Fort Clatsop. Mercury served as a cure. The subject of sexual intercourse once led Lewis to speculate about human affairs in terms of cultural differences between red and white people as well as between Indian nations. More often than not, the captains kept their silence, although on one occasion the sexual relations of the men with Indian women became public.

Years before the arrival of the expedition at the Great Bend of the Missouri, the Mandan had incorporated white males into one of their rituals. In the ceremony, these men, mostly traders, served as sources of power, like famous Mandan. During the ritual young Indians offered their wives to the traders and soldiers and to accomplished Mandan hunters and warriors to ensure the transfer of experience through intercourse. The soldiers participated extensively in the ritual, according to one trader's caustic comment about their devotion to the custom.[58]

The cultural complexity of the ritual must have severely taxed the ethnographic knowledge of the captains, who did not record their reaction. In general they preferred to use exhortations to deal with problems stemming from sexual relations. On August 19, 1805, Lewis asked his men to give Indians "no cause of jealousy by having connection with their women" without their husbands' knowledge. With Indians, he counseled, "strange as it may seem," such relation "is considered as disgracefull to the husband, as clandestine connections of a similar kind are among civilized nations."[59] During the previous winter, at Fort Mandan, Clark had tried to solve a case of confusion and jealousy arising from the relations between the soldiers and village women with the rather farfetched claim that he believed the men would not "touch a woman if they knew her to be the wife of another man."[60]

The captains' understanding of their mission was adaptable enough to encompass the complex issues surrounding the killing of Indians or the intercourse with their women. The explorers' duty to work for peace between the Indian nations and themselves ensured that they maintained a considerate attitude towards Indians, despite their ignorance about the cultural differences between red and white people. The task called for establishing and maintaining friendly contact with diverse groups of strange people. Furthermore, the explorers were charged with instructing the Indians about the Great White Father in Washington, the advantages of trade relations, and the need for intertribal peace. The sufferings of the sick placed the complex task on a practical level. Clark's skill as a healer and the strong constitution of his patients, more often than not, guaranteed an initial success. The explorers' sexual intercourse with Indian women expanded relations into the realm of personal contact and tribal ritual, emotions and lust. Against that complex set of experiences, the official task of diplomatic and trade relations needed to be carried out.

The singlemindedness of purpose that characterized the expedition also guided the explorers through the stress and strain of their own situation. Their commitment eased the hardships the topography and the climate of the Rocky Mountains had in store for the explorers. At times emotional reactions were stirred entirely by accident. Their return in June, 1806, to Weippe Prairie, the western end of the Lolo Trail leading over the Bitterroot Mountains, illustrated the interaction. The experience exemplified the power of the elements when the chance encounter with an enchanted landscape of spring flowers lifted the explorers' depression, suffered in the face of barriers of snow blocking the advance of the expedition.

"In order to prepare in the most ample manner in our power to meet that wretched portion of our journy," the expedition stayed about seven weeks among the Nez Perce before attempting to tackle the Lolo Trail again.[61] The explorers traded for supplies and tried to regain control of their horses, which had become so wild that the men could not round them up in the morning without Indian help. With the exception of the hunters, the men "have had so little to do that they are geting reather lazy and slouthfull," Lewis observed on June 8, when foot races and games with Indians provided some exercise.[62]

The captains had no control over the delay, because the expedition had arrived among the Nez Perce far too early in the year for the return trip over the Lolo Trail. Repeatedly the Nez Perce warned them to wait for the snow of the Bitterroots to melt enough for game and grass to reappear and to permit a crossing with horses. Spurred by the captains' growing impatience to move on, the expedition set off on June 10 for Weippe Prairie. It was a happy destination for everyone, because there, the last fall, they had first met the Nez Perce after the difficult crossing of the Bitterroots.

A daylong ordeal took the explorers on switchbacks into steep canyons and over tall ridges. That night the expedition made camp on a field of camas, an edible root of the lily family and an important part of the Nez Perce's food supply. Here the explorers planned to hunt for a few days, to lay in meat, and to wait for the trail to clear. Their spirits rose at the sight of a beautiful scene. Covering about two thousand acres, the camas or quawmash "at this time looks beautiful," Sergeant Gass recorded in his journal, "being in full bloom, with flowers of a pale blue colour."[63]

For four days, the expedition camped on the border of an "extensive level and beautifull prairie," Lewis wrote on June 12. "The quawmash is now in full blume and from the colour of its bloom . . . it resembles lakes of fine clear water," he noted. "So complete is this deseption that on first sight I could have swoarn it was water."[64] About thirty years later, Father Nicolas Point, who in the 1840s worked as a Catholic missionary and draftsman among the Flathead, Blackfoot, and Nez Perce, got a similar impression when he saw the beautiful blue flower of the camas that "makes the plain on which it abounds look like a lake."[65]

With the magnificent illusion of a beautiful week of mountain spring on their mind, on June 15 the explorers made their first attempt to recross the Bitterroots on the Lolo Trail. As the road took them deeper into the mountains, they found the valleys still covered in snow. The condition of "this comparatively low region," Clark admitted, "augers but unfavourably with rispect to the practibility of passing the mountains."[66] Two days later they found themselves "invelloped in snow from 12 to 15 feet deep," Lewis wrote on June 17. "Here was winter with all it's rigors; the air was cold, my hands and feet were benumbed." The captains "conceived it madness . . . to proceed without a guide," and resolved to "procure an indian to conduct us over the snowey mountains." Nothing but a retreat remained, but the return to the magic of the blue camas flowers ameliorated their disappointment. "The party were a good deel dejected tho' not as much as I had apprehended," Lewis acknowledged. " This is the first time since we have been on this long tour that we have ever been compelled to retreat or make a retrograde march."[67]

Lewis's faith in a benign nature working on behalf of the expedition was a corollary of his perception that doing one's duty answered all problems. He simply ignored some of the experiences that conflicted with his faith. Two weeks earlier, the captain had reflected in his journal on several retreats nature had forced on the expedition. He failed to recall an earlier sequence of adventures, however, because his anxiety about the crossing of the Bitterroots absorbed his attention. No one had yet "forgotten our suffering in those mountains" during the east–west transit, Lewis observed on June 2, 1806, "and I think it probable we never shall."[68] In the face of the threatening mountains, Lewis forgot to mention the fear tinged with respect that the grizzly had earned from the explorers.

The expedition's encounters with the grizzly exemplified one extreme of the confrontation between nature and culture. The clashes surprised the explorers, because they had heard details about the grizzly only from the Indians. Reports of early sightings of the animal did not circulate among the European newcomers. Francisco Vásquez de Coronado probably saw the grizzly on his expedition in the Southwest in 1540. The first recorded sighting occurred at the turn of 1602. While Sebastían Vizcaíno anchored at the site of Monterey, bears came down to the beach at night to feed on the carcass of a whale. They could only have been grizzly because black bears were not native there.[69] In the eighteenth century the journals of some explorers of Canada alerted only a few white people to the existence of the grizzly, and the American explorers had quite a surprise waiting for them.

Amazed at the size of the bear, the members of the Lewis and Clark expedition could neither leave the animal alone nor control their eagerness to kill it. The grizzly seemed to challenge hunter mentality of the explorers directly, who responded by emptying their rifles into the huge animal. So the explorers never saw the peaceful giant; they only encountered disturbed and provoked bears, cornered or wounded, maddened by fear or pain, and their stories about the experience created the reputation of the grizzly as a ferocious beast.

Their adventures were even more frightening as the firepower of their Kentucky rifles was limited. Even when a ball pierced its heart, the grizzly often lived on. Only several well-placed bullets in vital areas could bring the animal down. The explorers often depended on their wits and agility to get away from an enraged grizzly. The culture of the hunter and the technology of firearms warped the bear's true nature. Distorted tales did the rest and created a monster.

Stories about the hunters' adventures may have contributed to the scientific term for the grizzly. George Ord, the naturalist and philologist, chose *Ursus horribilis*, "horrible bear," in his formal description of 1815. The common name took hold only slowly. The animal's color, which differed much with individual bears, explained the variety of names Lewis and Clark used for the grizzly. Theodore Roosevelt, the big-game hunter among the presidents of the United States, did not like "grizzly" because it means "grizzled" or "gray." He argued that "grisly," meaning "ghastly" or "horrifying," suited the animal better.[70] His comment also reflected the respect the bear had generally gained in the nineteenth century.

The tribute that the Lewis and Clark expedition learned to pay the grizzly contributed to changing the status of the bear in Anglo-American culture. The new outlook coincided with the growing concern of late eighteenth-century England about the treatment of animals in general. In the colonies, one attitude toward the bear appeared to be a variation of some notoriously cruel English practices. Colonists referred to bears to ridicule people and the animal itself.

A story from the Carolinas at the end of the seventeenth century, strongly disputed and denied, related that wicked men tricked a minister of the Church of England "who was too great a Lover of Strong Liquor" into baptizing a bear.[71] In the first half of the eighteenth century, William Byrd of Westover collected many references to bears in his writings. Although generally sympathetic to the animal, he tended to mock its appearance, walk, and courage. A barking dog decided the "romantic adventure" of one of Byrd's men with a bear that had come to the rescue of a cub; the dog diverted the bear so the man got away.[72] By contrast, the experience of the Lewis and Clark expedition gave dignity to the bear.

The weight of the cultural heritage worked against the grizzly, but slowly the bear gained the respect of the explorers. Even after Lewis first killed a grizzly on April 29, 1805, he still treated lightly the Mandan's warning about an enraged bear's ferocity, although the badly wounded animal had chased him and a companion eighty yards before their repeated firing killed it. Indians might well fear the grizzly, the captain noted, but to " skillfull riflemen they are by no means as . . . dangerous as they have been represented."[73]

A few days later, Lewis's opinion about the grizzly changed. On May 5, Clark and another hunter killed the largest grizzly the explorers had yet seen. The bear was "extremely hard to kill," Lewis reported, and kept roaring tremendously from the moment he was shot. "Nothwithstanding he had five balls through his lungs and five others in various parts," the grizzly swam to a sandbar in the middle of the Missouri, and "it was at least twenty minutes before he died." Clark commented at a length that spoke volumes: "A turrible looking animal . . . which we found very hard to kill. We Shot ten Balls into him before we killed him, & 5 of those Balls through his lights."[74] A reader unfamiliar with the language of the hunt will find the last line of the quote even more terrifying until learning that the lungs of animals are called "lights" on account of their lightness.

On the following day, when the explorers noted a grizzly swimming across the Missouri above them, Lewis admitted that the "curiosity of our party is pretty well satisfied with rispect to this animal." Size, appearance, and "the difficulty with which they die when even shot through the vital parts, has staggered the resolution of several" men, while others still seemed "keen for action with the bear."[75]

Without directly owning up to his feelings, Lewis himself seemed to have had enough of the grizzly. In the next sentence of his journal he identified the bear as a dangerous enemy and resorted to ridicule as one way to bolster his courage to face the animal. He called the grizzly "these gentlemen," employing the same language he used for Indians he considered either difficult to manage or outright hostile. At times his ridicule recalled the bear-baiting streak in Anglo-American culture: They "will give us some amusement shortly as they soon begin now to coppolate"; and with the sexual slur he hoped to denigrate the grizzly's symbolic potency.[76]

Before the week had passed, Lewis feared the grizzly more than the Indians. On May 11, a private who had permission to walk ashore chased after the flotilla for help. Several minutes after he caught up, the exhausted man was able to tell Lewis that he had badly wounded a grizzly. It pursued him a long way, but could not overtake him. Lewis took seven men "in quest of the monster," and killed it.

The hunters found that the grizzly had run almost two miles with a ball through the center of his lung, dug a bed in the underbrush, and "was perfectly alive . . . 2 hours after he received the wound." The bear's strength shook Lewis. "I must confess," he wrote, "that I do not like the gentlemen and had reather fight two Indians than one bear." The raw power of nature manifest in the bear's struggle unnerved the captain. The bear, he said, "being so hard to die rather intimidates us all."[77]

"So hard to die": his tribute to the bear's stamina stayed with the thirty-one-year-old Lewis for his few remaining years. Even after the return of the expedition and his appointment as governor of the Territory of Louisiana in 1806, the words remained in his mind, despite the changes in his life. His sense of mission gave way to land speculation, political fights, hard drinking, and emotional turmoil. His correspondence with Jefferson lapsed.

Then, in the last hours of his life, in his thirty-fifth year, when he lay dying in an inn on the Natchez Trace in Tennessee, he "often said, 'I am no coward, but I am *so* strong, *so hard to die.*' "[78] So the innkeeper's wife told Alexander Wilson when, during a field trip in Tennessee, the ornithologist inquired about his friend's end. The emphasis Wilson added to the words suggests that he may have heard them before, perhaps while Lewis was on the East Coast after the expedition. To the dying Lewis, on the run from detractors and creditors, his own death throes evoked the grizzly's death at the Great Falls of the Missouri.

Lewis had been on the way from St. Louis to Washington, D.C., to account for his use of government money. During the eleven-day trip down the Mississippi, he reportedly tried and failed twice to kill himself. He suddenly decided to go overland on the Natchez Trace instead of by ship via New Orleans. During his last hours on the Natchez Trace he did not fear death, but the end came slowly, although he had shot himself in the head and chest. The suffering man may have recalled how many bullets it took to bring down the grizzly. One of Lewis's last utterances, the words seemed to confirm Clark's fear expressed after Lewis's death that "the weight of his mind has overcome him."[79]

The explorers' experience with the grizzly and the tales circulating about their adventures coincided with the growing respect nineteenth-century Americans extended to the bear. The different attitude became visible in 1846. The animal appeared on the banner of the Bear Flag Revolt, which briefly established the Republic of California on the eve of the conquest of the Mexican territory by the United States. The flag, designed by William L. Todd, a nephew of Mary Todd Lincoln, showed a grizzly facing a brownish star in the upper left-hand corner above the word, "California Republic," and a red stripe at the bottom. In 1911 the California State Legislature adopted a modified version as the state flag.

In 1849, the grizzly had already found its way onto the Great Seal of the State of California. In the design the grizzly as the symbol of strength guards Minerva, the goddess of wisdom, who sprang full-grown from Jupiter's brow; like California, which joined the Union as full-fledged state without having been a territory. In 1868 Bret Harte assigned a special place to the grizzly in the literature of the Far West when he placed a picture of the bear serenely walking away from a railroad track on the cover of the *Overland Monthly*, a regional magazine published in San Francisco. At the beginning of the twentieth century, the teddy bear appeared, named after big-game hunter Theodore "Teddy" Roosevelt. The popularity of the children's toy completed the animal's rehabilitation, which gained momentum through the stories about the encounter of the Lewis and Clark expedition with the grizzly.

The respect the explorers learned to extend to the grizzly represented another step towards a balance between nature and culture and was one of the striking achievements of their trek. Their experience made them see that survival could be ensured without the destruction of nature. The insight touched on the precarious balance shaken early on in human history by the truism that people's interference with nature was the first evidence of culture. With that new awareness it ought to have become essential to keep the advances of culture in harmony with nature's ability to regenerate the resources damaged by people.

As long as the hunters' mastery of their Kentucky rifles provided just enough game to sustain the expedition, the explorers kept the precious balance. The adventures with the grizzly challenged the assumption that all game had to be fired at or that the hunt ended only with the slaughter of all animals within reach. "Altho' game is very abundant and gentle," Lewis had written earlier on April 27, 1805, at the confluence of the Yellowstone and the Missouri, "we only kill as much as is necessary for food." Clark wrote on the same day: "Altho the game of different kinds are in abundance we kill nothing but what we can make use of."[80] The captains recognized the importance of keeping the killing of animals within limits. They saw the carcasses of buffalo driven by Indian hunters over the cliffs of the

Missouri, and the sight confirmed the explorers' determination to exercise restraint while hunting.

Irrespective of resolutions and experiences, the urge to shoot remained strong, particularly if the target was large or looked unusual. After all, in the early nineteenth century it was also the most convenient way to get acquainted with and study the animals of the strange world the explorers traversed. Behind almost every description or etching of a bird published by Alexander Wilson or John James Audubon was a dead animal, which provided an opportunity to see and describe any bird accurately. These considerations explained the expedition's reaction to the California condor. Before its extinction on the open range the huge vulture soared far beyond the narrow realm it was later reduced to.

On November 18, 1805, after the party had reached the Pacific Ocean, one of the men shot a "Buzzard of the large Kind," which was feeding on a dead whale on the beach. It "measured from the tips of the wings across 9 1/2 feet," Clark reported carefully, "from the point of the Bill to the end of the tail 3 feet 10- 1/4 inches, middle toe 5- 1/2 inches, toe nail 1 inch & 3- 1/2 lines, wing feather 2- 1/2 feet long & 1 inch 5 lines diamiter, tale feathers 14- 1/2 inches, and the head is 6- 1/2 inches including the beak."[81] The explorers took the head back with them, and it reportedly found its way into Peale's Museum in Philadelphia, one of the period's notable collections of materials from the arts and the sciences.

Clark's meticulous measurements indicated one form of regard for animals. The language the explorers used for the grizzly spoke of a similar attitude, after their final encounter during the return trip. Respect for the grizzly was then mingled with reflection on Providence. When Lewis's party again reached the Great Falls of the Missouri, in July, 1806, Private Hugh McNeal rode to the portage to check on the condition of the equipment the party had cached on its outward voyage. Unawares, he approached to within ten feet of a grizzly, when his frightened horse "threw him immediately under the bear."[82]

The startled animal raised itself, while McNeal quickly recovered from the fall and clubbed the bear with his musket over its head. The stroke stunned the grizzly but broke the rifle. The bear now scratched his head with his feet, and the soldier used the opportunity to climb a willow. When the grizzly gave up waiting at the foot of the tree, late in the evening, McNeal caught his horse and returned to camp. "These bear are a most tremendous animal," Lewis summed up in his report; "it seems that the hand of providence has been most wonderfully in our favor with respect to them, or some of us would long since have fallen a sacrifice to their farosity."[83] The private had gotten within ten feet of the bear before his horse threw him, but Lewis did not take that aspect of the incident as evidence of the grizzly's peaceful nature.

Other adventures produced sobering thoughts about the limits of technology in the face of nature. On several occasions, some of the explorers barely survived their experiences. At times, their narrow escapes spoke less for their resourcefulness and more for bountiful nature providing succor. On one of these occasions, the youngest member of the expedition nearly starved to death, living for twelve days on wild grapes and a rabbit that he shot using a stick as bullet because he was out of ammunition.

The nineteen-year-old Private George Shannon had been detailed to move the horses while the expedition sailed up the Missouri from the Vermilion River to the Teton River. When he charged far ahead with his *remuda,* the expedition lost touch with him for sixteen days. The captains, who considered him just an average hunter, sent a man after him with provisions. He failed to catch up, because Shannon, afraid that he had missed the boats, rushed along as fast as he could. When Shannon became feeble, he decided to wait for the trading boat, which the expedition expected to follow the flotilla, "keeping one horse for the last resorse," as Clark put it on September 11, 1804. "Thus a man," the captain reflected, "had like to have Starved to death in a land of Plenty for the want of Bullitts or Something to kill his meat."[84]

The most dramatic failure of technology in the face of nature occurred after the expedition had portaged the Great Falls of the Missouri in eleven days, from June 22 to July 2, 1805. While Clark and his men were moving supplies and equipment, Lewis and his men were assembling his folding iron-framed boat, to be covered with skins and caulked with pitch or tar. The eighteen-mile portage was particularly grueling because the captains had understood the Mandan to say that the portage would be only one-half mile long. Despite great efforts by the men who could be spared to get it afloat, the attempt to float the boat failed so drastically "that any further experiments in our present situation seemed to me madness," the inventor conceded on July 9.[85]

The experiment was Lewis's brainchild; his heart was in the project, which became an extension of himself. In the spring of 1803 he had spent six weeks at the United States arsenal at Harper's Ferry supervising the construction of the frame of the iron boat. The pieces of the frame, weighing ninety-nine pounds, could be transported conveniently, assembled, and covered with bark or skins wherever the Missouri became too shallow for heavy boats like the pirogues. When fitted together, Lewis estimated, the iron boat would be able to carry a cargo of 8,000 pounds. It promised to answer admirably a predictable need of the expedition.

In the legends of classical antiquity the fate of the boat would have been sealed by the intervention of the gods, punishing the explorers' hubris expressed in the clever design of the boat. At the beginning of the nineteenth century the elements of nature seemed to have conspired to defeat the ingenious craft. Time and season worked against the project and filled the explorers with anxiety about their schedule and sustenance. The Missouri increased the dilemma; for the expedition the unpredictable river was a time-consuming riddle and an exhausting obstacle that contributed its share to the disaster of the iron-frame boat. Altogether, the explorers spent three weeks mastering the riddle of the Marias River and portaging the Great Falls.

The confluence of the Marias and the Missouri presented a

puzzle. It seemed impossible to say which river was the right one. Both rivers disguised their relation to one another—their size, sediment, color, and current contradicted the descriptions the captains thought they had obtained from the Indians. Making the right choice was further complicated because it would not be immediately obvious that the wrong one had been chosen. Any mistake could have been recognized with certainty only after the Corps of Discovery had reached the Rocky Mountains without coming across the Great Falls of the Missouri along their route.

The puzzle over the Missouri and the Marias helped defeat the iron-framed boat by increasing the explorers' anxiety about travel time and the season. Lewis and Clark spent crucial days persuading the men when all of them firmly believed that the Marias was the right course to take. The expedition's arrival at the cataracts validated the captain's decision, but the exhausting portage around the falls caused further delays and demoralized the men. The drudgery of moving boats, supplies, and equipment was increased by the prickly pear plants. The thorns shredded the men's moccasins and injured their feet. Furthermore, "sharp points of earth as hard as frozen ground" cut the soles of the men's feet because the hooves of buffalo had pounded the prairie during the rainy season.[86] Afterwards the sun had baked the hoof prints into their rigid summer shape.

The buffalo, overgrazing bluffs and bench lands, had sculpted the ground and helped to make room for the prickly pear. When additional experiments with the iron boat might still have turned it into a useful craft, however, the buffalo began their seasonal movement away from the falls. Hunting for meat now became uncertain, which reminded the explorers how hazardous further delays could be. The absence of the elk also jeopardized the experiment.

The elk, Lewis felt, had already deserted him earlier, when his crew faced the task of replacing those skins of the frame cover, ruined during the winter or by the water of the river. Reluctantly, Lewis decided to piece out the original elk skin cover of the boat frame with buffalo hide. Inspecting the craft after the failure of the project, he must have felt chagrined about hesitating to use buffalo hide as substitute when he noted that the part of the boat covered with singed buffalo hide had not leaked.

Tar and pitch could now have made the difference between failure and success, but what must have struck Lewis as an alliance of natural forces in their struggle against his technology held tight. There were no pits from which to distill tar. The barren land supported only a few trees, and the men had trouble finding bark and lumber for the ribs, stays, and lining. The scattered cottonwoods yielded no resin, and the pine-covered mountains were distant. No trees floated down the river and no driftwood was handy from which pitch could be made. Finally, the waters of the Missouri, churned by a sudden storm, washed off the mixture of tallow, beeswax, and charcoal that Lewis's crew had smeared over skins, hides, and seams to waterproof the cover. The combination of natural forces triumphed over the iron-framed boat.

After the disaster with the iron-framed boat, the explorers began to search for trees to make two canoes. The iron boat had been intended as substitute for the two pirogues left behind at the falls, and the expedition now lacked transport. Clark and eight men went ahead, found two big cottonwoods, and shaped them into dugouts. Sergeant Ordway and eight men followed with four loaded canoes. Lewis remained behind and "deposited the iron fraim" of the boat, "as it could probably be of no further service to us."[87] Appropriately, Sergeant Gass wrote that they "staid to take the boat asunder and bury her, and deposited her safely under ground."[88]

Lewis was "mortifyed."[89] After "all our labour," as Gass carefully called the drudgery, the victory of cottonwood over iron was galling.[90] For almost thirty months Lewis had longed for the day he could test the invention. Many entries in his journal from the Yellowstone River to the Great Falls showed his growing impatience. He detached men to search the very few trees of the plains for bark and timber. Others he sent after elk for skins and buffalo for hides. When the captain inspected the cargo of the pirogue beached at the Great Falls, he found all the parts of his iron boat complete, "except one screw," which one of his men could replace.[91] On the following day, Lewis had the frame "cleansed of rust and well greased."[92] Finally, on June 6, a man finished sewing together twenty-eight elk skins and four buffalo hides with rawhide thongs to cover "my leather boat," as Lewis called it.[93] Up to that date he had used "leather boat" and "iron boat" randomly, but the closer he came to launching his craft, the more he called it his "iron boat." His struggle to make his experiment river-worthy had convinced him that he had mastered only the iron technology, not the techniques of his experiment that depended on nature, particularly the stretching of skins and hides over the iron frame.

During the final stages of its assembly, the thirty-six-foot-long and four-and-a-half foot-wide boat turned from an obsession into a nightmare. On July 1, when everything was ready for putting the parts of the boat together, Lewis unburdened himself. "The difficulty in obtaining the necessary materials has retarded my operations in forming this boat extremely tedious and troublesome," he admitted. "As it was a novel piece of machinism to all who were employed," he emphasized, "my constant attention was necessary to every part of the work."[94]

On the Fourth of July, 1805, Lewis gave up hope of getting hold of tar. The holes made in sewing the skins left spaces around the thongs, but no pitch could be made to daub the seams. Despite that "serious misfortune," the men completed all the work, save for caulking the boat.[95] They now turned the boat upside down and started small fires underneath to dry it out, but frequent showers kept the boat wet.

As if to steel himself for the next disappointment, Lewis took comfort in the accomplishments of the expedition and described in his journal the men's determination to go on with the voyage. "All appear perfectly to have made up their minds to succeed in the expedition or purish in the attempt."[96] While the wooden horizontal stays dried slowly, the captain set a couple of men to pound charcoal, beeswax, and buffalo tallow, and they covered the outside of the boat with this concoction. The mixture worked fairly well in sealing the seams of regular canoes. The seesaw of Lewis's emotions was up, and he hoped the concoction would do the trick, but his optimism would vanish immediately and he feared it would not. "The boat in every other rispect," he said, determinedly looking at the brighter side of things, "completely answered my most sanguine expectation."[97]

On the "fair and pleasant" morning of July 9, the explorers launched the boat: "she lay like a perfect cork on the water," Lewis exulted. "I now directed seats to be fixed in her and oars to be fitted"; but a sudden storm whipped the water all day and by evening had washed the caulking off the skins and hides covering the iron frame.[98] Facing the leaking craft and the advancing season, Lewis "relinquished all further hope of my favorite boat and ordered her to be sunk in the water."[99]

Sergeant John Ordway recorded the sequence of events on that fateful Tuesday slightly differently. In the morning, "we put the Iron Boat which we covered with green hides in to the water." In the afternoon, "we loaded the 6 canoes but did not load the Iron boat as it leaked considerably." Soon after they had taken care of the canoes, thunder and high wind forced them to unload again. "Our officers concluded to . . . burry the Iron boat," because the expedition could not get tar or pitch to cover the outside of the skins. "The time is So far expended that they did not think proper to try any more experiments with it."[100]

Clark recorded the events of that Tuesday with understatement. The "Leather boat," when launched, "leaked a little." He saw no chance to succeed without tar to caulk the skins, hides, and seams. "This falur of our favourate boat was a great disappointment to us," he admitted, but his regret was followed by a very practical calculation. The explorers suddenly had more baggage than their canoes could carry, and Clark responded quickly: "Concluded to build Canoes."[101]

The defeat of the iron-boat technology by nature affected Lewis more than the other members of the expedition; however, everyone acutely felt the hardships produced by the cultural misconceptions about the distance separating the Missouri from the Columbia. It took eleven exhausting days to cross the awesome mountain ranges between the two water systems. Following the geographic speculations of his day, Jefferson had hoped that it could be done "possibly with a single portage" in his confidential message to Congress on January 18, 1803.[102] Alexander Mackenzie had crossed the Rocky Mountains over a low pass near the fifty-fifth parallel in 1793 and assumed that to the south the passes would be even lower and that a short portage would close the gap between the waters of the Atlantic and the Pacific.

Clark handled the disappointment about the length and the hardship of the portage or the crossing of the Bitterroots in his own way. After the party had reached the Pacific Ocean, Clark recorded in his journal on November 18, 1805, that while checking on an Indian report about an anchorage used by traders, he found Captain Lewis's name on a tree. "I also engraved my name," he noted, "& by land the day of the month and year, as also Several of the men." Five days later Clark made a similar entry about cutting his name into a beech tree, again adding the information "By Land."[103] Perhaps he wanted to mimic the message Mackenzie had left on a rock in sight of the ocean.

Clark had to make do with trees to record that the Corps of Discovery, and not the earlier Mackenzie expedition which in his view relied on the canoe, was the first party to come by land to the Pacific Ocean. The arduous eleven-day crossing on horseback of the towering Bitterroots must have seemed longer than it was. Like Jefferson, the explorers had expected a short portage between the water systems of the Missouri and the Columbia. Clark's conviction that the Corps of Discovery actually came "by land" showed how deeply the strains of the mountain crossing must have affected him, as well as how long he could conceal that fact.

No American had envisioned the width of the enormous range of the Rockies in the path of Lewis and Clark. Mackenzie, who had reached the Pacific north of Vancouver Island, had crossed the Rocky Mountains on several relatively short portages. His experiences, published in 1801, supported the hope that Lewis and Clark, wedded to the existence of a feasible Missouri–Columbia route, might encounter even less-formidable mountains. These ranges of the Bitterroots had their own magnitude, however, which was particularly difficult for those explorers who may have farmed, logged, mined, soldiered, or traveled in the Appalachians and thought they knew mountains. They had not figured them as an obstacle in their daily calculations, and when they thought about them as mountains they saw them only in those familiar proportions, which suited their plans.

When Jefferson received a letter from the French naturalist Bernard Lacépède in July 1803, he translated the parts bearing on his project and sent them on to Lewis, who was preparing the expedition. The president's letter mixed fact and fantasy. He told the captain that from the lower reaches of the Columbia "Mount Hood is seen . . . , which is probably a dependence of the Stony mountains, . . . and the source of the Columbia is probably in the Stony mountains."[104] All speculations about the Stony Mountains made sense in the absence of specific knowledge, but they failed to prepare the explorers for the reality of the Rocky Mountain ranges.

The ragged cliffs and the steep canyons, the heights and the distances they encountered staggered them. There are few observations in the journals of the expedition about the beauty of the mountain scenery. Strained to the limits of their resources, the explorers made only perfunctory entries in their journals. References to geological and geographical phenomena rarely appeared. The ordeal of surmounting the monstrous mountains subdued any speculation or curiosity about their formation and composition.

In their encounter with the mountains, the explorers faced a powerful nature that challenged the mission of the expedition. The experience strained their cultural resources to the breaking point. Nature reduced their stamina, exhausted their supplies, and humbled their pride during the eleven days they struggled across the Bitterroot Mountains. These 150 miles from the Bitterroot Valley in western Montana to the foot of the mountains on the Clearwater River in Idaho epitomized the encounter of the Lewis and Clark expedition with the Rocky Mountains.

The ordeal began on September 10, 1805, when the expedition left Traveller's Rest, about ten miles south of present-day Missoula, Montana. On their way to that campsite, pushing northward along the North Fork of the Salmon River and the valley of the Bitterroot River, the party had its first exposure to travel in rugged terrain. In many places a path through the thickets of heavy timber had to be cleared with axes. Horses slipped and several fell on slopes wet with sleet or rain. There was nothing to hunt, and salt pork carried along from St. Louis took the place of game.

To be sure, the men had faced hardships and adventures before, but they had traveled predominantly the Missouri River route or on open plains, which provided game for their needs. Clark's reconnaissance of the turbulent water and rugged gorges of the Salmon River had crushed their hopes of quickly finding a river suitable for travel and a convenient way to cross the mountains. There was no room on the edge of the Salmon to move men or horses and no timber for building canoes. His findings had convinced the captains they should follow Indian advice and reach the navigable water of the Columbia drainage by crossing the mountain barrier farther north with a Shoshone guide and packhorses. It had meant moving about one hundred miles in northerly direction to the beginning of the Lolo Trail leading across the Bitterroot Mountains.

For more than a week, the explorers had seen the saw-toothed, snowcapped Bitterroots to the west. The Indians had told them about the hardships that went with following the harrowing path across the mountains, the Lolo Trail. One Shoshone chief had described it to Lewis as the trail used by the Nez Perce to get to the Missouri for the buffalo hunt, and added that the road was "very bad." He also related that the Nez Perce had told him they "suffered excessively with hunger . . . as there was no game in . . . the mountains, which were . . . so thickly covered with timber that they could scarcely pass." Lewis reflected on the report and added: "I felt perfectly satisfyed, that if the Indians could pass these mountains with their women and Children, that we could also pass them."[105] During the ordeal of the Lolo Trail, the memory of this hasty prediction might have kept Lewis from contributing journal entries detailing the crossing of the mountains. The eleven days of the harrowing journey tested Lewis and his companions to the utmost.

An awesome sight threatened the explorers' advance. A maze of bewildering ridges, studded with high peaks, made up the lateral spurs of the north-south range forming the divide of the Bitterroots. Deep saddles alternating with craggy peaks and sharp hogbacks marked the beginning of large canyons. Some of the lofty, snowcapped summits towering in the west went up to 10,000 feet: most of the peaks averaged between 8,000 and 9,000 feet. Although it was September, fields of old snow still lightened the dark rock. The explorers' eyes fastened on the lower saddles (around 6,000 feet high), searching for passes over the range.

The steep sides of deep canyons and the rugged crags of the gigantic walls dominated the scenery. Long ago, great glaciers had cut and fissured some of the slopes. For centuries there may have been a path across, but at the beginning of the eighteenth century, when the horse first reached the Nez Perce and the Flathead in its northward migration from the Spanish settlements, the Lolo Trail across the Bitterroot Mountains most likely gained the shape encountered by Lewis and Clark. A view of the crests of the major ridges, which Indian mountain trails often followed as nearly as possible, gave the explorers a foretaste what the Bitterroots had in store for the Corps of Discovery.

Hunger, thirst, fatigue, and despair reduced the life of the explorers to the level of a poverty culture of survivors. The hunters found no game or if they did, they could not shoot it because the game moved quickly out of rifle range. Seven times Clark's rifle misfired when he aimed at a mule deer. It had never happened to him before, but when he examined the gun he "found the flint loose."[106] The bears, which had chased the aggressive hunters relentlessly at the Great Falls, now ran away from them. The hungry Sergeant Ordway took it as sign of doom. "The hunters chased a bear up the Mountain but could not kill it," he reported on September 17. "We hear wolves howl," he added ominously, "some distance a head."[107]

The starving men killed several colts and ate them. As a kind of homage to the colts they named a camp Killed Colt Island and a river fork Colt Killed Creek. Water was not always within reach, and the party melted icy clumps from old snow banks to cook horse meat or to prepare portable soup, a dried soup mix. In the halcyon days of the expedition, during the planning stage in 1803, Lewis had obtained about 200 pounds of the dried soup in Philadelphia. The men had dragged the food along because they were ordered to. They did not like the concoction until hunger changed their minds. On September 18 they had for supper portable soup, a little bear oil, and twenty pounds of candles. They had exhausted their provisions, with the exception of the packhorses, which they did not dare to butcher because the animals carried the equipment and the trade goods of the expedition. "There is nothing upon earth" here, Lewis tersely reported.[108] On that Wednesday, Clark and his men, who had gone ahead to hunt and restore morale, spent the night on a small stream they called Hungry Creek.

Despair sharpened their hunger. Gloom fed on the harsh terrain and the elusive trail. Most trails develop branches over the years, and the Lolo Trail could boast its share. The Shoshone guide who accompanied the expedition was far from his familiar turf. With only vague knowledge of the path, he strayed from the main trunk for a day. The explorers stumbled down a fishing path after him and ended up in a river. On the evening of the following day they finally regained the main trail on a divide 7,000 feet high. They all panted and sweated: some horses gave out. Whenever the men looked up, they saw nothing but towering mountains holding them captive.

The next day, September 16, dawned with a snowstorm. It continued to blow all day and by evening had dumped eight inches of new snow on the old. The men staggered along, cold, wet, and hungry, with freezing fingers and toes. Clark summed up the agony: "I have been wet and as cold in every part as I ever was in my life."[109] The blinding snow disguised the trail, and the explorers felt relieved when they could spot the rubbed tree trunks scarred over decades by the packs of Indian horses.

Horses and trees helped the explorers, but they also sapped their strength. Fallen trees and trunks charred by forest fires obstructed the path and blocked some of the canyons entirely. Skirting or cutting through the windfalls took time and energy. They found little level ground and almost no pasturage, and whenever the party came across a meadow, they all rested because the horses needed to feed. The delays, however, proved costly because they prolonged the trek through the rugged mountains. In camp at night, the men could not hobble the horses but had to let them run free so that they could find what little grass was there. Continuously the expedition feared that the animals would wander off and scatter widely. The party got off late every morning because the roundup took time.

On the wet and snow-covered paths the horses slipped, fell, and injured themselves, and several tumbled down the slopes. The falls of the exhausted horses led to accidents that suggested that nature had taken command of the expedition. On September 15, a packhorse crushed Clark's writing desk when the animal rolled forty yards down a slope and lodged against a tree. The horse "appeared but little hurt," Clark emphasized, but the fall had destroyed another vestige of white culture dragged into the terrible Bitterroots.[110] Clark continued to keep a journal, but Lewis seemed to have stopped writing already, before the expedition entered the Bitterroots, after he had received Clark's message on August 26 that the Salmon River route was impassable and that they had to find their way through the Bitterroot Mountains.

Within a speculative context, which envisions nature holding culture at bay, it is tempting to argue that the threatening mountains embodying the elements had silenced the most articulate of the explorers. However, Lewis did return to his journal again on January 1, 1806, with entries written in the winter quarters of the expedition at Fort Clatsop, at the Pacific Ocean. With the exception of four entries on September 18, 19, 20, and 22, and three entries on November 29 and 30, and December 1, Lewis remained silent for such a long time that one may assume that many of his notes got lost. Perhaps both explanations of his silence could be valid if taken in reasonable proportions.

Lewis briefly began writing again on September 18. On the previous day, the captains had decided that Clark, with six of their best hunters, should charge ahead into prairie country, find game, and send food back to Lewis, who would follow with the main party. "The want of provisions together with the difficulty of passing those emence mountains dampened the sperits of the party," Clark explained on September 18, "which induced us to resort to Some plan of reviving ther sperits."[111]

After seven days on Indian trails running west to the Clearwater River, the explorers seemed lost in a maze of mountains. "We . . . proceeded over the most terrible mountains I ever beheld," Patrick Gass stated bluntly, who had never seen tall mountains before.[112] The eerie mist of the high altitude heightened the sensation of being out of touch with reality and lost for good. Sergeant Ordway felt on September 16 "as if we had been in the clouds all . . . day."[113] The constant hunger did the rest. "Set out without anything to eat," Private Whitehouse recorded in his journal on that Monday.[114] The explorers' low morale called for bold measures.

The separation from Clark jolted Lewis back to writing. Despite hunger and thirst, discouraged men and tired horses, he now recorded the eagerly anticipated signs promising an end of their tribulation. Lewis, who had taken the suffering of the horses as a sign of doom, suddenly shook off his anxiety after a spectacular accident. One evening, on an "excessively dangerous" stretch of the journey, the trail ascending and descending "several steep mountains," a horse slipped on a "narrow rockey path . . . on the side of a steep precipice." The animal rolled down an "almost perpendicular" cliff of large, irregular boulders "with his load near a hundred yards into the Creek."

Although everybody expected the horse to be dead, the packs seemed to have cushioned the tumble, and when they were taken off, the animal got on its feet and in twenty minutes stumbled along again with the load. "This was the most wonderful escape I ever witnessed," Lewis marveled. He was not inclined to let the miraculous accident go unremarked after the day (September 19) had already begun with another miracle. In the morning of that Thursday, to their "inexpressable joy," the party had seen in the distance a great tract of prairie. The Indian guide promptly identified the sight as the Columbia River.[115] On the next day, Lewis and his men found in a tree parts of a horse, put there by Clark's party, which had killed the animal when it strayed into the explorers' path on September 19.

The stray horse not only fed the starving explorers but also signaled the presence of an Indian village to Clark. His laconic observation of September 18 that his party had passed over country "similar to the one of yesterday" reflected the weariness produced by the hardships of the mountains. Clark had left the Shoshone guide with Lewis because Clark assumed that even a guide unfamiliar with the trail provided some measure of encouragement to the main party, which needed all available support. Rushing along with the hunters, his eyes eager to get away from gullies blocked with fallen timber and ridges exposed to blowing snow, Clark saw from "the top of a high . . . mountain . . . an emence Plain and *leavel* Countrey." Although the men of the advance party could not yet detect any signs of deer, their revived optimism renewed their resilience, and that night they called their camp site "*Hungery* Creek." Clark must have felt hopeful enough about impending change, because he added factually: "We had nothing to eate."[116]

Three days after Clark's party had killed and butchered the

stray horse, the hospitality of a Nez Perce village reunited the Corps of Discovery on September 22. As soon as he had made contact with the Nez Perce on September 20, Clark had sent back dried salmon, roots, and berries, which speeded Lewis's party onto the last leg of its journey. "The pleasure I now felt in having tryumphed over the rockey Mountains and descending once more to a level and fertile country where there was every rational hope of finding a comfortable subsistence for myself and party can be more readily conceived than expressed," Lewis noted with relief, "nor was the flattering prospect of the final success of the expedition less pleasing."[117]

The Lolo Trail across the Bitterroot Mountains left its mark on the explorers. A good rest with the Nez Perce took care of hunger and fatigue and healed cuts and bruises. It took longer to get over the painful stomach disorders. The emotional impact lasted. The dreaded mountains haunted Lewis at the Pacific Ocean as he prepared the expedition for the homeward journey. Although advice and help from the Nez Perce cut down the time for the return crossing to seven days, the Lolo Trail again confounded and exhausted the explorers. In 1806, the winter lasted into the summer in the Bitterroots. When the impatient captains, against the warnings of the Nez Perce, moved too early into higher altitudes to start the return transit, they found the feed for the horses covered and the path blocked by deep snow. On June 17, 1806, the horrible Bitterroots forced them to retreat to the safety of the Nez Perce settlements.

When they eventually crossed the range between June 24 and July 1, the snow had melted nearly four feet in some places since June 17 and was down to about seven feet. Indian guides, who intimately knew the twists and the shortcuts of the trail, the saddles and ridges, kept the explorers out of deep snow and on top of the divide, which the sun had freed from snow. "These fellows," Lewis wrote in tribute to the Nez Perce guides, "are most admirable pilots," finding "the road wherever the snow has disappeared."[118] The return journey produced other strains than hunger and despair, however. "I was taken yesterday with a violent pain in my head," Clark recorded on June 26, "which has tormented me ever since most violently."[119]

The awareness of being again at the mercy of the powers of nature did not only feed frustration: it provided the explorers with a new insight into their relation with the elements. On June 27, the party reached a summit that had been marked by the Nez Perce with a pine pole embedded in a tall mound of stones. Three days earlier, at the outset of the journey, the Indians had set the dry limbs of firs on fire in the hope that the tall trees, blazing from bottom to top, would bring fair weather for the crossing of the mountains. With their goal within reach, and reassured by the big cairn on the ridge, they called a halt to smoke the pipe.

The ceremony enabled the explorers to see one of the mounds of stone that served as trail markers for the Nez Perce. On the westward journey, due to the vicissitudes of the Lolo Trail, the explorers camped near, but may not have seen, the other mounds, which later came to be known as "Indian Post Offices."[120] Smoking the pipe on the summit also allowed Lewis to catch "an extensive view of these stupendous mountains." They "were entirely surrounded by those mountains," the captain said, "from which . . . it would have seemed impossible ever to have escaped." The intimidating scene forced him to concede: "Without the assistance of our guides I doubt much whether we who had once passed them could find our way to Travellers rest in their present situation."[121] The company of the Nez Perce, providing safety and mitigating the threat of the mountains, encouraged him to admit that the marked trees, which the expedition had intended to use as trail markers on the return trip, were fewer and more difficult to find than he had anticipated. "My head has not pained me so much to day as yesterday and last night," Clark noted on the same day.[122] He may have gotten used to the altitude sooner, or finally gotten over his anxiety when he saw that his Indian companions knew what they were doing.

The Bitterroots released the expedition on June 28. No one but the diarists may have noted that it was a Sunday, because one day followed another in the routine of the Corps of Discovery. There was something special about the day, however. The explorers had crossed the final divide and camped at Lolo Hot Spring. While they relaxed, reentering a more familiar world, the Nez Perce guides grew tense because they found themselves in alien territory; and they wanted to retrace their steps immediately. However, before explorers and guides parted company, they soaked together in the hot springs; Lewis remaining in the pool for nineteen minutes and Clark for ten. "Most of us bathed in its water," Sergeant Gass commented with restraint.[123] On the following day Clark knew that they had left "these tremendous mountains behind us, in passing of which we have experienced cold and hunger of which I shall ever remember."[124]

The strenuous crossings of the Bitterroot Range impressed the explorers with the power of nature. The hardships of the crossings had reduced their lives to a struggle for existence. They lived on four colts and a soup concentrate, drank the melted snow of the previous year, and stumbled through clouds in search of a trail. The maze of ridges shattered the longstanding expectations of a convenient portage between the Missouri and the Columbia. Despite the harrowing days and nights on the Lolo Trail and the crushed hopes for an easy passage, the discovery of the huge obstacle marked the high point of the expedition and the crossing of the Bitterroots the explorers' finest hour. That outlook made reaching the Pacific Ocean an anticlimax to the great adventure. Furthermore, the party already knew the relation of the coastline at the mouth of the Columbia to other landmarks of the Pacific Northwest.

"*Ocean in view!* O! the joy," Clark wrote delightedly on November 7, 1805, when he thought he saw the Pacific Ocean. His premature outburst was not echoed in the other journals.[125] Sergeant Ordway finally acknowledged the Pacific on November 18: "Capt. Clark myself and 10 more of the party set out in order to . . . see the passific ocean."[126] The captain commented about the small turnout in his journal: "All others being well contented with what part of the Ocean . . . could be seen from the vicinity of our camp."[127] Ordway's description of a California condor that one of the men had shot took up as much space in the entry as his account of the difficulties of getting to the water. At last the Pacific came in sight. "Towards evening we arrived at the . . . Sea Shore . . . where we had a handsom view of the ocean."[128]

The Lewis and Clark expedition's mission brought them to the shore of the Pacific Ocean, after they had penetrated a range of awesome mountains and resolved one of the mysteries of the continent. The Corps of Discovery failed to find a convenient waterway through the continent, but it demonstrated that no passage linked the Missouri with the Columbia. The explorers' resilience and commitment enabled them to solve the last remaining riddle of the gigantic mountain range. Their answer put to rest all speculations about the existence of a Wilderness Passage. Lewis and Clark placed before their countrymen an enormous chain of mountains stretching from the Arctic Ocean to Central America, dividing the woodlands and the prairies of North America from the plateaus and the Pacific littoral.

The encounter with the gigantic mountain ranges separating the drainage systems of the Missouri and the Columbia also taught the explorers some of the limits of their culture. The collapse of the iron-framed boat and the turbulent waters of the Salmon River gorges seemed to presage defeat. The help from Indians, however, who shared with the explorers the ways their cultures coped with nature, enabled the party to survive the ordeal. In the course of the struggle the explorers were pushed to the edge of their own culture. They learned to interact with powerful nature in ways that broadened their view of humanity and increased their respect for other forms of life.

For a brief time, the size and the attitude of the Corps of Discovery struck a balance between culture and nature. With the return of the party, the accord vanished. The discoveries of Lewis and Clark, eagerly welcomed by a nation on the move, in part sustained industrialization and urbanization. Their reports about the resources of the Far West molded nineteenth-century America into a country built on the utilization of nature, even to the point of its destruction.

The dedication of the expedition to its mission was one of the influences that extended the Founding Fathers' spirit of obligation to mankind into the nineteenth century. The apocalyptic triad of nationalism, urbanism, and industrialism converted the explorers' utilitarian sentiments into a destiny that exploited the resources of the continent to build a modern nation. The awareness of the potential of the continent for empire-building set in motion generations of Americans who abused nature to the point of destruction by adhering to a destiny they saw manifested in their conquest.

In the nineteenth century, the exploitation of resources, the annihilation of Indians, and the destruction of nature went hand in hand with the creation of exalted images of American scenery. The contradictory activities diluted the intimate contact with land and people achieved by Lewis and Clark. Above all, few of their words attesting to that directness of life reached nineteenth-century Americans. The sudden death of Lewis was "a great loss to the world," Jefferson wrote in 1810: "no pen can ever give us so faithful & lively an account of the countries & nations which he saw, as his own would have done, under the guidance of impressions made by the objects themselves."[129]

The History of the Expedition under the Commands of Captains Lewis and Clark, which appeared in 1814, confirmed Jefferson's prediction. The "interesting narrative," as Jefferson called it, was the work of Nicholas Biddle, a Philadelphia lawyer and litterateur.[130] As a frequent contributor to the *Port Folio*, which considered pride in American writing obligatory, Biddle embellished with a nationalistic pen the journals' concern for humanity and respect for nature. Paul Allen, another *Port Folio* contributor, gave the book a few final touches when other obligations demanded Biddle's attention. Allen's name alone appeared as editor on the title page.

Biddle cast the traveling journals into literary form with splendid effect. His elegant prose celebrated the success of a distinctly American venture. Biddle, an author who had never left the Eastern Seaboard, had the help of Clark, the custodian of the captains' writings; of David Shannon, a member of the Corps of Discovery; and of Ordway's journal. Their assistance gave the publication "the ring of truth," in the opinion of Reuben Gold Thwaites, the editor of the first edition of the *Original Journals of the Lewis and Clark Expedition.*[131]

Biddle's marvelous accomplishment towered for almost a century over several counterfeits as the only legitimate Lewis and Clark edition. The nationalistic tone and romantic sentiment of his language suited nineteenth-century Americans well. His sentences corresponded with other lofty literary and artistic statements that thrived on Romanticism and Transcendentalism, the visions of the Hudson River School, and a nascent environmental movement. These literary and artistic works enshrined nature, but failed to save it. Only in the city, which had arisen by eradicating forest and meadow, did democratic impulses engender the engineering of nature as well as culture and create park cemeteries and urban parks. City parks sustained in the emerging modern society the practical spirit supporting the continuing search for a balance between nature and culture.

»» THREE ««

Engineering Nature—Engineering Culture

THE DISCOVERIES OF the Lewis and Clark expedition turned a western wilderness of guesswork and rumor into a distinct part of the continent. They opened a new world to Americans, who eagerly responded to the promise of a vast new field for their cultural mission. Their attempts to harvest the fur resources and their efforts to make over forest, prairie, and savannah in the image of field, meadow, and city warped their view of nature and almost blinded them to the natural world.

"Europeans think a lot about the wild, open spaces of America," Alexis de Tocqueville observed in the 1830s after his tour of the United States, "but the Americans themselves hardly give them a thought. . . . The American people," the French philosopher of government explained, "see themselves marching through wilderness, drying up marshes, diverting rivers, peopling the wilds, and subduing nature."[1]

The respect for nature in the Lewis and Clark expedition, such as it was, vanished during the ensuing contest for the spoils of conquest. The lure of land, the urge of commerce, the design of empire, and the destructiveness of war erased the concern for the wilderness and its inhabitants. The pillaging of the continent increased the tension between nature and culture in American civilization, but the bounty of a vast continent obscured the disastrous consequences for a while.

Meanwhile, a new understanding of nature emerged in those parts of the United States where city life threatened the remnants of forest and prairie, hill and valley. The rapid disappearance of natural sites in the big cities woke urbanites to the enormous loss. They responded by making park cemeteries and municipal parks parts of their urban world. By re-creating natural areas in the cityscape, they curbed an insidious aspect of the triumphant city: its exclusive orientation to cultural convention.

A digression is in order lest the argument be misunderstood. Although almost eliminated from sight in the modern city, nature continued to influence city life. Fire and flood, rain and snow, drought and dust, light and darkness were always ready to check the hubris of nineteenth-century Americans in building a city removed from nature. An environment dominated by culture means an urban setting steadily stripped of noticeable remnants of nature—until the residents recognize the need to reintroduce trees and meadows into their lives.

The interaction of various influences contributed to the engineering feats that ensured the return of nature to the nineteenth-century city in the form of the park cemetery and the municipal park. Their sudden creation well fitted the impulsive development of American cities, which grew fast within decades, in contrast to European cities, which had grown slowly over centuries. Spiritual and secular motives created the park cemetery and the city park. The demands for each of them were equally pressing.

The park cemetery appeared before the municipal park in the American city because the new burial ground offered to its supporters personal benefits that could be easily understood. Although the builders of the park cemetery were deeply concerned with what they considered the proper care of the dead, it is rather difficult to suppress the thought that they had in mind not only reform and economy, but also their own future, when they laid out a park cemetery. They created a natural setting that would lure their fellow-citizens to promenade on shaded alleys lined with monuments carrying their names. Clusters of trees sheltered their graves in a setting of meadows and lakes, and they could rely on the visitors' respect for the dead to protect the re-emerging natural setting.

A new relationship to nature contributed to the rise of the park cemetery; and the new form of burial ground, in turn, introduced respect for nature into the modern city. The founders of the park cemetery evinced feelings for nature similar to the sentiments of the Lewis and Clark expedition. While the attitude of the explorers had been fostered by their actual exposure to pristine nature in its majestic forms, however, the builders of the park cemetery venerated trees, foliage, and lawns through their reverence for the dead and the reflection that death restored people's harmony with nature.

American Romanticism encouraged the idea of the park cemetery as the embodiment of nature and death as the return to it. "Enter this wild wood / And view the haunts of Nature," the poet William Cullen Bryant advised the stranger reading "Inscription for the Entrance to a Wood" (1815). To his alluring invitation the poet added what he may have considered an irresistible promise: "Thou wilt find nothing here / Of all that pained thee in the haunts of men, / And made thee loathe thy life."[2]

Romanticism directed attention to the woodlands in the vicinity of quickly expanding cities as accommodations for the dead. The idea of converting patches of forest and meadow into cemeteries also appealed to the thinking of urban reformers. This new type of burial ground, they hoped, might reduce the hazard of epidemics spreading from unsanitary, crowded city graveyards that endangered the health of rich and poor alike.

Other influences reinforced temporal and spiritual considerations and focused attention on the new significance of nature in the lives of city people. The Enlightenment in America had weakened the bond between the individual and a specific church and freed his descendants from the obligation to commit his corpse to a family gravesite. Intensified urbanization had increased the physical mobility of Americans and severed the migrants' attachment to the family churchyard. Finally, the rapid disappearance of open land in the city had alerted urbanites to look elsewhere for the remnants of nature in their world. They accepted the park cemetery, not only as an alternative to traditional church graveyards, but also as a substitute for the formerly nearby pleasure grounds in forests and fields that now had been pre-empted by urbanization and industrialization.

The park cemetery returned nature to the American city. The new relationship between nature and city in the United States appeared clearly in light of the role of the park cemetery's European antecedents. They anticipated some of the features of the American park cemetery, with the significant exception of the strong influence of nature on the new graveyard in the United States. Europe in the eighteenth century contributed two outstanding characteristics of the new kind of cemetery. They stemmed from the rise in Georgian England of natural landscape gardening and the demand in Revolutionary France for an adequate graveyard for Paris.

Broadly stated, English traditions inspired the creation of a park with groves of trees, winding paths, meadows, lakes, and rural scenes evoking those vestiges of rural beauty untouched by farm work. From France came the idea of a burial ground decorated with funerary monuments, statues, sarcophagi, obelisks, and pyramids.[3] Traces of the English and French characteristics influenced the return of nature to the American city and the westward migration of the park cemetery from the Atlantic to the Pacific.

The English and French influences came to be modified on the East Coast, as well as during their migration across the continent. The changes affected the relationship between nature and culture in American society. In the course of that interchange, at times, nature seemed to appear as if it were a cultural construct due to people's preoccupation with concepts of nature such as the sublime or the picturesque. In all its cultural contexts, however, even during the engineering of nature in the city, nature dominated in its elementary form, as a life-giving or life-taking power in animate things, independent of and external to human design.

The introduction of the park cemetery in the city and its westward movement across the United States modified the relationship between nature and culture that the European contributions to the new form of burial ground had achieved. The ascendancy of culture over nature that could be observed in Europe, in the United States gave way to a growing subordination of culture to nature in the new park cemetery. It foreshadowed a compromise between nature and culture in the American city in form of the big city park, which became an example of civilized life struggling for harmony with the natural environment. The outcome was a cultural accomplishment that briefly allied people's aspirations with the fragile natural environment that was besieged by the modern city.

Although culture frequently overshadowed nature in the park cemetery, it was the natural scene and the informal layout that set the park cemetery apart from other graveyards. The presence of nature as a force external to culture accounted for the ever-changing appearance of the park cemetery. The contrasting images of luxuriant and decaying nature distinguished the park cemetery from earlier modifications of conventional burial fields. Death spoke from the solemn, vaultlike tombs set in tiers at New Orleans' first St. Louis Cemetery, which had been laid out near the city in the late eighteenth century. Everlasting life spoke from the trees and shrubs that changed with the seasons, that grew and decayed regardless of any gardener's artistic desire to defy the constant changes, and made the park cemetery a monument with a life of its own.

Americans were attuned to change because it was part of their lives in the New World. Furthermore, their English heritage had exposed them to a fascination for well-ordered landscapes. In England, the return to nature that marked the Georgian age had its roots in the age-old search for a balance between nature and culture. The change in taste and design in the early part of the eighteenth century linked ideas from antiquity to the daily affairs of English aristocrats, and provided a setting that made possible Christian burial in a park, outside the confines of a narrow churchyard. The newly built landscape united the tomb with the sources of a nobleman's wealth—with land and agriculture. The fashionable setting of the garden evoked "the genius of the place," an idea derived from the ancients to identify a setting distinguished by the harmony of scene and taste, of nature and culture.

For centuries, or so it seemed, the arts had prepared the ground for the mausoleum of Charles Howard, third Earl of Carlisle. In the 1720s Alexander Pope erected an obelisk commemorating his mother in his garden at Twickenham. Only a decade later, Charles Howard's coffin was placed in his mausoleum in the park of Castle Howard, an English country seat in Yorkshire. Within that span, the monument as place of burial appeared in the English landscape garden, while the "Natural Style," to use David Jacques's phrase, modified the geometry of the Palladian landscape.[4] The desire for the irregularity of nature eroded the ideal of symmetrical design.

Early eighteenth-century England was a good time and place for moving the tomb into the park. The age fostered the late flowering of baroque architecture, clung with that slowly fading spirit of the Baroque to the mystique of the tomb, and glorified nature's reign in its Georgian gardens. The English concern about the natural environment, gaining inspiration from Dutch, French, and Italian influences, displayed itself well in the first great eighteenth-century poem about nature, James Thomson's "The Seasons" of 1730.

Thomson's poem was set in the English countryside, but other influences came from farther afield: from Surat, India. It was the most important seaport in India for seventeenth-century Englishmen and, until 1687, the administrative seat of the English East India Company. At Surat, the death rate, the climate, and the influence of the Indian scene led Europeans to develop a form of park cemetery. At the beginning of the eighteenth century, the Surat contribution to burial was recognized by some English architects as an alternative to ugly, unhealthy, urban churchyards. A few decades earlier, such churchyards had roused Christopher Wren, the architect, and John Evelyn, the scientist, to campaign for a large cemetery outside of London after the plague of 1665 and the great fire of 1666. They had been moved by bones rising in the soil of crowded churchyards and frightened by the prospect of plagues and epidemics rising from churchyard miasmas. They considered the rebuilding of London after the Great Fire an opportunity also to solve the problems of the burial grounds.

A specific recommendation to establish handsome cemeteries on the outskirts of London, with lush trees and lofty mausoleums, in the "manner of Internment . . . practiced by the English at Suratt" emerged early in the eighteenth century.[5] This phrase was part of a memorandum to the Commission for Building Fifty New Churches sponsored by Queen Anne. The suggestion was an attempt to free the projected churches from the burden of providing burial places. Written in 1710, the document is in the hand of John Vanbrugh, the architect who worked on Castle Howard. His collaborator, Nicholas Hawksmoor, designed the Howard Mausoleum in the garden of Castle Howard. The thoughts and works of these men may also have influenced their patron, Charles Howard, third Earl of Carlisle, and encouraged him to place his tomb in a garden.

The American park cemetery was also indebted to French influence, which enlarged the awareness of the interaction between nature and culture in an urban setting. By way of the cemetery of Père Lachaise, opened in 1804 on a former country retreat in Paris, the French contribution reached the United States. To avoid the aura of the graveyard, that perennial midwife of somber reflection; and to obscure and mitigate the absence of a church, the administrators made Père Lachaise a cemetery of monuments, decorating the grounds with obelisks and statues. The superintendents even built sepulchers that were said to hold the remains of famous French men and women, including for the delectation of all romantic hearts the tomb of the twelfth-century lovers Héloïse and Abélard.[6]

The appeal to sentiment contributed to the success of Père Lachaise and stimulated a new vogue of funerary architecture. The success of the fashion depended on the emotional response to a heritage of burial monuments laden with the cultural accretion of millennia. The vogue soon touched the pictorial arts. Ferdinand Quaglia, one of the painters of the Romantic Age, made an ancient necropolis visible once again, graced with the new monuments of Père Lachaise. He derived the inspiration for his fanciful drawing from the etching of an old Roman cemetery street by Giovanni Battista Piranesi. In Quaglia's etching, his romantic vision expanded the cobblestone-paved lanes of the Parisian cemetery into a spectacular French Via Appia, lined with the temples of the dead displaying the illustrious names of famous French scientists and artists.

When the new style of funerary architecture reached the United States, the reality of nature in America overwhelmed the European vision of the necropolis. The streets and houses of the dead, the cenotaphs and sarcophagi created in Père Lachaise, were reduced to a natural scale, one less obviously intruded upon by the hand of man. Furthermore, in the United States burial in a natural setting had cultural antecedents in the country's colonial past.

Necessity, in the form of poor roads, distant churchyards, and bad weather, at times forced colonials to bury the dead near their homes. The Bishop of London reported in 1677 that Virginians insisted on the "profane custom of burying in their gardens, orchards, and other places."[7] Irrespective of his admonitions, the custom continued. Poems celebrated the locations of the graves of some illustrious dead. The poem "Burk's Garden Grave" celebrated the site in the garden of a villa near Petersburg, Virginia, where the dramatist and poet John Daly Burk had been buried in 1808.[8]

The practice of burying the dead near the living was sanctioned and perpetuated by family burial grounds, with Washington's tomb at Mount Vernon the outstanding example. In 1796, to ensure the continued existence of a final resting place for his family, Senator James Hillhouse of Connecticut built the Grove Street Cemetery in New Haven, which would give his family plot the measure of permanence he sought, even if his lands were sold after his death.

The New Haven cemetery and the family burial grounds lacked the dimensions and design of a park cemetery. These features first appeared in 1831, when the English idea of putting a tomb in a landscape garden and the French solution to urban burial came together in a park like setting near Boston, in Cambridge, Massachusetts. There a tract of land struck a few eminent Bostonians as a good place to begin tackling the city's problems with crowded burial places and with vanishing natural sites. The creation of Mount Auburn Cemetery on some seventy acres of woodland brought the phrase *garden cemetery* into vogue. Its founders had allied themselves briefly with the newly organized Massachusetts Horticultural Society, the proprietor of an experimental garden, in an attempt to ensure the success of the novel idea.[9]

The new term *garden cemetery* appealed to diverse groups of people. It attracted those who were pleased to link the daring idea of creating a big park to the manageable task of making a garden. The phrase consoled those mourners who associated gardens and death because of the link of the Garden of Gethsemane to Calvary. There, at the Garden, Christ suffered the Agony and was taken prisoner; at Calvary, near the cemetery, he was crucified. To others, burial in a park cemetery represented a return to the bliss of the Garden of Eden before Adam and Eve had brought death into the world. An age that first recited the poems of William Cullen Bryant cherished his equating of nature's grove with God's manmade temples. The association of grave and garden also seemed to supply a lost divinity at least for those believers in the Age of Romanticism who thought that although God had abandoned his church he still resided in nature.

Doubtless, too, the young nation, recalling its colonial past considered the word "garden" a fitting republican substitute for the aristocratic "park." In England the park had developed from a game preserve held by royal grant into a large, ornamental piece of enclosed ground, with woods and meadows for cattle and sheep, surrounding a country house. In the United States a bountiful nature and a brief history, a tiny work force of trained gardeners, and the absorbing task of building a nation had blocked the spread of parks.

In the 1830s, the image of the haughty aristocrat had less appeal for many Americans than the ideal of the earthy farmer, and the planners of Mount Auburn came up with yet another name. They proudly called their new suburban burial ground a "rural cemetery," favoring the distinction offered by the English poet William Cowper in *The Task*: "God made the country, and man made the town." Backed by the attractive associations that rural life evoked, the phrase "rural cemetery" found its way into the language of American lawmakers, beginning in 1831 when the Massachusetts General Court passed an act authorizing the Horticultural Society to give land for a "rural cemetery."

Nature indeed served as a setting for the graves in Mount Auburn Cemetery, instead of the "immense city of the dead" that Charles Sumner (as determined a friend of nature as a foe of slavery) had seen at Père Lachaise during his European grand tour in 1838. "Nature has done as much for Mount Auburn as man has done for Père Lachaise," he wrote from Paris to his Harvard Law School professor Joseph Story, "and I need not tell you how superior is the workmanship of Nature."[10] Story, an associate justice of the U.S. Supreme Court, was also the president of the Proprietors of the Cemetery of Mount Auburn.

The concern of Americans for nature as the crucial element of the new burial ground puzzled Europeans who shared de Tocqueville's view of the predominant American attitude towards nature. Europeans marveled at the contradictions in American behavior. They noted that the European stereotype of the hectic American life rarely left time for a walk in field and forest or for any appreciation of nature. They also noted, however, that in contrast to the narrow, crowded European graveyards, Americans had created park cemeteries that looked like paradise and gave Americans the satisfaction of seeing their dead slumbering in the shade of lush stands of tall trees. In 1853, the author of a report on Mount Auburn Cemetery in *Meyer's Universum*, which annually published descriptions and pictures of novelties and curiosities from all over the world, could not help but search for the moral in his observation: "Freedom rules the infinite spaces of the cosmos, freedom rules according to any American's precept, and therefore free nature shall be the guardian and heir of his dust," he concluded from his visit to Mount Auburn Cemetery.[11]

The power of nature in park cemeteries along the East Coast inspired James Smillie, an outstanding engraver of American landscapes. His engravings of park cemeteries became the favorites of a public that was drawn to many aspects of funerals and burials. The views accentuated the rural scene and the patches of forest and meadow with vistas of solitary graves, lofty monuments, and tree-lined entrance gates. His art captivated the editor of the *Protestant Churchman* on September 19, 1846, to such an extent that he found it needless to describe the "varied and beautiful scenery" and merely referred his readers to the engravings.

Despite America's preference for burial in a natural landscape of the dead, the influence of Père Lachaise was not entirely lost. Fashion shaped the new graveyard like any other cultural expression. Mourning was the vogue in the United States until the death toll of the Civil War began eroding a state of mind—one rather foreign to ours today. Poems, pictures, weeping willows, and fancy black dresses inspired bereaved people who expressed their feelings by taking long walks among tombs. Mark Twain's artful satire of Emmeline Grangerford and her devotion to the funerary cult in *Huckleberry Finn* showed just how prevalent was the interest in burial. If new inspirations for mourning fashion came from Père Lachaise in Paris, so much the better.

There was something in the name of the famous Parisian cemetery that struck American hearts. The memory of the country's debt for the French help in the American Revolution reinforced the appeal of the graveyard from France. In the 1820s the popularity of the Lafayette bonnets, gloves, belt buckles, gingerbread, and cakes during the Marquis de Lafayette's visit to the United States reflected one aspect of the emotions linked to the French connection, symbolized by Lafayette's services during the Revolutionary War and the young general's friendship with George Washington.

Quite apart from nostalgia and fashion, Père Lachaise was a practical and progressive project, credited with providing a solution to the sanitary problems of the crowded burial grounds that reeked in the old cities of Europe. To emulate Père Lachaise was to display, not only fashionable taste, but also an indication that one was in step with new ideas and enjoying economic success. These considerations also added to the appeal of the name. In 1839, in Boston, the first published guide to Mount Auburn suggested that the cemetery, despite its natural setting, "may be called the Père la Chaise of America." [12] In Philadelphia that wave of fascination broke in 1837, when the press killed a suggestion to call a new project the "American Pere Lachaise." The stockholders chose "Monument Cemetery" as the new name.[13] Inadvertently the action betrayed their view of the French original as a place where art dominated nature.

In spite of the homage paid to French leadership in the design of an urban cemetery, Americans remained committed to the idea of a natural park for the dead. The appearance of the parklike setting suffered, however, because the venture had to pay for itself. That austerity somewhat diminished the appearance of the new cemetery as a park, because it affected the layout of the grounds and the arrangement of lots and graves. A considerable number of avenues and lanes, hugging the contours of the hills and winding through the vales, was required to provide convenient access to the lots. Their sale, after all, financed the experiment. Even so, maintaining the grounds turned into a financial burden, and the management came to view the curves of the popular serpentines looping up steep hills as a waste of space and funds. Initially these budgetary considerations did not cause the trustees to disturb the harmony between nature and culture that the park cemetery had achieved.

The landscape of the Cambridge tract, called "Stone's Wood," appeared so idyllic and parklike in its natural state that Harvard students, attracted to it in their rambles, had named it "Sweet Auburn," inspired by Oliver Goldsmith's poem "The Deserted Village."[14] The vision of fair, dappled lanes and bosky dells may also have stimulated thought, and it remains pleasing to think that the name "Sweet Auburn" might have reminded some students of the analogies between the poet's village, ruined by the enclosure movement, and the trees and meadows of Stone's Wood, threatened by the sprawling city and suburban development.

The novel burial ground saved dells, hills, and forest from the onslaught of urbanization to such an extent that in 1859, in form of a "cautionary suggestion," Dr. Jacob Bigelow, the Boston botanist, physician, and guiding spirit of Mount Auburn, considered the "multiplication of trees . . . " a serious evil. From the tower that had been built to grace the highest point, the cemetery looked "like a dense, impenetrable forest."[15]

The fleeting moment that saw nature and culture in concord in the new type of cemetery did not extend far beyond Mount Auburn. And there it ended even before its gardeners responded to Dr. Bigelow's warning. The luxurious foliage obscured the increasing number of memorial sculptures, which enjoyed a growing popularity after Bostonians began placing them in the park cemetery. Branches and leaves interfered with the display of funerary art designed to honor the dead and to satisfy the self-esteem of the living. The trustees undoubtedly thought that a curb on nature would please any patron of the arts who had embellished a grave with an elaborate sarcophagus and a fine sculpture.

The rise of ostentatious cemetery art also provided sculptors with a large urban audience. These visitors could not help but see the sculptures because they combined a stroll through the park cemetery with remembering the dead and assessing the cost of the monuments. "If those who have lots in Mount Auburn will employ the genius of American artists, undoubtedly the first in the world," a correspondent of the Boston *Evening Transcript* exaggerated in the 1840s, "they may soon make it as remarkable for the treasures of art collected there, as it is now for scenery."[16]

Neither a devotion to nature nor a concern for equality could block the spread of funerary art. Nature lost its eminence, and equality rarely gained currency. Since the middle of the eighteenth century, antiquity exercised a growing influence on the forms of funerary architecture. Inspiration came from Rome, Athens, Memphis, and Thebes. Chinese and Gothic models added to a cult of monuments that through exotic and intricate designs defied the image of death as the great equalizer.

Charlotte, one of the heroines in a Goethe novel from the opening decade of the nineteenth century, anticipated the development of funerary art in the park cemetery. She remonstrated with an architect that he had shown her nothing but a small obelisk, a broken column, and an urn. The promised thousand innovations in design turned out to be a thousand repetitions, Charlotte felt, and she drew her conclusions. She leveled the mound of the grave, planted clover, and achieved one goal: "the pure feeling of a final great equality."[17]

Charlotte's inspired solution did not alter the growing creed of an emerging park cemetery etiquette that funerary art should be displayed so that it could be seen or, better yet, so that it could not be ignored. Trees and shrubs obstructing the view were pruned back to suit the fashion. The love of natural solitude and the desire for a final resting place hidden from view lost out to the craving for social distinction offered by a prominent grave close to a popular promenade.

The demands of elaborate funerary architecture and the need for an economical ground plan joined with other considerations and constantly threatened to dethrone nature in the various park cemeteries that Mount Auburn inspired on the East Coast. The second park cemetery opened in 1836 on the eastern banks of the Schuylkill River north of Philadelphia at Laurel Hill. The ground had been part of "the country seat of a gentleman who, fully appreciating its many and remarkable beauties, had left the river front to the care of nature."[18] Commissioned by the proprietors of Laurel Hill, John Notman, one of Philadelphia's innovative builders in the second quarter of the nineteenth century, turned the estate into the country's first park cemetery designed by an architect.

The plans of one of America's first landscape professionals for the grounds and the Palladian entrance he designed showed similarities to the first English park cemetery, Kensal Green, established outside of London in 1831–1832.[19] Those plans attest to the continuity of European cultural influences on the American park cemetery. In addition, cultural artifacts and ideas employed routinely kept nature at bay, quite literally. "They are building the wall & will make a handsome place of it," Sidney George Fisher noted in his diary in November, 1836.[20] It was the first reference to Laurel Hill by Fisher, one of the few great nineteenth-century American urban diarists, after he had made an excursion to see the new project.

The relationship between nature and culture in the early East Coast park cemeteries is complex because all these experiments in urban burial intended to bring back nature into the rapidly growing cities of mid–nineteenth-century America. That goal was foremost in the minds of the directors of Greenwood Cemetery, established in 1838 on Brooklyn's Gowanus Heights, overlooking New York Bay and lower Manhattan. The planners shaped the 480-acre site, chosen for its beautiful appearance and its design potential, to resemble a rural scene. Instead of the name *necropolis* which conveyed to them "an ideal of *city* form and show," the proprietors chose "Greenwood" because it evoked "rural quiet and beauty, and leafiness and verdure."[21]

In order to echo accurately the prevailing spirit, in January

1843, the author of the poem "Greenwood Cemetery" in *The Knickerbocker* ignored his imagination and turned to the safety of a quote when he introduced the scene: " 'Here is the unshorn forest.' " Once he had evoked the desired image of the locale, so illusive in an urban context, his inspiration followed the poetic conventions that kept his lines in touch with nature quite effortlessly. "Man, as yet, / Has left untouched the handiwork of God"; he went on, "no art is here—'tis Nature's own domain."[22]

Although extolling Greenwood's affinity to nature, the poet's timely reservation about the absence of art—"as yet"—also seemed to foreshadow the coming profusion of funerary architecture that made the cemetery New York's most fashionable nineteenth-century burial ground. In 1849, Andrew Jackson Downing described the ten-year-old Greenwood Cemetery as "grand, dignified, and park-like."[23] The horticulturist, landscape gardener, architect, and editor of the *Horticulturist* estimated that many of the 60,000 people who visited Greenwood Cemetery during the summer came solely to enjoy trees and lawns.[24]

The popularity of the park cemetery as a country promenade eroded the magic of the graveyard as a retreat to nature. Man's hand showed itself quickly in Baltimore's Green Mount Cemetery, a sixty-acre former country estate on the northern boundary of the city. John Pendleton Kennedy, author, politician, and popular orator, made the praise of nature the center of his address at the dedication ceremony in 1839. He saw "the space, the quiet, the simple beauty and natural repose of the country" as prerequisite for a park cemetery. Its natural setting was for him the natural home of the dead.[25]

To keep all that naturalness safely inside cultural bounds Robert Cary Long, Jr., Baltimore's leading architect in the 1830s and 1840s, drew up two designs for an entrance gate—one Egyptian, the other Tudor—and the latter was accepted and built in 1840. The elms along Oliver's Walk, which had become the major thoroughfare of Green Mount, were removed in 1848 when disease was killing them. Tobacco juice as a cure for the ailing trees was considered too expensive, the *Green Mount Report* of that year indicated. In addition, its use threatened to stain the fine tombstones of Baltimore County marble.[26]

A triumph of nature over culture, if it would be at all conceivable to speak about such a feat, occurred in the Spring Grove Cemetery of Cincinnati. Dedicated in 1845 on some 170 acres four miles north of the city, the beauty of forest and meadow, hill and dale, lake and brook, made plausible the opening prayer to the God of Nature by the Reverend Dr. Brook. In the best of what was rapidly becoming a tradition of dedicatory oratory for graveyards, John McLean's speech acknowledged dutifully the many contributions to burial mankind had made since antiquity, singling out in recent decades specifically Père Lachaise, Mount Auburn, and Greenwood. After his tribute to the precedents, McLean, an associate justice of the U.S. Supreme Court, was ready to hold forth on the distinct contribution of Spring Grove as a park cemetery. Essentially, he found its characteristic, the combination of symbols of mourning with signs of hope, emanating from the unspoiled landscape. "Nature, in all her luxuriance," the Justice stressed, "should be here preserved and so cultivated as to expand her wildest beauty." He urged the building of plain memorials as the only way to shield the natural splendor of Spring Grove from the destructive forces of elaborate funerary monuments. In people's sincere responses to unadorned nature he professed to detect the restraint that would protect trees and wild flowers.[27]

The idea of simplicity as a characteristic of nature dominated the development of Spring Grove after the traces of John Notman's design for the cemetery had been eliminated in favor of a rural Ohio Valley scene. Presumably the Cincinnati proprietors found the cultural weight of the Philadelphia architect's plans too burdensome or the scheme too expensive for their ideas and means. Perhaps some had seen his work at Laurel Hill and recognized that there was not much left of natural simplicity. The classical features in the Palladian design of the entrance and the rigid geometry of the central circle had put the picturesque layout of the grounds into a straitjacket. Any marks Notman may have made on Spring Grove were erased by local gardeners who determinedly kept the setting of the cemetery more natural.[28]

The changes in the architecture of the cemetery entrance reflected this goal. *Cemetery of Spring Grove,* an early pamphlet published by the proprietors in 1849, contained the blank of a "Certificate of Ownership" as a promotional gadget. Engraved by the Cincinnati firm of Harrison & Jewett, the top of the document was embellished with a drawing of the entrance, a barnlike carriage gate with a cupola. Identical structures flanked the gate on each side. A passage for pedestrians linked the carriage entrance to a plain, two-story farmhouse set parallel to the main gate, with a single-story wing protruding at a ninety-degree angle and providing the connection with the picket fence encircling the cemetery. The appearance of the gate buildings measured up well to John McLean's admonition about ostentation, but at best it marked only the halfway point between nature and culture any ordinary farmstead occupied.[29]

Roughly a decade later, in October 1857, F. G. Cary published in his farm journal, *The Cincinnatus,* an account of Spring Grove. The article was accompanied by a lithograph, "View of the Entrance to the Cemetery," done by the Cincinnati firm of Ehrgott and Forbinger after a photograph by J. P. Ball & Thomas. The barnlike gate flanked by the two farmhouses was gone. The road approaching the entrance had been lowered and now led into the cemetery through an underpass. Its arch served as bridge across the entrance road for the cross traffic of the graveyard. On a much smaller scale, the arrangement was like the sunken crossroads, underpasses, and bridges, used at roughly the same time by Frederick Law Olmsted and Calvert Vaux to facilitate Manhattan's east–west traffic through Central Park. All traces of the fence enclosing Spring Grove Cemetery were gone, replaced by trees, bushes, and shrubbery forming a natural enclosure. On the masonry of the arch a sign facing the oncoming traffic attempted to curb an age-old human impulse with the warning, "No fast driving."[30]

Spring Grove also did away with the guardrails, iron chains, posts, and bars that frequently surrounded the graves in park cemeteries on the East Coast. The monuments remained, however, and over the years gained in magnitude and pretentiousness. They responded to people's seemingly irrepressible urge to use a monument as a device that would present the dead in an image best suited to the survivor. The appearance of statues, obelisks, and tombs produced a monotony of sculptures that contrasted starkly with the ever-changing shapes and colors of trees and shrubs, flowers and grasses. A publication of the Philadelphia Laurel Hill Cemetery Corporation condemned the seemingly irreversible trend. "Obelisk succeeds obelisk . . . with only slight variations," the writer stressed. "A correct idea, expressed in marble, may be very beautiful," he added wryly, "so long as it is unique."[31]

The conspicuous monuments gained added significance during the subsequent stages of the migration of the park cemetery. As the park cemetery moved farther west, a threat became clear that had been hidden by the luxurious forest of the East Coast. Along the Atlantic littoral, trees and meadows indeed reinforced belief. They conjured up the vision of a traditional country setting that supported the notion of death as return to nature. There, the changes of the clearly defined seasons seemed to invite drawing an analogy with the cycles of human life, with the promise of an equally ordered, rejuvenating afterlife.

The westering of the park cemetery heightened the emotional discomfort of people who sensed that the changing climate and soil could not evoke immortality in the park cemeteries through leafy trees and lush lawns. As a result, the emphasis on the natural component of the park cemetery, which had flourished in the favorable stages of the migration, came to be matched by a concern to erect durable memorials that promised the kind of immortality a different natural environment seemed no longer able to provide. In May 1850, at the dedication of the Bellefontaine Cemetery in St. Louis, Dr. Truman Marcellus Post, Congregational minister, educator, and orator, urged letting "pyramid, column, and statue with heavenward hand, and slab with graven cherubim . . . speak of immortality and point to God."[32]

The name of the new St. Louis cemetery also bespoke the changing outlook. Instead of evoking an aspect of nature, as the earlier park cemeteries had done, the 138-acre burial ground of the St. Louis Rural Cemetery Association linked itself with history. Located on the west side of Bellefontaine Road, it received its name, "Beautiful Fountain," from the road, which in turn was called after old Fort Bellefontaine in the northeastern corner of St. Louis County. It stood near the mouth of the Missouri, roughly opposite the Illinois shore of the Mississippi River where in the winter of 1803–1804 Lewis and Clark had gathered the members of their expedition at Camp Dubois. The name of the cemetery evoked memories of St. Louis's ties to the conquest of the West, and in 1850 that association with the extension of the republic to the Pacific Ocean pleased the residents of the "Gateway of the West" immensely. They had made the nation's leap from the Missouri to the Pacific in the 1840s their affair, and now found in the march of history and the name of their park cemetery yet another substitute for immortality.[33]

The report of St. Louis *Intelligencer* about the opening ceremony reflected the re-emerging dichotomy between nature and culture. In part the newspaper story read like the account of a land rush in a new Western settlement: "The lines are run. The stakes are set. The site of the Great City of the Dead is marked off and dedicated." After emphasizing that the projected improvements of the grounds would be extensive and "in admirable taste," the paper's junior editor (credited with writing the report) set out to prove that he had mastered the appropriate vocabulary to pay tribute not only to Mississippi Valley culture but also to Mississippi Valley nature: "The sun shone brightly; the oak and the elm trees opened their bursting buds and unfolded their young leaves to the genial sun; the green grass sprung fresh and glistening under feet, enameled with the delicate blue bell and wild heart's ease; the birds sang sweetly their springtide songs, and the zephirs dallied over all the happy scene."[34]

Only when the park cemetery reached the Pacific Ocean in 1865 did the paradox inherent in the westward migration of the park cemetery come to be resolved. At San Francisco Bay, the idea of death as a return to the nature of the East Coast, with the implication of rebirth conjured up by seasons changing with the coming and going of familiar indicators, faced the bleak, barren Oakland Hills. The lack of leafy trees and lush meadows, or regular rainfall to sustain both, made them an unlikely place for the cultivation of the kind of faith that nature seemed to sustain on the East Coast. Without fall colors and snow, people accustomed to well-defined seasons had to wait until the engineering of nature had been perfected in the making of the big-city park to provide the proper nature for the park cemetery in California.

After the modern city developed thoughts and methods for the engineering of nature, which made possible the reintroduction of nature in the urban setting, the clash between the available natural resources and the cultural expectations about proper care for the dead could be resolved. The necessity, willingness, and ability of Americans to engineer nature in the inhospitable environment of the modern city provided the answer. It changed the outlook on the relationship between nature and culture, which guided the final stage of the westward migration of the park cemetery.

The use of ideas and know-how developed in the making of the big-city park for solving the problem of the park cemetery on the West Coast reflected the reciprocity between big-city park and park cemetery. The exchange began roughly two decades earlier, when the initial success of the park cemetery on the East Coast contributed to the building of the municipal park. That interaction also stimulated the development of the rationale and the technology that decisively changed the relationship between urbanites and nature in the United States.

The creation of New York's Central Park encouraged this reversal of attitudes. Unlike the support for the park cemetery, which almost automatically came from people concerned with their obligations to the dead and their own future, the advocates of the municipal park needed to enlist a considerable body of social philosophy to back their project. They also faced a slightly different task in physically landscaping the site. While the proprietors of the early park cemeteries could build on and work with an existing stand of trees, with hill, vale, and meadow, the backers of the city park faced a large plot of land so unattractive that developers had bypassed it as a building site. Only ragged remnants of stunted nature had escaped casual destruction by squatters. Engineering methods to transform these areas had yet to be developed. Work crews needed to be educated to the novel responsibility of raising, instead of destroying, nature in a city. Eventually, technique and workers would introduce in the city a pleasing natural landscape as an expansion of the cityscape, appealing to the diverse interests supporting the project.

Aesthetics and politics, art and money worked together to fuse nature and culture for urban purposes. Visionaries who regarded a park as a work of art that would produce primarily psychological and aesthetic benefits joined businessmen who calculated the rise of real estate values in a park neighborhood, or the income from streetcars bringing visitors to the rural oasis in the cityscape. Petty politicians, attuned to speculations in franchises and land, recognized the park project as a source of jobs for faithful voters out of work in depression years. Since outsiders (that is, those who did not share in the graft of the big city) viewed most official expenditures as signs of municipal corruption, local politicians welcomed the growing support for spending money on parks. They must undoubtedly have been delighted by such comments as the San Francisco *Real Estate Circular*'s observation in 1873 that "no public money has been more economically or usefully expended" than on the making of Golden Gate Park.[35]

The municipal park, as a leisure space and a country retreat in a predominantly work-oriented urban society, brought citizens and reformers together. Some of the most respected spokesmen of the age heartily approved of outdoor recreation of all kinds as a worthwhile use of leisure for all segments of society. Henry

Ward Beecher, whose service as pastor of the Plymouth Church of Brooklyn from 1847 until his death in 1887 made him the most conspicuous Congregational clergyman in the United States, supported the changing outlook on work and leisure early on. In the 1850s he explained to his readers the pleasures of daydreaming and of the "industrious laying down" he frequently practiced on his farm while his neighbors worked diligently.[36]

The municipal park had the potential of enlarging the realm of leisure for city dwellers by becoming the rural world of the multitude chained to the city. That possibility quickly attracted urban reformers, who examined the project with practical eyes. They regarded areas of trees, grass and lakes as the lungs of the city that would breathe fresh air into a congested, disease-ridden social organism. Their hope that a healthy environment could ensure hygiene matched the yearnings of other urbanites for an attractive one. While the pursuit of the beautiful cityscape, the healthy environment, the profitable real estate scheme, and the harvest of the novel political plum continued to lead to division among the project's advocates, many people of different interests could unite behind a park venture.

Behind these specific hopes for the municipal park lay a public conscience that united groups with widely ranging goals as supporters of the project. Concerned about the quality of urban life in general, the cosmopolitans among them had been inspired by the English park models during their tours of the British Isles and the agitation for public gardens in Europe after the Napoleonic wars. Some drew conclusions from a talk between a traveler and editor Downing about the French and Germans, which Downing published in his *Horticulturist* in 1848. Despite their objectionable politics, Downing from his perspective as landscape gardener argued at the conclusion of the conversation, these Europeans seemed greater practical "republicans" than the Americans. The French and German cities had parks and gardens "provided at public cost, maintained at public expense, and enjoyed daily and hourly by all classes of persons."[37] Finally, to a few cosmopolitans, a park seemed to promise relief from the gridiron's "deadly uniformity of mean ugliness" that the novelist Edith Wharton recalled from her New York childhood.[38]

Over the years, the reaction of visitors to the park cemeteries as pleasure grounds had changed. When first laid out, they could have been considered parks, with "here and there, a monument or tombstone half seen among the trees," as the author of an early history of Central Park recalled. Later on, when the number of burials increased, "it was not easy even for the lightest hearted . . . to get much cheer out of a landscape set so thick with sad suggestions." Visitors turned away, the author concluded, and "fashion and pleasure looked about for a garden where death was not so frequent a visitor."[39]

In an age that saw the editor replace the minister as spokesman of the community, William Cullen Bryant of the New York *Evening Post* played a considerable role in giving park planners a sense of urgency. The poet editor warned in 1844 that "commerce is devouring inch by inch" the city's harbor, shore, and land. "If we would rescue any part of it for health and recreation," he emphasized, "it must be done now."[40] In the next decade the various groups advocating a large municipal park for New York found in Frederick Law Olmsted the Superintendent and Architect-in-Chief to create Central Park.

Olmsted seemed unprepared for the task, unlike Downing, who would have been the most likely candidate for the position until he drowned in a steamboat accident on the Hudson River in 1852. At the age of twenty-two, Olmsted had decided to become a scientific farmer, instead of a civil engineer, a merchant, or a ship captain. His wide reading brought him in touch with Downing, who impressed upon him his concern for the practical and the beautiful in all areas and forms of life. His studies and his work as farmer convinced him that cultivating a rural taste mattered as much as raising a crop.

Having a restless mind, Olmsted shared many concerns of the outside world, but his idea of the virtuous life kept him from losing sight of his obligations to others. His extensive travels had reinforced these ideas. As an enthusiastic traveler Olmsted had seen the Far East, England, the Continent, New England, Canada, and the South. He published his impressions of England and his experiences in the South before he was called to New York. When he made Central Park it became abundantly clear that his entire previous life seemed to have been a preparation for the task, and his ability to learn and grow did not end with his appointment as superintendent. While creating the park Olmsted continued to absorb new knowledge. He learned much about drainage work as a part of engineering, and architecture as a part of landscape design, from his fellow workers during the building of the park.

Olmstead brought to the task of constructing Central Park a vision of the park as a place where trees, lawns, and lakes would bring the diverse groups of city people together. His travels through the South had alerted him, not only to the pernicious effect of slavery on everyone, but also to the shortcomings of the free society in the North. In a letter to his friend the philanthropist Charles Loring Brace, Olmsted summed up the conclusions he drew from a stirring conversation with a wealthy Nashville slaveholder, a classmate of his brother. The knee-deep-in-the-cotton aristocrat had relied callously on blatant self-interest to explain and justify the social system of the South. As a "Socialist Democrat," Olmsted felt strongly that "government should have in view the encouragement of a democratic condition of society as well as of government."

His exposure to the selfish thoughts of slaveholders, he explained to Brace, convinced him that in a free society, "the poor & the wicked need more than to be left alone." The "low, prejudiced" people of the North, enslaved by party politics and material interests, needed to be uplifted by enlarging education with devices "so attractive as to force into contact the good & bad, the gentlemanly and the rowdy." Among these mechanisms for helping people, Olmsted listed the park first.[41]

Democracy's defense of people's natural freedom through the attractive arrangement of trees, lawns, and lakes in a city set the municipal park apart from other public places that had existed in American towns since the beginning of colonization. The design called for more land than a common, a market, or an exclusive retreat from the hustle of the city. The need for a park came to be felt at a crucial phase determining the future character of American urban society.

The idea of the park as an essential component of the modern city took hold in an era when urban development drastically reduced the amount of open space, concentrated large, diverse groups of people in a limited area, and severed most urbanites' ties with the countryside. Irrespective of similar trends in European countries, these distinctly American interactions between urbanization, industrialization, and immigration allowed Olmsted to view the movement for the municipal park as an independent development of the United States, spontaneously engendered by the "Genius of Civilization."[42]

In Olmsted's perspective the movement for a park appeared to be an outgrowth of a steadily expanding democracy that depended on the modern city for its developing institutions and ideas. The growth of the city, in turn, became one of "the natural fruits of democracy," in the words of Henry W. Bellows, head of the First Unitarian Church in New York and one of the leading intellectuals of the Civil War era. The demand raised by city people for equal opportunities, in his view, stimulated the rapid rise of communication systems as diverse as the railroad and the press. Apart from the profit motive shaping innovations in a democracy, Bellows felt that innovations "are as much the products of social rivalries" as a response to "an ineradicable democratic instinct for popularizing all advantages." With the creation of a park, city people linked their individual pursuit of money to a communal effort that built a monument to their majesty.[43]

Central Park in New York made the links between democracy and nature visible. Bellows called the park "the most striking evidence of the sovereignty of the people yet afforded in the history of free institutions."[44] The city's most popular poet, the editor William Cullen Bryant, had educated two generations of his fellow citizens about the crucial bond. His verses rekindled in the urban reader the feeling that nature was the necessary complement of human existence. To bring back that yearning for nature into the city as embodiment of large numbers of people, Bryant hoped to instigate a public call for some contact with nature. Viewing the city as a place that fostered popular democracy, such a public demand found a direction and an outlet in the municipal park.[45]

An awareness that the beginnings of the park reached back to the yearning of the urban democracy for its share in the advances of American civilization spoke from various statements reflecting the diversity of the city. Bellows felt that the complex origins of Central Park could only be understood by those steeped in the workings of popular government. "It is a royal work, undertaken and achieved by the Democracy," he argued eloquently, "and developing in its creation and growth, in its use and application, new and almost incredible tastes, aptitudes, capacities, and powers in the people themselves." He extolled the virtues of magnanimous people willing to concentrate their authority in hands capable of building the park. In April 1861, with the beginning of the Civil War, these actions threw "light and cheer upon the prospects of popular institutions, at a period when they are seriously clouded from other quarters."[46]

In 1859, an editorial writer in *Harper's Weekly* celebrated the success of the park movement as the symbiosis of democracy and nature, the joint product of town and country. He felt that the newly forged community of city and nature strengthened the people's constructive ability and brought out the best in them. "The more parks we plant," he emphasized, "the more we promote refinement of soul by the increasing influence of beauty, the more we shall find that faith in the people is justified and deepened."[47]

Nobody could claim credit for New York's splendor but the people, an editorial in the New York *Tribune* stressed in 1862, when it compared the creative energies of people ensuring the growth of the city with the beautification of Paris engineered by Louis Napoleon. "We have no great men," the editorial writer asserted. In Europe "men are great because the people of communities are small," he explained. "Here are all great, . . . all devise, all work." The beauty of Paris, Rome, Vienna, or any other famous city simply showed him how little freedom, room for initiative, and chances for organized projects their residents had if a single individual could get credit for all accomplishments.[48]

Henry W. Bellows reasoned similarly when he expressed his trust in the constructive abilities of large numbers of people. He saw the difference in the functions of public buildings and their grounds in Europe and in the United States. In the Old World these monuments sought to link the loyalty of common people to aristocratic regimes by a lavish appeal to people's pride as citizens surrounded by the splendid exhibits. At the same time, the spectacle of the magnificent architecture and the enjoyment of spacious parks and gardens served to drain off popular restlessness and defuse dangerous designs. In the New World, he stressed, it had not yet been necessary to provide distraction for popular discontent or to stimulate patriotism through bribes.[49]

"Demopiety," the faith in the constructive vitality of ordinary people, gained enormous strength during the Civil War period.[50] Demopiety thrived on the demonstrated ability of ordinary people—not royalty, princes, or government officials—to build an attractive and beautiful cityscape. The belief found ample support in the visual evidence provided by hotels and theaters, palatial department stores, and other imposing business buildings. They served legions of customers and answered the need of countless people for a useful as well as beautiful urban environment. There, individuals adrift in the tides of the modern city became part of communities. These physical creations of city people also visibly strengthened the spirit of a generation rallying to the support of popular government. Lincoln, when dedicating a cemetery for soldiers killed in the defense of popular democracy, found at Gettysburg the words that immortalized that belief and gave meaning to their death.

Demopiety antedated Central Park as a specific American element of urbanization. The belief in the ability of diverse groups of people to build the good life in the big city emerged when intensified urbanization began to leave its mark on the United States. As early as 1826, the missionary Timothy Flint articulated the fundamental component of the faith after his travels in the Ohio Valley. He compared the rise of Cincinnati, which took place before his eyes, to the founding of the Russian imperial capital, St. Petersburg, roughly one century earlier. There, at the Neva, he saw "the will of the sovereign, who made the same use of men that the mason does of brick and mortar." Here, at the Ohio, he saw "the fostering efforts of liberty. . . . The people build and multiply imperceptibly . . . city comfort, beauty, and opulence."[51]

Central Park, as the creation of city people, embodied the relationship between democracy and nature. The city dwellers longed for the promise of grass and trees that could bring them in touch with nature for a few leisure hours. In Central Park they could identify with nature as a component of the cityscape, much as other Americans could greet the grandeur of the pristine mountains and valleys as components of their country.

The beauty and extent of the extravagant, unsullied nature of the continent had filled the heart and mind of some of the spectators with awe for the power of the Almighty. They found their bond with nature reinforced by the feeling of "geopiety" that they experienced in their encounter with the mountains and the valleys not yet defaced by them.[52] Geopiety, the awe for the power of the Almighty or the power of Nature evoked by spectacular scenery, had special dimensions for the generation of Emerson and Thoreau, which deepened the association with nature.

Seeing a mountain gorge in New Hampshire called the Franconia Notch, the painter Thomas Cole noted that "the silent energy of nature stirred the soul to its innate depths."[53] After a visit to Yosemite Valley in California, the editor Samuel Bowles wrote in 1865 that in this "confrontal of God face to face . . . all that was mortal shrank back . . . as we reined our horses sharply out of green forests, and stood upon high jutting rock that overlooked this rolling, heaving sea of granite."[54] Following the lead of that spirit of geopiety, urbanites incorporated nature into their lives as an essential component of leisure in the urban environment.

Central Park flourished with the spirit of demopiety because the magician who constructed the park had the ability to ignore everything but the public vision of a natural landscape in a big city. Olmsted played no part in the initial phase of the project.[55] Neither the crusade for the park nor the debate about the site involved him; but from the summer of 1857, when he joined the project as superintendent, he played a more important role in the making of Central Park than anyone else. In the following year he prepared a plan for the design competition together with Calvert Vaux, a London-born architect who since 1850 had assisted Downing in his growing practice as landscape gardener. The plan provided a unified design for the roughly eight hundred acres in central Manhattan, a strip of land half a mile wide and two-and-a-half miles long. Both men joined their talents so auspiciously that it seems prudent to follow their explanations of their individual contributions.

In later years, Olmsted and Vaux agreed to share equal credit for the overall design and for the sunken crossroads, which directed the Manhattan cross-traffic through the park without disturbing its ambience. Vaux received specific credit for the architectural features and his technical skills in general. Olmsted's individual contributions consisted of the organization and management of the work force constructing the site, the administration of the area, and the education of the public to the use of the park.[56]

The division of credit that the two men devised for their work on Central Park suggested that Olmsted functioned as the creator of the park's role as a joint venture in democracy and nature. To achieve that end, people and nature needed to be changed: the one educated, the other engineered. Olmsted stressed the immense satisfaction he gained from administering the park and preparing the public for its use. "It was in this," he wrote to Vaux on November 26, 1863, "that without any exertion or labor but by fact of natural gift that I have been worth most to the park."[57] Vaux, in a letter to Henry W. Bellows on February 25, 1864, added to Olmsted's elaboration the significant observation that Olmsted was nature's man in a special way. In "his knowledge of agriculture in its finer sense," Olmsted balanced Vaux's artistic and technical competence as professional architect.[58]

The creation of an enchanted world called for the introduction of pastoral and picturesque nature in central Manhattan. It usually required the destruction of the remaining forms of indigenous nature. The preparation of lakes, meadows, wooded areas, tree-lined promenades, foot paths, and carriage drives required blasting of rock ridges, laying pipes to drain the swampy glens, moving tons of soil, and planting mature trees and shrubs. In 1873 Olmsted estimated that his work force constructing the park, which on the average numbered about three thousand men, had moved 4,825,000 cubic yards of earth and stone. That amounted to "nearly ten millions of ordinary city one-horse cart loads, which, in single file, would make a procession of thirty thousand . . . miles in length."[59]

The public funds for the project and the natural potential of the site were limited. These factors shaped Olmsted's ideas on the making of Central Park. During the travels of his New England childhood he had learned from his father to think of landscape more as scenery and less as an assemblage of hills, valleys, and rivers. The concept of landscape as scenery fitted well the spirit of their prize-winning park design, which Olmsted and Vaux called "Greensward." The expanse of green turf created an impression in a viewer's mind analogous to that made by the wide-open spaces and vague borders of the pastoral style of landscape gardening.

Olmsted's experience as a practical farmer and nurseryman enabled both architects to vary the sweeping rural vistas with patches and stands of divers foliage, providing the variety of impressions characteristic of the picturesque style. Olmsted added another dimension to the calm, comforting effect of the pastoral scene and the mysterious character of the rugged and vivid woods of the picturesque. He took conventional picturesque scenery and expanded it by adding lush, exotic vegetation. The tropical plants, Olmsted hoped, would impress the park users with splendid examples of nature's variety and vitality.

On his voyage to China in 1843, Olmsted had also visited parts of southeast Asia and experienced its luxuriant, tropical vegetation. He returned convinced that tropical plants should be included in the design of a picturesque landscape. This idea was just one example that reflected the intellectual audacity that enabled Olmsted to build Central Park. Although Olmsted lacked training in any specific field that would qualify him as superintendent and architect-in-chief, he brought to the task great intelligence, an open mind, and personal integrity. To these qualities he added the fruits of his twenty years in varied occupations. He also drew on insights acquired from his eclectic experiences and his widespread acquaintances. Like him, many of them considered it their obligation to serve others by serving society.

Olmsted's travels had broadened his personal identification as a social democrat, and Olmsted the Republican cherished that commitment. As a conscientious citizen he regarded it as his task and the duty of democratic government to help destitute and suffering people. He viewed the building of schools, parks, and whatever other public institutions were needed as the best way to uplift poor people to the level of the group he had the good fortune to be born into: the gentry.

Olmsted's exposure to Downing's thoughts strengthened the rationale that linked Olmsted's view of social responsibility to the task of building the big-city park. Downing, who had agitated for a large park in New York in his *Horticulturist* in October 1848, buttressed Olmsted's belief that society could be improved and civilization enhanced by cultivating a popular taste in architecture and landscape design.

Olmsted, the self-styled socialist-democrat who voted Republican, lived up to the promise of the Greensward plan. His intellectual, artistic, and technical eclecticism gave physical form to the moral intentions of the design. In the words of Olmsted and Vaux, it offered "to the hundreds of thousands of tired workers, who have no opportunity to spend their summers in the country, a specimen of God's handiwork."[60]

Working the pillaged ground of central Manhattan in the language of the New England landscape, Olmsted engineered nature by blending color, shape, size, and texture into unified impressions. He fused the contours of the land with distinct modes of scenery into a setting that appealed to people's timeless respect for earth, trees, and shrubs to bring out their better qualities in a communion with nature.

The natural resources of Central Park, as used by the people of New York, matched the expectations the city had attached to the project. Nature and culture joined in harmony for a fleeting moment before various interest groups could usurp segments of the park for their aims. Olmsted changed the rocky hills, swampy meadows, and broken valleys of a dreary site in central Manhattan to suit his generation's faith and hope for nature in the city. Educating his fellow citizens systematically to the virtue and use of their municipal park, he resolved the conflict between the meager natural resources and the great cultural expectations.

Central Park itself provided the most persuasive argument for protecting nature in the city. The awareness that the last disparaged remnants of nature would soon have been lost to more buildings also enhanced the magic of Olmsted's solution. The re-creation of nature exposed the unattractive character of the original site and obscured the surrounding city behind shields of foliage. The success of the project assured city people that the engineering of nature provided the answer to the need to keep nature an integral part of the urban experience.

As soon as the meticulously transplanted trees showed their first fresh green, crowds of people eagerly took advantage of the carefully planned "natural" scenery. The imagination of the sheer number of park users began the slow process of inadvertently amending the original ideas of the supporters of the project. With the recognized importance of the park in city life and its increasing use by large numbers of people, there appeared a "strong tendency" to convert it "into a great, perpetual metropolitan Fair Ground." The additions disturbed those who saw the park as a work of art, "framed upon a single, noble motive"; as well as those who regarded the park as a device to convert their fellow men to their own concepts of leisure.[61]

The obvious steps in the engineering of culture that accompanied the engineering of nature in the city park aimed at protecting the fragile creation. In an age that encouraged the exploitation of natural resources, appropriate public behavior in city parks was reinforced with signs and guards who kept people on walks, lest they injure new grass, budding plants, and young trees. While these measures were accepted as necessary, disagreements arose about other aspects of the uses of the park for leisure. Specific preferences often clashed with general norms or infringed on the modicum of nature being developed. Suggestions came for playing fields and parade grounds, for monuments and restaurants, for a zoo and a museum—to mention but a few of the special interests that different groups of people put forth.

The layout of paths, promenades, carriage drives, and horse trails served as constant reminders that although all people were created equal, some were more equal than others. A democratic society, assiduously seeking ways to express distinctions between people without violating its own professed creed, would use a fashionable promenade terminating in a set of grandiose steps just for that purpose. After all, the stairway provided a convenient setting to make an impression: the spectacular descent of a smartly dressed couple of social climbers to the lake shore below framed with the hoi polloi seeking rather ordinary pleasures. The superficial attempts to engineer culture with the engineering of nature did not, however, diminish the enjoyment city dwellers found in the many uses of the park.

The considerate and extensive use the residents of New York

made of the park indicated clearly that they endorsed it as an addition to city life. In 1865, when Olmsted urged San Franciscans to build a large municipal park without delay, he summed up both aspects of success. "Notwithstanding the bad reputation of the New York populace," he wrote in a San Francisco newspaper, "there is no park in Europe that is made as good use by the people, none where the proportion of offenses against good order and good taste is so small, or the respect for the regulations necessary for the best use of the park, so great as in the park of New York." While still "in an incomplete state" and "comparatively bare of trees," the park attracted annually about three million visitors.

On special occasions, one hundred thousand people walked in the park on a single day. On an average summer day, five to ten thousand people came to the park on foot. About one thousand carriages were driven through the park each summer day. The largest number of carriages on a single day was 9,460; of saddle horses, 1,540. "It is beyond all question," Olmsted emphasized when he used the figures as evidence of the success of the project, "that the influence of the park is exceedingly favorable to moral as well as physical health, and that it exerts a highly civilizing effect upon the population of the city."[62] He considered the number of visitors the best indication of the wide range of response Central Park had achieved.

A public-spirited physician and one of the first reviewers of the history of parks and public grounds in the United States argued in 1869 "that apart from considerations of sanitary economy public parks may be regarded as an unerring index of the advance of people in civilization and refinement."[63] Among all the manipulations of the environment in the modern city, the municipal park alone preserved public spaces for leisure, free from commercialism or pietism, in an urban context predominantly oriented toward work. In their attempts to ensure the uses of the park in socially acceptable ways, the designers relied on people's timeless respect for earth, trees, and water to bring out their best disposition and temperament in their communion with nature.

Central Park became the model for urbanites seeking ways to reintroduce nature to the city and to integrate trees and meadows with the daily lives of city people. The park demonstrated the city's potential as source of civilization and provided for all Americans an inspiring example of how to restore and protect selected nature effectively. However, various interest groups trying to shape the large city park to their needs weakened the cohesion of the design and reduced the magnitude of a project dedicated to few, specific purposes. The onslaught of diverse demands for uses of the park diminished the harmony between nature and culture Central Park had radiated during the early years under Olmsted's direction.

Created in response to a more uniformly shared single task—the age-old obligation of the proper care for the dead,—the design of the park cemetery managed to retain the harmony between nature and culture for a while. The park cemetery provided an ideal field for the realization of that utopian dream, because its occupants, unlike the members of an ordinary utopia, could not object to the vision of the planners. In the final stage of its westward migration, the planners of the park cemetery relied on insights drawn from the Central Park experience to ensure a visually harmonious blend of nature and culture.

Facing the Golden Gate across the expanse of San Francisco Bay, the Mountain View Cemetery in Oakland marks the place where, in 1865, the park cemetery as a new type of burial ground reached the Western rim of the continent. Until people began shaping the scene with trees, tombs, and water from irrigation ducts and watering cans, the appearance of the 200-acre site about two miles east of the center of the city had been determined by topography, climate, and animals. The original shrubs and trees had long since given way to ranch land. The grassy slopes of the sandy hills that embrace the flatlands along the bay formed a narrow valley enlivened only by those live oaks and bushes that had escaped the roaming cattle. The wind, incessantly sweeping the fog off the foliage and shrouding it again in mist, stunted the growth of the scattered trees and shrubs, intensifying the struggle of scant vegetation in poor soil against a climate characterized by summer drought and winter rain.

Struck by the stark setting, the future builders of the new burial ground contrasted the barren hills with the glades and groves of park cemeteries they had known in the East. They sought a proposal for a similar cemetery from Frederick Law Olmsted, who recognized the restraints nature would place on any attempt to build an "eastern" park cemetery on the shore of San Francisco Bay. Each leap in its westward migration had moved the park cemetery further from the soil and the climate that favored its existence, its creation, its maintenance.

Although the natural conditions of the barren Oakland Hills differed from the lush forest of the East Coast, the cultural framework of the park cemetery reached the West Coast intact. Mount Auburn Cemetery had produced guidelines that became part of the intellectual heritage of Americans moving west. The California Rural Cemetery Act of 1859, which followed the Massachusetts and New York precedents, provided the legal framework, while experiences and insights gained from Spring Grove and Bellefontaine cemeteries broadened the knowledge of designing and operating park cemeteries.

Taking a lead from the "tasteful cemeteries of the East," the first pamphlet of the Mountain View Cemetery Association in 1865 announced a ban of wooden railings as well as stone and iron fences. The brochure defended this policy by referring to the views of an anonymous Cincinnati landscape gardener and one of the country's great men of letters, Washington Irving, who had opposed the use of fences in the park cemetery. In case these voices were ignored and fences deemed necessary, local pride considered it out of the question that the grounds would be grazed by cattle or that visitors would be "incapable of conducting themselves properly."[64]

Although the barren Oakland site was far different from the parkland of the East in 1865, nineteenth-century Californians were eager to match national models, and in the previous year the Board of Trustees had asked Olmsted to draw up a plan for the cemetery. The trustees hailed Olmsted as "landscape architect" and "architect of Central Park," referring to his best-known accomplishment to buttress their ambitious hopes.[65] They assumed that this very ability to turn the rocks and wastes of central Manhattan into Central Park guaranteed that he could turn their barren Oakland site into a park cemetery the equal of any that other cities might boast about.

Olmsted, shortly after the outbreak of the Civil War, had taken a leave from his work at Central Park and gone to Washington as general secretary of the United States Sanitary Commission, the forerunner of the American Red Cross. Exhausted from his exertions, in 1863 he resigned from the Commission and from Central Park. In order to restore his health he accepted an invitation to administer a California estate, a large gold-mining property, for New York financiers. Olmsted soon became disillusioned with the prospect of the mines. He took on several tasks that brought him back to landscape architecture, among them the request to design Mountain View Cemetery.

After an initial survey, he wrote a report explaining his approach to the task, and in the introduction explained his solution, which aligned the trustees' expectations with the potential of their land. A strong argument backed his reasoning: "Scarcely anywhere in the world," he emphasized, "except in actual deserts, is the indigenous vegetation so limited in variety as in the country about San Francisco."[66] With that assertion made, he shrewdly guided the trustees to his view.

Olmsted argued that any design serving the purpose of a park cemetery must necessarily mar any purely natural landscape. Furthermore, he insisted that the stubborn pursuit of the cultural goal would exhaust resources. He ridiculed the notion "that in a cemetery the gardener's art should only appear as if used in a humble waiting on Nature."[67] Finally, he crowned his arguments with the observation that, first and foremost, the purpose of creating a burial ground was not to make a beautiful landscape garden but to make a place to honor the dead.

To capture the trustee's sympathies for his plan more firmly, Olmsted reinforced their perception of themselves as a civic elite. The trustees were agreeable. The thirteen men stood out in an area that had attracted outstanding men. They came from the East Coast, predominantly from New England and New York. They were merchants, bankers, politicians, judges, and lawyers. Two were clergymen. One had been a brevet brigadier general in the Quartermaster's Department during the Civil War. They must have dealt with and competed with each other, but Mountain View Cemetery struck them as a suitable diversion for hard-driving men, not far from what their obituaries later would call their abiding interest in the community. Undoubtedly they deeply felt their obligation to the dead, but they were also concerned about their own future when they began thinking about a park cemetery.

Olmsted may have felt an affinity with these men who were cast momentarily into the mold of a community by an awareness of the fate nature held for all of them. He let them know that it required men of distinguished understanding to comprehend the soundness of his suggestion and that it was their duty as civic leaders and guardians of public taste to safeguard the venture. Olmsted highlighted his argument by skillfully comparing the difficulties of the natural climate of the cemetery with those of the social climate of the Bay Area. In the face of a rootless population, he stressed the immediate need for a firm policy linking nature and culture into a single unit of operation. That idea of integrating nature and culture would guide the mechanism to fulfill Olmsted's view of Christian care for the dead in a terrain that lacked the natural features of other park cemeteries.

The design and the subsequent landscaping reflected the extent of the compromise between nature and culture. The level grounds of the cemetery, "far . . . from being suggestive of picturesque treatment," Olmsted bisected with a straight, tree-lined avenue, which under the circumstances he considered to be the "simplest and most natural course."[68] On the slopes of the five or six hills skirting and flanking the avenue, he constructed curved lanes and paths to ease ascent and descent, like the twisting roads of the park cemeteries in the East.

Ultimately, Olmsted turned from engineering nature to engineering culture. He expounded moral principles in arguing what in his view would be appropriate and beautiful for Mountain View. To defend his combination of straight and curved lines, Olmsted insisted that the simplest approach was also the most natural one. He acknowledged that "the cemeteries to which we are accustomed in the East are laid out entirely in curved lines," but he dismissed the assumption that curved lines were natural, while straight lines were unnatural because they were artificial, the work of man.[69]

On behalf of his design, Olmsted drew upon the moral propositions that distinguished Emersonian transcendentalism to argue that both man and nature are God's work and that His hand is to be seen in trees planted by gardeners as much as in those rising from seeds sown by birds. As long as man's purpose is good and pure, Olmsted concluded, the so-called natural scene cannot be more beautiful than a man-made landscape designed with the "single purpose to manifest Christian tenderness and care in the presence of the dead."[70]

Appealing to the obligation of the trustees as an elite and evoking the unity of nature and culture as God's agents, Olmsted's explanations suited his belief as well as those of the like-minded members of his generation. His acceptance of an elite as a fact of life was qualified by his insistence that its members, living in the midst of a democratic society, should avoid the stigma of a privileged group by sharing their knowledge and accomplishments with others. In addition to Emerson as the herald of the divine presence in nature and humanity, Olmsted drew particularly upon the teachings of those Protestant preachers at mid–nineteenth century who, like Horace Bushnell, emphasized moral conduct more than rigid theology as key to Christian life.[71] From such a perspective, Olmsted and thousands like him had adopted an outlook that made moral principles crucial to the assessment of the beauty of a scene.

Olmsted's argument appealed to the trustees' idea of a graveyard. His description enabled them to envision the foliage that would cover the barren hills after adding the transplanted Italian cypress, Lebanese cedar, and Italian stone pine to the landscape of the California live oak, which in a few places had escaped destruction by grazing cattle and reached maturity. Simple in form and color and distinctive in composition and appearance, the trees established a scene reminding people of their obligation to venerate the dead. In protective shelters of low-ranging cedars, with the spires of cypresses venturing to the sky above them, Mountain View exhibited simplicity and unity through the fusion of nature and culture.

Momentarily the hills of the San Francisco Bay area had joined a revolution in taste that Alexander Pope, the English poet, expressed in *The Guardian* on September 23, 1713. He identified "the amiable simplicity of unadorned nature" as the ideal of the garden in antiquity and of that distinct measure of civilized people: nature and culture in harmony. The ideal briefly characterized the park cemetery on the shore of San Francisco Bay. The regularity of ordinary graves, their location and sequence of placement, upheld the balance, and the first large tomb reflected the spirit of the builders. It was a trustees' catacomb dug into a hillside in 1866, blending with terrain and design.

Less than a decade later, unity and simplicity gave way. Disagreements about money and methods, as well as about the men running the cemetery, stirred the trustees. The clash of opinions culminated in a spirited controversy that was carried to the public by Samuel Merritt, a physician, former mayor of Oakland and president of the Mountain View Cemetery Association. He exposed the diverse views in a pamphlet in 1871.[72] Underlying what seemed to be a discussion of personalities was also the question of greater freedom to use elaborate funerary architecture. The debate touched on the advantage of the park cemetery as a utopia over other utopian experiments: unlike the living, the dead are silent on any planner's solution for their resting place. In due time silence was rewarded on Mountain View Cemetery in the form of a city of the dead.

The elaborate monuments, the mixture of mausoleums, obelisks, chapels, pyramids, and columbaria overwhelmed the transitory harmony of nature and culture. The additions undermined the unity of the design and created the need for regulations to ensure the "harmonious improvement" of the cemetery. "Monumental Lots," those in prominent places or along the main avenues, were only sold "on conditions providing for their improvement and for keeping them in perpetual repair."[73]

There remained traces of the contribution of Mountain View to the westward migration of the park cemetery and to the interaction between nature and culture in American history. The grandeur of the necropolis that sprang up on the Oakland hills also attracted palm and eucalyptus trees, which earlier seemed out of place; however, the feathery shape of their leaves and the whirling motions of their branches enlivened the monotony of the gray granite and the white marble of the ostentatious structures. "In some places there is too much expensive and grandiose glitter," Charles Howard Shinn, historian and conservationist, reported after a visit in 1891, "but for the most part good sense and modesty prevail."[74]

Sections of the cemetery preserved the accomplishments of Mountain View. The settings of these graves reflected a mixture of tradition and innovation in a unique location. There the power of nature challenged the transmitted cultural assumptions about observing the elemental task of proper burial; there the creative impulse of the builders of Mountain View checked the westering culture's search for mastery over nature. For a moment it brought a measure of harmony to the relationship between nature and culture, between environment and people, and achieved in the Far West a distinct contribution to American civilization.

An application of the insights into the concord between nature and culture that Central Park and Mountain View provided faced great obstacles in the building of San Franciso's Golden Gate Park. The extraordinary conditions of the site were at the root of the difficulties. Sand dunes moved from place to place by the ocean breeze made up the largest portion of the thousand-acre site, which the city acquired in 1868. Their constantly shifting appearance formed a striking contrast with the models of urban pleasure grounds Americans had in mind. The drifting sand hindered the development of a great park in San Francisco to such an extent that the early stages of the project re-enacted aspects of the classic conflict between nature and culture. In 1876, when the drifts had been somewhat stabilized with a long brush fence holding off the encroaching sand, a journalist commenting on the success of the bulwark expressed what must have been the prevailing sentiment: "Thus nature has been made subservient to science, and her frowns converted into smiles."[75]

The characteristics of San Francisco culture reinforced the influence of the natural obstacles that complicated the making of a large park. As residents of an "instant" city, San Franciscans were on the point of compressing the ordinarily protracted growth of a settlement from wilderness to city into the experience of a single generation.[76] The rapid pace of urbanization, which widened the gulf separating them from their unprepossessing natural environment, also deepened their commitment to purely urban ways of life. The comments about the miserable site run like a red thread through the early history of the San Francisco peninsula.

In the 1790s Pedro de Alberni, commanding a company of Catalonian volunteers at the San Francisco presidio, considered the San Francisco peninsula "the worst place" for settlement in California, without timber or water, pasturage or irrigable land.[77] In the 1860s Olmsted could not find a single "full grown tree of beautiful proportions in San Francisco."[78] Except for the waters of the bay, "the surroundings of San Francisco are not at all impressive," a visitor wrote to the Springfield *Illinois State Journal* in 1875. "The hills and depressions are utterly bare—no trees, no shrubs, no grass. All are arid and," he stressed, overcome by the dreary sight, "cheerlessly bare."[79]

The dry summer months, together with the rising value of real estate, made gardens a rarity and increased the residents' fascination with skillfully arranged flower beds. Nothing came of a detailed proposal for metropolitan parks in 1866. In accordance with their city mentality, San Franciscans considered an urban amusement park called Woodward's Garden their city park. Every man, woman, and child in San Francisco, a newspaper report exaggerated, and more than two-thirds of the residents of California, had visited its playground, zoo, conservatory, and art gallery often, by the end of the 1870s.[80]

A long legal struggle for the windswept sand dunes that became Golden Gate Park also interfered with the immediate satisfaction of the urban need for nature in the form of a big-city park. In the early decades of San Francisco, the desolate area was part of the Outside Lands, so called because they lay outside the city charter lines of 1851, but within the limits of the four-square-league site of the old Spanish or Mexican *pueblo* that supposedly had occupied the actual site of San Francisco on the bay as well as the area on the tip of the peninsula reaching to the Pacific Ocean beyond the city site. When the Spaniards colonized California, each civilian settlement or, to use the Spanish term, each pueblo received land from the crown according to the Laws of the Indies, and in later years these grants were generally confirmed by the Republic of Mexico. The future ownership of the Outside Lands depended on the solution of the protracted dispute over pueblo land rights, which dated back to the Mexican War.

As the successor to the Mexican pueblo, San Francisco claimed the pueblo lands from the United States, which in turn contended its right to them on the basis of the 1848 peace treaty with Mexico. There was doubt that a Mexican pueblo had existed as a legal entity, but the city's claim was strengthened when state courts decided that there had been some sort of pueblo at San Francisco. Federal and state courts heard and adjudicated the cases involving pueblo lands, which became the daily bread of some lawyers. The dispute over the pueblo lands also kept politicians and editors occupied. The public attention focused on the matter, and the uncertain legal status of the Outside Lands attracted speculators, settlers, and squatters who all hoped to gain from the wrangle.

In 1860, the decision of the California Supreme Court in the case of *Hart* vs. *Burnett* placed San Francisco in the position to assert its ownership of the pueblo lands.[81] Although conflict and litigation continued for eight years, the sequence of subsequent court actions offered an opportunity to work out a compromise with the private parties who held parcels of Outside Lands. They gave up fractions of their holdings and received clear titles to the remaining lands. Charges of municipal corruption and claims of political wisdom accompanied the transactions.

In the end, the city avoided yet another legal maneuver that seemed to presage interminable litigation. San Francisco obtained as a park site land covered by sand dunes stretching four and a quarter miles long by half a mile wide, from the Pacific towards the built-up sections of the city. With the projected park went a city-block-wide strip of land, commonly known as the Panhandle, which pointed in the direction of the projected city hall. It was relatively good land, and speculators considered the land and its neighborhood well suited for a variety of real estate projects. They managed to hang on to much of the land in their deals with the city. That explained the limited length of the Panhandle, which for most of the remaining decades of the nineteenth century did not effectively bridge the gap between the park and the built-up city streets.

The cultural ambience of San Francisco as an instant city shaped the creation of Golden Gate Park. In the face of the natural obstacles to a project of such mammoth proportions, a unified plan was far more expensive than San Franciscans were willing to spend for a park. They had little knowledge of landscape gardening, if it concerned them at all, and none in reclaiming sand dunes. Patient reclamation did not agree with the spirit of the instant city. San Franciscans had used steam shovels and lorries to dump the sand dunes blocking the spread of their urban site into the bay. The fabulous rise of the city absorbed their interest, and most of them thought that San Francisco had done well with chance and accident.

San Franciscans had strengthened the cultural fabric of their lives with an impromptu mix of innovation and borrowing that they applied to the solution of public tasks. They expected the park to do likewise and to thrive immediately. Solutions to any civic problems served only the present moment. In the absence of a common past, they could not readily conceive of a common future. Thus, Golden Gate Park was the most unlikely enterprise undertaken by nineteenth-century San Francisco.

One basic characteristic of San Francisco life, however, supported the idea of a big park. The creation of such a park was a part of the "metropolism" that distinguished some residents of the instant city: the tendency to emulate the patterns of older cities in the East, regardless of their vast distance from San Francisco. The attempt to inaugurate a style and tone of life typical of great cities made residential parks a part of the San Francisco cityscape early on. The outstanding early example of metropolism was South Park on the shoulder of Rincon Hill. In 1854, George Gordon almost singlehandedly laid it out after the pattern of a residential square of his native London and then gave the park to the city. The gift paid off when South Park attracted wealthy San Franciscans as buyers of Gordon's fashionable house lots encircling the park. From the profits of the real estate scheme, Gordon built a sugar factory that inspired a poet's barb: "First man then sugar he refined."[82]

The spirit of metropolism spoke clearly from a memorial signed by many residents and presented to the San Francisco Board of Supervisors in 1865. "The great cities of our own country, as well as of Europe, have found it necessary," these citizens emphasized, "to provide large parks, or pleasure grounds, for the amusement and entertainment of the people. . . . No city in the world needs such recreation grounds more than San Francisco."[83]

The board consulted Olmsted, who looked at San Francisco and saw a windblown desert. He found neither trees nor grass, the elements essential for the type of park he had created in New York. Instead, he found little flower gardens in the city in sheltered areas, and since he assumed that handsome trees would not grow, he suggested designing "pleasure grounds" with compact ornamental sections, protected from the wind, and linked by an elaborate system of walks, promenades, and drives. He did not look at the exposed sand dunes of the Outside Lands, because he favored the protected location of a valley for growing plants near the present Fillmore district. The public response to his practical ideas was mixed: some support came from park advocates, but the costs defeated the plan.[84]

The opposition of various city districts also contributed to the defeat of Olmsted's project. There were enough rival residential sections with choice locales to ensure a stalemate about the location of the park. The "Mission Crowd" vied with the "North Beach Clique," who "advocated the use of the Presidio as a park."[85] While both groups now relied on Olmsted's authority to campaign against a park in the sand dunes, they forgot that expediency was also one of the components of the instant-city mentality. When San Francisco needed level land for its downtown, the space between the wooden piers stretching over the shallow waters of Yerba Buena Cove was filled with beached ships, debris, and sand. This solution was resorted to several times when level ground was needed for factory construction, convenient street connections, and large railroad yards. Steam shovels excavated dunes and hills, and horse carts and railway lorries moved the sand to the bay and cast it into the deep.

The wresting of land from nature was a distinct feature of San Francisco's development. The bay had been pushed back steadily and had yielded new waterfronts. San Francisco Bay might soon have shrunk considerably more had not the State of California, by 1863 in control of San Francisco's waterfront, blocked further encroachment into the bay. The advance of the shoreline into the bay and the grading of several hills sustained the hopes of people who fervently believed that one day San Francisco would be a big city. Some recalled the profits that had been made by the sale as well as the purchase of so-called water lots. Others were firmly convinced the sand dunes towards the Pacific would one day yield to real estate development attracted by a magnificent park and conveniently linked to the downtown area with streetcars operated by companies in the hands of "the right people."

One of the staunchest supporters of a park in the sand dunes was Frank McCoppin. He became mayor of San Francisco in 1867 when the Democratic Party, recovering from the Civil War, swept the state. He had served four terms as a member of the Board of Supervisors, with street railroads as his field of interest. When Washington turned the pueblo lands over to the city in 1866, McCoppin's endorsement of the transaction earned him the animosity of those who had hoped to claim parts of the Outside Lands from the federal government. A compromise between these squatters and the city, worked out by the Outside Lands Committee of the Board of Supervisors, took this trouble off his back. In May 1869, the board approved the selection of the sand dunes as the park site, and in April 1870, the California State Legislature passed an act creating Golden Gate Park, managed by a board of three commissioners appointed by the governor.[86]

McCoppin lost his bid for re-election in September 1869, but not his interest in the park. As the major stockholder of the San Francisco Grading Company, he regarded the hills of shifting sand as a source of handsome profit. McCoppin thought that his various connections with the project would bring him a contract, if not for creating a park, a least for grading the sand dunes. These he intended to dump, for additional profit, as fill into the tidelands of the Mission District. Up to then he had been filling the swamps and lagoons of the Mission District with dirt hauled from the hills around Lone Mountain at the edge of the built-up city (as if intent on justifying the name of the mountain).

McCoppin may also have hoped that other connections would

allow him to profit from the park project. He had come to San Francisco relatively late—in 1858. Although of poor origin, he had done well in the instant city, which recognized outstanding men immediately. As a successful businessman and an aspiring politician McCoppin married into a well-known San Francisco family with a tenuous link to the park.

His father-in-law, James Van Ness, as mayor had worked out what appeared to be a farsighted planning ordinance for San Francisco in 1855. Such a measure would have been quite unusual for an instant city in the nineteenth-century American West, had it not served to mask the legalizing of some "notorious frauds."[87] Among its accomplishments, the ordinance reserved a considerable part of the Outside Lands for public use, and in the late 1860s a project like Golden Gate Park could be linked to the ordinance, with some stretch of imagination.

In later years, McCoppin was at times referred to as "the Father of Golden Gate Park" by San Franciscans (who managed to gloss over how dubious or accidental fatherhood can be). In nineteenth-century San Francisco many residents thrived on ingenuity as well as chance, and accident played quite a remarkable role in public life. The making of Golden Gate Park was no exception, as the dismantling of McCoppin's scheme illustrated. William Hammond Hall, who became the first superintendent of the park, later related how he foiled McCoppin, recalling in guarded language the "interested motives" of "a big grading company" in obtaining a contract.

"The idea was," Hall explained, "to cut things down to a plane like a public square," and "hills, valleys, and undulations, were to be done away with." In the nick of time he related McCoppin's strategy to General Barton S. Alexander, an officer with a distinguished Civil War record in the Corps of Engineers and with a background in dune management. During his San Francisco assignment Alexander had gained additional experience with battling sand drifting into gun emplacements on the coast. The general's qualifications and judgment convinced the Park Commissioners that grading the dunes would endanger, not only the park, but also the city, if these natural bulwarks against the afternoon winds, the westerlies, were removed.[88]

The Park Commissioners also benefited from Alexander's knowledge about the most effective way to hold sand dunes in place. He was familiar with the centuries of European experience, as well as with the contemporary methods of stabilizing drifting sand that building the Suez Canal had produced.[89] However, as an outsider Alexander could only briefly interest the instant city's freewheeling government in the idea of long-range park planning as an approach to problems. To William Hammond Hall fell the task of directing the practical work to ensure a balance between nature and culture, unusual in an instant city.

As a practical man, Hall suited the task and the temper of the city, which called for immediate, inexpensive solutions. As an honest man, he did not last long in office after the "real boss" of San Francisco, an eminent railroad corporation lawyer pulling strings in Sacramento, blocked further development of the park for ten long years. As a modest and reserved man, Hall was satisfied when the startling success of Golden Gate Park spoke for his work. Born in Maryland, he had come with his family as a four-year-old to San Francisco in 1850. Shortly afterwards, as result of losses suffered in a fire, the family moved to Stockton, where Hall was educated in a private academy.

In 1865 Hall began his professional career with the United States Corps of Engineers and come to know General Alexander. For a number of years he worked as draftsman, surveyor, assistant engineer, and chief engineer on various jobs. In August 1870, his low bid won the contract for a survey and a topographical map of Golden Gate Park. A year later he became superintendent and engineer of Golden Gate Park, and in the five years before his resignation in 1876, he got the project well under way by attracting many San Franciscans to their distant city park.

While the work of stabilizing the dunes went ahead slowly, Hall found arable soil at the eastern end of the park and on several north–south ridges in the park. Here and there, hills of red rock, suitable for making roads, relieved the desolation. To obtain mature trees was difficult and expensive, and in order to cut costs he began raising trees from seedlings in a greenhouse in a corner of the park. His enterprise disappointed San Francisco horticulturists who had hoped to find the park a steady customer for their products. In areas sheltered from the ocean breezes, he sowed grass and planted trees interspersed with beds of flowers.

The green blades of grass and the leaves and colorful blossoms of the flowers provided the immediate gratification that the residents of the instant city craved. Flower beds were out of place in the woodland park that Hall had envisioned; however, he planted and incorporated them in Golden Gate Park because he knew they pleased San Franciscans enormously, more so than the ornamental fountain, the rustic shelter, and other compromises he struck with public taste. "We doubt the existence of a superior floral display anywhere in the world," the *Pacific Rural Press* bragged in 1881, "and a 30-year-old city being the possessor of it must commend, abroad, our admiration of the beautiful, as well as the public spiritedness of our citizens."[90]

At the same time, Hall's workmen patiently experimented with soaked barley and lupine to stabilize the dunes. The future of Golden Gate Park as a big-city park hinged on the swift growth and the well-timed interaction of the growing cycles of barley and lupine seeds. The quickly sprouting barley lasted just long enough for the slowly growing lupine to sink roots and hold the shifting sand in place. Hall had known that the local lupine was the best vegetation for the main reclamation project of the park, but he came across the usefulness of the barley accidentally in November 1870.

A saddle horse, during the survey of the park, spilled its nosebag with soaked barley into the sand at the shore of one of the little ponds that since have been made into the Chain-of-Lakes. Ten days later, when Hall saw the area again, the barley had sprouted vigorously, "as thick as hair on a dog's back."[91] He realized that the promptly sprouting barley would protect the hard shell of the lupine seed from the blowing sand during its weeks of germination. Hall's innovation—planting barley and lupine together to hold the dunes down—solved the primary reclamation problem of the park.

The section of the park near the Pacific Ocean called for a different method of reclamation. From Europe Hall boldly borrowed the solution for stabilizing the western dunes of the park close to the ocean. He used the seeds of European beach grass in 1871–1872 as a substitute for barley and lupine, which could not tolerate the salt in the recently washed-up sand. "There was nothing original in this work," he stressed in his memoir of the park. "We were simply following directions," derived from long years of experience "along hundreds of miles of sandy coasts of Europe." He had anticipated the need for the beach grass seeds and had sent for the seeds at the outset of the work.[92]

If nothing else, the engineering of Golden Gate Park in itself distinguished it among American city parks. The enormous project of converting the sand dunes into parkland lasted three decades. The temper of the residents, the limits of financial resources, the complexities of the project, and the lack of political support precluded a unified design for the park. Accustomed to the constant change produced by the rapid growth of their city, San Franciscans were frequently inclined to believe that almost nothing really mattered but the present. Consequently, if there was to be a park, they wanted it *now*.

This attitude influenced the making of Golden Gate Park, which despite Hall's farsighted plan became a piecemeal undertaking. The execution of parts of his design (frequently modified) moved the western boundary of the park only slowly towards the Pacific Ocean. Hall concentrated most of his resources on the part of the park closest to the expanding city. There, in the East Park, he built a kind of showcase for those San Franciscans who wanted a park instantly.

While the builders worked on various projects through the long years it took to guide the reclamation project to fruition, the pressing demands of the moment required their careful attention. Manure to fertilize the parkland came daily from the sweepings of the stables and needed to be distributed according to plans that ensured adequate coverage for the sections under cultivation. Provision was made for water storage, irrigation, and drainage; for incorporating several natural lakes into the park; for grading and filling; and for the moving of topsoil.

These were enormous tasks in the face of a very limited budget and a very difficult natural terrain. Under these conditions, to work successfully, at times, meant to work slowly. Necessity placed a considerable degree of restraint on the work of Hall and his men. That moderation, so to say, prevented them from turning the entire site upside down in a single day, and ensured the making of a park that from the beginning reflected a balance between nature and culture.

Several projects, of course, called for the application of Hall's skills to specific areas where visitors could actually follow the making of the park and see for themselves evidence of its progress. Hall used the developed sections of the East Park to entice San Franciscans to the scene with carefully nurtured tree plantations and flower beds. As dividing line between the East Park and the West Park he selected the Great Transverse Ridge, running across an elevation covered with wild strawberries and soon called Strawberry Hill. The West Park he left to the future, but he kept people aware of its potential by constructing two long carriage drives leading through the entire park to the Pacific.

The design of the northern and southern drives through the park was Hall's master stroke. The carriage drives provided travelers with good road connections to the Ocean Beach Road, running from the Cliff House north of the Park along the ocean front of Golden Gate Park, to the Ocean Side House two miles south of the Cliff House. The arrangement immensely pleased all those San Franciscans who considered a drive to the Cliff House or the Ocean Side House the outer limit of their contact with the nature of the peninsula. Inadvertently, the drive through the park enlarged their exposure to nature. The construction of the carriage drives also appealed to instant-city residents who recalled building their city on land they were reclaiming from the bay, or wresting construction sites from the hills while their houses and business blocks rose.

If building a great city park amounted to engineering nature, the construction of the three-mile-long Northern Drive showed Hall was in control of the complex task of building a road through the drifting sand. While making Central Park Olmsted had demonstrated the potential of the city park to ensure the balance between nature and culture with the relatively lush vegetation of an old American city on the East Coast. Hall accomplished a like balance between culture and nature in the relatively arid climate of a new American city on the opposite side of the continent, when he engineered the Northern Drive through what wags had called the "great San Francisco sand drift."

Hall's success surprised his fellow residents. The achievement particularly delighted San Franciscans when the Park Commissioners reported that the cost of the road had been less than six cents per square foot, and that the expense included grading, claying, macadamizing, shaping, and covering the side slopes. "We believe," the San Francisco *Evening Bulletin* stated, "there is not a piece of macadamized road within the city limits that did not cost twice that sum."[93] The efficient work impressed the reporter of the San Francisco *Chronicle* so much that his summation of the completed job was not only enthusiastic but also accurate.[94]

The work, begun in the winter of 1873 and completed in the summer of 1874, required a kind of engineering management that went beyond the work of a landscape gardener. The construction of a roadway through moving sand dunes was a feat in itself, but it was only half of the work. The other half involved securing the shoulders of the carriage drive and coordinating the stabilization of the banks with the daily progress of the crew constructing the road.

These undertakings needed to be skillfully integrated to take full advantage of the growing seasons of the San Francisco peninsula. The calculations of when and where to work had to ensure that there would be cover vegetation on the banks to hold the sand. Otherwise the sand would drift onto the roadbed and bury a just-completed section. The effect of the drenching rainstorms of the San Francisco winter on men and animals had to be weighed against the benefits of the rainwater's fostering plant growth as well as soaking the sand and keeping the kernels in place. The need to irrigate the seedlings along the banks on sunny summer days when the fog stayed away, somewhat diminished the relief from the drudgery that such an unusual day would bring.

The making of Golden Gate Park called for the successful completion of a variety of complex tasks. Hall thrived on the challenge. He considered the diverse demands an opportunity for the development of "the highest type of landscape gardening—this successful blending of the artificial with the natural." Hall used the phrase in a note on a plan he proposed for the improvement of the campus of the University of California at Berkeley in 1873. Analogous to his approach to the problems of the site of Golden Gate Park, Hall's plan for the Berkeley campus suggested links between landscape gardening and "many important engineering works" to ensure "a complete example of the art of improving grounds to landscape principles."[95]

As was appropriate for a park for an incomparable city, Golden Gate Park acquired a unique character. The balance between nature and culture, which Hall had achieved with barley and lupine protecting his road, supported the impression of the growing woodland park he had envisioned. The records of the gatekeepers of Golden Gate Park for 1880 reflected the popularity the park had enjoyed within a decade. About 780,000 visitors, who came in 260,000 carriages, enjoyed the park, together with 38,000 equestrians and 835,000 pedestrians.[96]

The steadily growing number of visitors, as in the case of New York's Central Park, reflected the success of Golden Gate Park. In San Francisco, as in New York, however, the presence of so many people increased the demands put on the park. New ways to use the municipal park eroded the original vision of the woodland park. While a park served as a humanitarian agency, the builders of a park were loath to consider pleasure the predominant purpose of the park. The park as a place for restorative recreation was a different issue. As soon as the park attracted a large number of people, it became necessary to find varied forms of leisure activities for many of them. Parade grounds, baseball diamonds, tennis courts, band stands, terraces, conservatories, museums, and monuments became a part of the big-city park. They were not essential parts of an ideal park, but Hall thought it necessary to have them somewhere in the city where people could enjoy them. The freedom of choice the modern city offered generally limited the role of the municipal park as a device for the kind of cultural engineering that went beyond evoking a concern for nature.

The presence of people burdens any segment of nature, especially a city park. For Hall as the maker of Golden Gate Park, however, people were far less abusive than venal city-park management. "It may be openly intent upon destroying a most valuable park area," he warned, "in order to build a track for the racing horses bred by one of the Park Commissioners—as was done in San Francisco."[97] Following a disastrous decade, which from 1876 to 1887 saw Golden Gate Park fall prey to the manipulations of corrupt politicians, a new superintendent, John McLaren, continued the work in Hall's spirit.

The park benefited from McLaren's gifts as a landscape gardener, and perhaps even more so from his persuasive influence over people. McLaren combined his professional expertise with the strength of his convictions to ensure the distinct character of the park. He struggled incessantly to keep at bay the multitude of cultural threats to the delicate balance with nature. Aware that the making of a big-city park never ends, he adhered to procedures that allowed him to continue Hall's work.

"The artistic direction of work on such grounds," Frederick Law Olmsted wrote to the park commissioners in 1889, "should be continuous when once found fitting." He had not seen the park in the two decades since the selection of the site was discussed, and the passage of time invited comparison. Returning for a visit to San Francisco, Olmsted recognized Golden Gate Park as "an achievement far exceeding all that I have believed possible." He felt assured "that if the work so well begun is as wisely carried on, no city in the world will have as good reason for taking pride in its Park as San Francisco."[98] His gracious words acknowledging the accomplishment put Hall's success in fine perspective.

Central Park and Golden Gate Park became the epitome of big-city parks. They were more accessible to New Yorkers and San Franciscans than the state parks and national parks that (with few exceptions) came later into existence. Central Park and Golden Gate Park invited visitors to enjoy the balance between nature and culture, to see one aspect of the multifaceted role of American cities as source of civilization. The achievements of cities, "the centers of all strong movements of civilization," strongly impressed the German geographer Friedrich Ratzel during his trip through the United States in 1873 and 1874. He felt that the essential achievements of civilization were concentrated in cities. There, people's lives became richer and more productive, and "their accomplishments present a lasting testimony to posterity."[99]

Some of the achievements of city people in the United States directly touched a distinct mark of civilization, the harmony between nature and culture. In the 1850s, the building of Central Park first gave concrete form to the search for a balance between nature and culture in an American urban setting. In the 1870s, the making of Golden Gate Park showed that the reward of the struggle for harmony between nature and culture was within reach, despite great obstacles.

The intricate political, financial, and social history of the parks, as well as the complex engineering feats in the citifying of nature, pointed to the role of the residents of big cities in the preservation of nature. Landscape architects and engineers would realize their ideas, but the people ensured the success of the plans. By using the parks, the people made them instruments of civilization that could open the minds of city people to nature, reminding them how fragile was life and its forms—including their own.

Experiencing nature shaped people's everyday behavior in favor of nature. Workmen executed the designs of the parks, contouring and planting the grounds, and in those settings the processes of nature carried on. Observing growth and decay intensified the encounter with citified nature that gave city people a feeling for different forms of life. Respect for nature was the outstanding mark the big-city park made on American culture. That engineering of culture made large-scale attempts to conserve nature in the United States an offspring of the city.

Epilogue: A Measure of Civilization

FOR THREE CENTURIES, the European invaders of North America sought to master nature in the New World. They were eager to use the resources and people of the continent for their own purposes, and their efforts to control nature overshadowed the brief moments of concord between nature and culture experienced by some of the newcomers. The most venturesome among the European conquerors led the way in the onslaught against nature. Unaware of the enormous size of the geographic obstacle in their road to the riches of the Far East, they charged into the heart of the continent, with Spaniards, Frenchmen, and Englishmen in the forefront.

Farflung schemes to get rich quickly spurred many of them on in their ventures. They believed their success depended on the discovery of global trade routes, the building of continental empires, or the tapping of North American resources. The lack of any substantial knowledge about the geography of the continent did not deter the invaders. Their ignorance and greed opened up fertile fields of speculation about possible shortcuts to reach the elusive goals.

The idea of a Wilderness Passage sent some of the newcomers on a protracted search for a convenient waterway through the continent, connecting the Atlantic with the Pacific. They hoped to find a route that would shorten the lengthy sea voyages from Europe to the Indies and the Far East around Cape of Good Hope or Cape Horn. The sheer dimensions of the mass of land, the enormous distances, the impenetrable forests, the implacable deserts, the unusual qualities of some of the menacing animals, the many groups of people speaking different languages—these and many other characteristics of North America combined to complicate the difficult pursuit of the Wilderness Passage and to heighten the impression that nature was powerful in the New World.

The vanguard of the invaders suffered severe culture shock as result of its exposure to the power of North American nature. At times the mental and technological support systems of the intruders proved inadequate for the tasks of conquest. The hardships experienced in their encounters with the New World invalidated familiar practices and demanded different forms of thinking and living. The Indian ways of life often seemed to be far better suited to meeting the hazards of forests, plains, rivers, and lakes.

Some of the invaders responded to the lessons learned from their struggle with nature by quickly turning their backs on their own culture. They began living with Indians and adopted their languages and customs. Tolerated and accepted by their hosts, these white men not only fathered children with Indian women but also married the children's mothers. Once some of these white men had mastered the Indian technique of woodcraft and their mode of travel, they used the detailed geographical knowledge of the Indian world to enter the Indian trade networks. Forest trails and river routes developed by Indians brought them farther into the continent.

Most of the other conquerors hoped to obtain similar advantages, but they resisted adopting Indian ways of life. As a defense against the inclination to return to nature they invoked a strident ethnocentrism and used it as an effective response to the tasks of survival and advance. They relied on Christianity, literacy, technology, and organization, as well as their hunger for riches, to shield themselves, the conquerors of North America, from the temptation to surrender to its nature.

The study of the search for the Wilderness Passage illustrates some aspects of the European invaders' experiences with North American nature. The explorers, soldiers, traders, and officials involved in the search were forced to make mental and physical adjustments in order to function in their respective roles in the changing environment. Together with the acquisition of new behavior and knowledge, there slowly appeared a realization of the crucial role of nature in people's lives; a realization indicative of the opening of new horizons and of the development of a new sense of humanity. Although expediency led newcomers to act counter to the dictates of their culture, the changes in action and outlook were few. Most of the explorers modified familiar practices and beliefs just enough so that they could be applied to solve a specific task or to pursue a distinct vision.

Only a few white people, mostly Frenchmen involved in the fur trade, the *coureurs de bois,* shook off their European culture entirely. Others, like the French aristocrat Louis Armand de Lom d'Arce, Baron de Lahontan, professed belief in the superiority of Indian ways; but after his service as officer in the Canadian forest he returned to the fold of his culture. In the 1680s, Lahontan scorned white civilization, extolled the wisdom of Indian ways, and among a group of Wisconsin Indians envisioned the creation of a brotherhood of all people. He spent the last twenty years of his life, however, drifting farther and farther away from the mystic land of his imagination, his distinctly American Arcady, and trying to re-establish contact with his heritage. Since he had broken with the king of France, Lahontan searched for a sinecure in the Low Countries, Denmark, and Great Britain, until he finally obtained a place as the philosopher Leibnitz's companion at the court of the Elector of Hanover.

In the closing decades of the eighteenth century, the Englishman Samuel Hearne also found his way back to his roots, despite the physical and emotional distance separating the Canadian High North, where he had encountered nature, from his native

London. A fur trader in the service of the Hudson's Bay Company, Hearne was sent out to find and explore the Coppermine River. In 1771, he journeyed under the leadership of the Chipewyan chief Matonabbee to the river's mouth in the Beaufort Sea of the Arctic Ocean. He was the only white man in the company of a group of Indians, and in the course of the trek through the Canadian North he came to feel deeply the humanity they shared. Yet after this moving experience, Hearne returned to his chores as a fur trader in the Hudson's Bay Company. In 1782, during the American Revolutionary War, he surrendered to the French the Prince of Wales's Fort at Hudson Bay, which he governed for the Company. Ten years later he died where he was born—in London.

Towards the turn of the eighteenth century, when the last riddles of the illusive Wilderness Passage were being solved, vastly changed circumstances contributed to a shift in the European invaders' perception of the balance between nature and culture in North America. France had retreated completely from North America, and Great Britain had retreated from a considerable part of it. A new country, the United States of America, had come into existence, and its nationalism challenged British Canada's in the struggle for an extension of their respective territorial boundaries from the Atlantic to the Pacific. Geopolitical and commercial considerations now fueled the American penetration of the last unknown areas of the continent. National pride, scientific curiosity, and romantic imagination combined to create the belief that nature was an integral part of the new nation's heritage.

In the United States, growing support for the young nation's newly perceived continental destiny made the Pacific Northwest an area of special interest. The Northwest's significance also derived from the continuing search for the Wilderness Passage and the growing speculations about a possible portage between the Missouri and the Columbia that might be a substitute for a genuine waterway from the Atlantic to the Pacific. President Thomas Jefferson, very interested in national aggrandizement and scientific discovery, used the acquisition of the Louisiana Purchase in 1803 as an added reason to send out an exploring expedition.

Between 1804 and 1806, the Lewis and Clark expedition made the round trip from the Mississippi to the Pacific Ocean by way of the Missouri and the Columbia. The explorers were the first official representatives of the United States in the newly acquired territory. Their advance across the Great Plains and the Rocky Mountains to the Pacific stimulated Americans' awareness of the Pacific Northwest. The reports about the farthest West, an area not yet claimed by Americans, evoked the vision of an empire reaching from the Atlantic to the Pacific. The explorers heightened that potential with the first reliable information about the land and the people of the Pacific Northwest.

The success of the Lewis and Clark expedition had special significance for the relationship of the young nation to the nature of the continent. While solving the last remaining riddle of the Wilderness Passage, the explorers also experienced for a brief time a balance between nature and culture. Though they were an isolated group of white people in an unknown part of the Far West, their resilience and courage, as well as their commitment to duty and to each other, sustained the expedition. For roughly two years, their sense of mission and their curiosity exposed them to the topography, flora, fauna, climate, and people of the Far West. The explorers' singlemindedness of purpose and their resourcefulness in action enabled them to endure the hardships, while the toil of travel intensified their contact with nature. At times the drudgery of the venture seemed to be reduced to a sequence of ordeals pushing cultural attitudes and behavior of the explorers close to their limits.

Under the inspired leadership of Captains Meriwether Lewis and William Clark, the explorers managed to sustain confidence in the successful outcome of their enterprise. With desperation at times reinforcing determination, the explorers managed to cope with nature on their terms, despite frost and heat, hunger and fatigue, doubts about success and blunders of judgement testing their stamina. They recorded the physical and mental strain, the discoveries and triumphs, in a language well suited to their acquired respect for the nature of the continent. Their vernacular shunned the artful phrases some of their contemporaries considered essential for describing stunning views or strange people.

The plain messages of the Lewis and Clark expedition about bountiful nature and unknown Indian nations presented the Far West, hitherto existing primarily in the imagination, as reality to other Americans. The explorers' experience of living briefly in balance with nature and culture towered over the nineteenth century when Americans built a nation on the development and exploitation of the natural resources of the continent. The strenuous task of realizing some of the promises of American democracy diminished the chances of living in harmony with nature.

Only a handful of Americans went against the powerful tide that swept away forests, prairies, and mountains. A few thinkers and artists, some explorers, mountain men, and settlers, as well as the pioneers of the emerging conservation movement—these were the kindred spirits seeking to foster in Americans a new feeling for the role of nature in their lives. They aimed at convincing their countrymen that in the wildness of nature, to paraphrase Thoreau, is the salvation of the world. To most Americans the logged tree, the plowed sod, the graded hill, and cattle grazing where the buffalo had roamed, were signs of progress. In general, during the nineteenth century, nature appeared to be a force threatening to block the attempts of settlers to transform the continent into the familiar images of fields, gardens, factories, and towns. Drought, locusts, and Indian raids all too often seemed to shatter the American dream.

More distant from the threats of nature than the frontier farmer, the miner, or the lumberjack, some city people began searching for a harmonious relationship with nature. Their impulse to restore nature in the urban world gained momentum when growing numbers of urbanites felt deprived of the restorative influence of trees and grass. Their search found expression in the making of park cemeteries and city parks.

The obligation to provide decent burial for the dead and the need to provide natural settings for the leisure of urban residents increased the haunting realization that intensified urbanization would soon destroy the remnants of nature. These considerations offset the tendency of American culture to subdue nature at all costs and stimulated the creation of park cemeteries and city parks. The westward migration of the park cemetery from Boston's Mount Auburn Cemetery to Oakland's Mountain View Cemetery, and of the city park from New York to San Francisco, brought great numbers of city dwellers into touch with selected nature: trees, meadows, lakes, and grass.

In the 1850s, New York, the nation's largest city, started the movement for the city park in the United States. As the first big-city park, Central Park demonstrated the potential of the American modern city as a source of civilization. Central Park was created by Frederick Law Olmsted, the great American landscape architect of the nineteenth century, and built by urbanites whose faith in the constructive abilities of the people made the park the symbol of the link between urban democracy and nature. Central Park "citified" nature and in the East Coast metropolis exemplified the balance between nature and culture.

In the 1870s, San Francisco built Golden Gate Park. Unlike New York, San Francisco had condensed the normally protracted growth from wilderness to city into the experience of a single generation. San Francisco's sudden rise as an instant city depended largely on the exploitation of nature. William Hammond Hall, the creator of Golden Gate Park, had to cope with that heritage of conflict. In addition, Hall, an outstanding environmental engineer of the nineteenth-century American West, faced working with the most difficult terrain of any big-city park in the United States. In order to succeed, he had to instill concern for the shifting sand dunes of the parkland in the residents of the instant city, who were used to filling San Francisco

Bay with the hills that stood in their way. Hall stabilized the dunes and turned part of the barren, windswept peninsula into a woodland park that brought San Franciscans in touch with trees, meadows, and lakes. Golden Gate Park showed that the struggle for harmony between nature and culture could succeed despite extreme odds.

The park designs of Olmsted and Hall enriched the lives of their fellow citizens in many ways. "Greensward," the name Olmsted and his collaborator, Calvert Vaux, had chosen for their plan of Central Park, identified one need of the congested metropolis, and Central Park introduced large fields of green grass into New York. Hall's design of the "Woodland Park" brought to the Golden Gate Park of San Francisco the stands of tall trees the city had never known.

For city people the exposure to the tranquil scene of a park, hedged round by the turmoil of the metropolis, was an extraordinary experience because the hectic pace of urban life had left little room for tranquillity. That delightful disruption of the routine of city life, the repeated encounter with meadows and lakes, molded the mentality of great numbers of people. Their contact with grass, shrubs, and trees instilled in their minds a concern for nature as a precious heritage.

The engineering of nature, which created the glens and groves of the metropolis, entailed an engineering of culture in a special way. The freedom of choice the modern city offered for many residents defeated most efforts to use the park as a device to engineer culture. The impact of the city park on city people went far beyond modifying forms of behavior, propagating norms of conduct, or exploiting landscape designs to reinforce distinctions between people. The big-city park introduced in city people's minds a respect for nature as an integral part of urban democracy. The engineering of nature in the big city amounted to an engineering of culture, which made the extensive efforts to protect nature in the United States an offspring of the city.

The interaction between nature and culture in the big-city park underlined the sobering thought that natural resources are finite. Enjoying a city park also produced an awareness of the damage people can inadvertently do to the environment by their sheer numbers. These and similar observations produced an appreciation of the constant efforts required to maintain the magnificent site. The park offered momentary relief from the cacophony of city streets and extended an elementary understanding of the need for a balance between nature and culture into the lives of countless people. The big-city park became a measure of civilization.

From the outset, the engineering of nature into city parks served the people. Through the preservation of nature, the city park mitigated the crushing effects of crowded houses and noisy streets. Citified nature enriched people's lives with the trees and meadows of the city park, a green open space in a desert of grey stone and brown brick. For the common good it was irrelevant whether winds and birds had sown the seeds or gardeners had planted the seedlings. In their role as agents of nature, gardeners were also servants of humanity.

The availability of lawns and lakes framed by stands of trees, created by their city's own political will, gave many people the chance to experience a balance of nature and culture. Perhaps with time they will understand the significance of that balance on a nationwide and worldwide scale for the future of civilization.

Sources

An inquiry into the relationship between nature and culture in the course of American history fosters an acute awareness of a dilemma. There is a wealth of evidence to illuminate the subject, but that very wealth tends to obscure the small portion of the topic one can hope to penetrate within a reasonable span of time. The management of sources, not the gathering of material, becomes the most formidable task. It is a task rendered quite palatable by the need to reread documents and reflect anew on evidence one may have met earlier for other purposes in quite different contexts.

For these reasons it is not meaningful to compile a formal bibliography. Furthermore, with the possible exception of one collection of manuscripts, the sources for my study are familiar to my fellow workers in various fields of American history. Consequently, this is not an exhaustive bibliography that might be read to glean so-called new material. Nor is it a discussion of all the items cited in the notes. It is rather an attempt to explain the usefulness of groups of documents and to delineate their role in this exploration of a complex subject.

I have focused my investigation on the search for the Wilderness Passage, the Lewis and Clark expedition, the creation of the park cemetery, and the making of the city park to keep in manageable bounds my discussion on the relationship between nature and culture in American history. This note on the sources generally follows that framework.

My investigation of the documents on the Wilderness Passage has profited from several great collections of sources pertaining to the early contacts of Europeans with North America. David Beers Quinn has reshaped the monumental compilation of *Voyages,* which Richard Hakluyt published in the closing decade of the sixteenth century, and has made parts of it easily accessible: Quinn, ed., *New American World: A Documentary History of North America to 1612,* 5 vols. (New York, 1979), is an inexhaustible resource. The Hakluyt Society Publications, that impeccable corpus of sources, contain another of Quinn's editorial achievements, *The Roanoke Voyages, 1584–1590: Documents to Illustrate the English Voyages to North America under the Patent Granted to Walter Raleigh in 1584,* 2 vols. (Cambridge, 1955). In the same collection appeared Eva G. R. Taylor, ed., *The Writings and Correspondence of the Two Richard Hakluyts,* 2 vols. (Cambridge, 1935); and Philip L. Barbour, ed., *The Jamestown Voyages under the First Charter, 1606–1609,* 2 vols. (Cambridge, 1969). George Best, an Elizabethan sea captain whose testimony I could have found also in Hakluyt's or Quinn's work, I quoted from Vilhjalmur Stefansson, comp., *The Three Voyages of Martin Frobisher,* 2 vols. (London, 1938), to show how many of these documents can be found in several places. That also holds true for the Newfoundland letter of a Hungarian poet, but in his case it would have been folly not to benefit also from the excellent commentaries in Quinn and Neil M. Cheshire, eds. and trans., *The New Found Land of Stephen Parmenius: The Life and Writings of a Hungarian Poet, Drowned on a Voyage from Newfoundland,* 1583 (Toronto, 1972).

Original Narratives of Early American History, published at the beginning of our century under the general editorship of J. Franklin Jameson, is still very useful. In particular I have relied on Lyon Gardiner Tyler, ed., *Narratives of Early Virginia, 1606–1625* (New York, 1907); and James Kendall Hosmer, ed., *Winthrop's Journal: "History of New England," 1630–1649* (New York, 1908).

One document needs to be singled out. In the early stages of my research it offered me the kernel of an idea of how to navigate in the sea of information surrounding me. I am referring to the account of the 1527 to 1536 journey of Álvar Núñez Cabeza de Vaca, a Spanish conquistador and the first European to cross North America. Stripped of the trappings of his culture during his arduous trek across the continent, Álvar Núñez discovered a common humanity with his Indian hosts in the Far Southwest, almost three centuries before the Englishman Samuel Hearne experienced it on his way to the Coppermine River in Canada's High North.

Álvar Núñez's account was first published in Spain in 1542. It went through several editions, was reprinted, and translated or paraphrased into Italian, English, and French. I have used primarily the new edition and translation by Cyclone Covey, *Cabeza de Vaca's Adventures in the Unknown Interior of America* (New York, 1961), which brought together some of the earlier scholarship on the subject.

Núñez's experience prompted me to relate my assessment of nature and culture in the American experience to the fleeting moments of harmony and to look at the secondary literature of exploration from a new perspective. Clues to potential sources came from Lawrence J. Burpee, *The Search for the Western Sea: The Story of the Exploration of North-Western America* (New York, 1908); John Bartlett Brebner, *The Explorers of North America, 1492–1806* (London, 1933); Carl Ortwin Sauer, *Sixteenth Century North America: The Land and the People as Seen by the Europeans* (Berkeley, 1971); and Samuel Eliot Morison, *The European Discovery of America: The Northern Voyages,* A.D. 500–1600 (New York, 1971). A monument of scholarship by a German iconoclast on the discovery and conquest of America, Georg Friederici, *Der Charakter der Entdeckung und Eroberung Amerikas durch die Europaeer: Einleitung zur Geschichte der Besiedlung Amerikas durch die Voelker der alten Welt,* 3 vols. (Stuttgart, 1926–1936), documented the circumstances and shadings of the contact between European cultures and American nature with a wealth of evidence.

Additional insights came from various directions. The works of Jacques Le Moyne and John White show that Europeans saw New World nature reflected in its people. Their drawings and water colors have been collected in two splendid publications by Paul Hulton, ed., *The Works of Jacques Le Moyne de Morgues, a Huguenot Artist in France, Florida, and England* (London, 1977); and *America 1585: The Complete Drawings of John White* (Chapel Hill, 1984). The verso of the Great Seal of the United States speaks eloquently about the Founding Father's perception of the continent. The historical background of the symbolism has been unravelled by Richard S. Patterson and Richardson Dougall in *The Eagle and the Shield: A History of the Great Seal of the United States* (Washington, D.C., 1976). Jeremy Moyle, trans., *Nature in the New World: From Christopher Columbus to Gonzalo Fernandez de Oviedo. By Antonello Gerbi* (Pittsburgh, 1985), relates the early Spanish author's search for words to do justice to the flora and fauna of America. The impact of the magic of water, one of the four classic elements of nature, on settlers in the English-speaking colonies is traced imaginatively by John Seelye, *Prophetic Waters: The River in Early American Life and Literature* (New York, 1977). Jessie L. Weston, *The Quest of the Holy Grail* (New York, 1913), stresses the unending quest as a religious impulse that gives perspective to the cultural context of the exploration for the Wilderness Passage.

In addition to Sauer and Morison, Roald Amundsen, *The Northwest Passage*, 2 vols. (London, 1908), provides a good perspective on the elusive waterway. Quinn, *The Voyages and Colonising Enterprises of Sir Humphrey Gilbert*, 2 vols. (London, 1940), attests to the change of direction from the high seas to the continent. Lawrence C. Wroth, *The Voyages of Giovanni da Verrazzano, 1524–1528* (New Haven, 1970), emphasizes the voyages significance for the European ideas about North American geography and the French involvement with the continent. The Spanish search on the West Coast of North America for a Pacific exit of the Wilderness Passage is discussed well by Warren L. Cook, *Flood Tide of Empire: Spain and the Pacific Northwest, 1543–1819* (New Haven, 1973).

For an understanding of the rapid penetration of the continent and the accompanying threats to the invaders' culture, Reuben G. Thwaites, ed., *The Jesuit Relations and Allied Documents*, 73 vols. (Cleveland, 1897–1899), is indispensable. Thwaites, ed., *New Voyages to North America. By the Baron de Lahontan*, 2 vols. (Chicago, 1905); Lawrence J. Burpee, ed., *Journals and Letters of Pierre Gaultier de Varennes de La Vérendrye and His Sons* (Toronto, 1927); and W. Raymond Wood, ed., *The Explorations of the La Vérendryes in the Northern Plains, 1738–1743: By G. Hubert Smith* (Lincoln, 1980), convey the imagined and actual encounters of Frenchmen with the heart of the continent.

Two multivolume histories of New France, published originally in the first half of the eighteenth century, contain clues to attitudes towards nature, which at times are obscured in the sources. Claude Charles Le Roy Bacqueville de la Potherie, *Histoire de L'Amérique Septentrionale*, 3 vols. (Paris, 1722), I saw in the original. Charlevoix's monumental history, published originally in 1744, I found in the translation by John Gilmary Shea of *History and General Description of New France. By Rev. P. F. X. de Charlevoix, S. J.*, 6 vols. (New York, 1900). In Francis Parkman's multivolume history, *France and England in North America*, two books— *La Salle and the Discovery of the Great West*, 12th rev. ed. (Boston, 1887) and *Count Frontenac and New France under*

Louis XIV, 17th ed. (Boston, 1887)—yielded the most insights on my subject. I have used the results of more recent scholarship as a corrective, however, particularly William J. Eccles, *Frontenac: the Courtier Governor* (Toronto, 1959). For details of Sir William Johnson's attitude towards Indians I found his first biography, William L. Stone, *The Life and Times of Sir William Johnson, Bart.*, 2 vols. (Albany, 1865), most useful.

John Parker, ed., *The Journals of Jonathan Carver and Related Documents, 1766–1770* (St. Paul, 1976), enabled me to find a way through the long-standing debate about Carver's contribution to the search for the Wilderness Passage and to see his *Travels through the Interior Parts of North America* (London, 1778) in a positive light. J. B. Tyrrell, ed., *A Journey from Prince of Wales's Fort, in Hudson's Bay, to the Northern Ocean in the Years 1769, 1770, 1771, and 1772. By Samuel Hearne* (Toronto, 1911), and E. E. Rich, *The History of the Hudson's Bay Company; 1670–1870*, 2 vols. (London, 1959), contain many clues to Hearne and provide a good understanding of the fur trade in the High North.

The subtitle of T. H. McDonald, ed., *Exploring the Northwest Territory: Sir Alexander Mackenzie's Journal of a Voyage by Bark Canoe from Lake Athabaska to the Pacific Ocean in the Summer of 1789* (Norman, 1966), should refer to the Arctic Ocean instead of the Pacific Ocean. Mackenzie hoped to reach the latter but he got to the former. The well-edited journal preserves Mackenzie's laconic language and shows the scant attention a great explorer accorded his interactions with nature. Much of Mackenzie's restraint is veiled by the ghost writer, who initially saw Mackenzie's journals of the voyages to the Arctic and the Pacific through the press: *Voyages from Montreal, on the River St. Laurence, through the Continent of North America, to the Frozen and Pacific Oceans: In the Years 1789 and 1793* (London, 1801). The definitive edition of Mackenzie's writings is W. Kaye Lamb, ed., *The Journals and Letters of Sir Alexander Mackenzie* (Cambridge, 1970).

The major source for the relationship of the Lewis and Clark expedition to the nature in the Far West is the journals of the explorers. They had a sad publication history, which is discussed extensively by Paul Russell Cutright in *A History of the Lewis and Clark Journals* (Norman, 1976). With that record in mind, I have relied on what is at the moment still the most authentic and complete edition of Meriwether Lewis's and William Clark's records: Reuben Gold Thwaites ed., *Orig-*

inal Journals of the Lewis and Clark Expedition, 1804–1806, Printed from the Original Manuscripts in the Library of the American Philosophical Society and by Direction of its Committee on Historical Documents, together with Manuscript Material of Lewis and Clark from other Sources, including Note-Books, Letters, Maps, etc., and the Journals of Charles Floyd and Joseph Whitehouse—Now for the First Time Published in Full and Exactly as Written, 8 vols. (New York, 1904–05). In addition to other material, Volume VII contains the journal of Sergeant Charles Floyd, the only man to die on the expedition, and the journal of Private Joseph Whitehouse.

The journals of two other members of the Corps of Discovery, Patrick Gass and John Ordway, have been published separately. David McKeehan edited the account of Private (later Sergeant) Patrick Gass, *A Journal of the Voyages and Travels of a Corps of Discovery, Under the Command of Capt. Lewis and Capt. Clarke of the Army of the United States* (Pittsburgh, 1807). Milo Milton Quaife edited *The Journals of Captain Meriwether Lewis and Sergeant John Ordway: Kept on the Expedition of Western Exploration, 1803–1806* (Madison, 1916), Volume XXII of the State Historical Society of Wisconsin *Collections*. Lewis's account covers his 1803 trip from Pittsburgh to Camp Dubois, the staging area of the expedition,—his so-called Ohio journal, which had not found its way into Thwaites collection. Clark's field notes, from Camp Dubois through the winter quarters at the Mandan villages, were edited by Ernest Staples Osgood, *The Field Notes of Captain William Clark, 1803–1805* (New Haven, 1964). Donald Jackson's commentaries make his edition of the *Letters of the Lewis and Clark Expedition with Related Documents, 1783–1854*, 2 vols., 2nd enl. ed. (Urbana, 1978), an excellent introduction to the general background of the enterprise.

Despite Thwaites's great collection, the printed records of the expedition are still rather scattered at present. Furthermore, additional material turns up once in a while, such as a revised version of Whitehouse's journal that is now in the Newberry Library of Chicago. Recently, the University of Nebraska Press began publishing a new edition of the journals of the Lewis and Clark expedition, edited by Gary E. Moulton. Bernard De Voto, ed., *The Journals of Lewis and Clark* (Boston, 1953); and John Bakeless, ed., *The Journals of Lewis and Clark* (New York, 1964), are two good selections that make it easy to grasp the outlines of the expedition.

There are several good commentaries on the Lewis and Clark expedition that clarify the official record. They also kept me from turning my investigation into yet another account of the explorers as naturalists. Elliot Coues, *History of the Expedition under the Command of Lewis and Clark*, 4 vols. (New York, 1893), tackled well many difficult questions about the geography, flora, fauna, and wildlife of the Far West. Thorough scholarship distinguishes Raymond Darwin Burroughs, *The Natural History of the Lewis and Clark Expedition* (East Lansing, 1961); and Paul Russell Cutright, *Lewis and Clark: Pioneering Naturalists* (Urbana, 1969). I shall always envy Olin D. Wheeler, *The Trail of Lewis and Clark, 1804–1904: A Story of the Great Exploration across the Continent in 1804–1806; with a Description of the Old Trail, Based upon Actual Travel over It, and of the Changes Found a Century Later*, 2 vols. (New York, 1904). He was still able to follow the expedition on trails that had not yet changed entirely. For most of us nowadays, John Logan Allen, *Passage through the Garden: Lewis and Clark and the Image of the American Northwest* (Urbana, 1975), is the best introduction to the geography faced by the expedition. James P. Ronda, *Lewis and Clark among the Indians* (Lincoln, 1984), provides good insights on the encounter with the Indians.

My views about the death of Lewis stem from his descriptions of the grizzly hunts and from Alexander Wilson, "Particulars of the Death of Capt. Lewis," *The Port Folio* VII (n.s., January 1812), 34–47. Jackson's *Letters* II, 574–75, discusses some of the evidence, endorsing the "verdict of suicide" by Dawson A. Phelps in "The Tragic Death of Meriwether Lewis," *William and Mary Quarterly* XIII (3rd ser., July 1956), 305–18. Recently Howard I. Kushner, "The Suicide of Meriwether Lewis: A Psychoanalytic Inquiry" *William and Mary Quarterly* XXXVIII (3rd ser., July 1981), 464–81, has broadened the focus of the discussion considerably.

Many questions of fact about the expedition were resolved by the scholarship of Donald Jackson. In particular I profited from *Thomas Jefferson and the Stony Mountains: Exploring the West from Monticello* (Urbana, 1981). My initial insights into Jefferson's attitude towards nature came from William Peden, ed., *Notes on the State of Virginia. By Thomas Jefferson* (Chapel Hill, 1955). A broad philosophical discussion, Charles A. Miller's *Jefferson and Nature: An Interpretation* (Baltimore, 1988), clarified specific points.

I read *The Port Folio's* issues from 1801 to 1815 while I was groping for an understanding of the cultural context of the Lewis and Clark expedition. The Philadelphia magazine, the first periodical designed to stimulate awareness of an American art, served my purposes well. I followed up the discussion on books and paintings by turning to commentaries on art and literature. Several catalogues of recent exhibitions I found particularly helpful. Theodore E. Stebbins, Jr., Carol Troyen, and Trevor J. Fairbrother, comps., *A New World: Masterpieces of American Painting, 1760–1910* (Boston, 1983), provided an overview. *Views and Visions: American Landscape before 1830* (Washington, D. C., 1986), edited by Edward J. Nygren, contracted my perspective. The Corcoran Gallery of Art's *Niagara: Two Centuries of Changing Attitudes, 1697–1901* (Washington, D.C., 1985), and the monograph by Elizabeth McKinsey, *Niagara Falls: Icon of the American Sublime* (Cambridge, Mass., 1985), helped me with Niagara Falls, the high point of Alexander Wilson's long poem "The Foresters." I had found the poem originally as installments in *The Port Folio* I (n.s., June 1809), 538–44; ibid., II (n.s., July 1809), 70–77; (August 1809), 141–47; (September 1809), 275–78; (October 1809), 367–73; (November 1809), 453–58; (December 1809), 561–65; ibid., III (n.s., February 1810), 159–68; (March 1810), 179–87.

Specific questions about Wilson as ornithologist and hiker were answered by Clark Hunter, ed., *The Life and Letters of Alexander Wilson* (Philadelphia, 1983), and Robert Cantwell, *Alexander Wilson: Naturalist and Pioneer* (Philadelphia, 1961). The world of letters at the turn of the eighteenth century, in its relation to scenery as a dominant form of nature, is well assessed by Robert Lawson-Peebles, *Landscape and Written Expression in Revolutionary America: The World Turned Upside Down* (Cambridge, 1988).

Two manuscript collections furnish the backbone for my discussion of citified nature: the Olmsted Papers and the Hall Papers. The progress of a splendid publication project made the use of the Olmsted Papers in the Library of Congress much easier. Five volumes have been published so far under the sagacious general editorship of Charles Capen McLaughlin: *The Papers of Frederick Law Olmsted,* 5 vols. (Baltimore, 1977–). In particular I benefited from the carefully edited details of Volume III: Charles E. Beveridge and David Schuyler, eds., *Creating Central Park, 1857–1861* (Baltimore, 1983). An older edition of parts of Olmsted's papers also proved helpful: Frederick Law Olmsted, Jr., and Theodora Kimball, eds., *Frederick Law Olmsted: Landscape Architect, 1822–1903*, 2 vols. (New York, 1922). In addition, some of Olmsted's writings particularly pertinent to my work have been published in pamphlets. His report on the Oakland Mountain View Cemetery is part of *Organization of the Mountain View Cemetery Association, Oakland, California: Officers of the Corporation, Rules, Regulations, and By-laws, Including a Preface to the Plan by Frederick Law Olmsted. Services at the Consecration of the Ground, Etc. Etc.* (San Francisco, 1865), 44–66. Olmsted, Vaux & Co., *Preliminary Report in Regard to a Plan of Public Pleasure Grounds for the City of San Francisco* (New York, 1866), contains Olmsted's views on San Francisco's limited potential for a large park.

Like anyone dealing with Olmsted, I am beholden to the thoughtful work of Laura Wood Roper: *FLO: A Biography of Frederick Law Olmsted* (Baltimore, 1973). From the comments on Olmsted's achievement by newspapers and magazines, which reflect the concept of demopiety, I should like to mention here: "City Improvements," *New York Times*, September 5, 1859; "The Central Park," *Harper's Weekly*, October 1, 1859, p. 626; Henry W. Bellows, "Cities and Parks: With Special Reference to the New York Central Park," *Atlantic Monthly* VII (April, 1861), 416–29; and "Growth and Grandeur of New-York," *New York Tribune*, November 26, 1862. For the broad context of demopiety, turn to my "Demopiety: Speculations on Urban Beauty, Western Scenery, and the American Discovery of the Cityscape," *Pacific Historical Review* LII (August, 1983), 249–66.

The William Hammond Hall Collection in the Bancroft Library at the University of California in Berkeley contains the papers of an outstanding civil engineer, the creator of San Francisco's Golden Gate Park. In addition to the diaries, notes, letters, maps, photographs, and clippings covering reclamation, conservation, and irrigation is also a substantial manuscript, "The Romance of a Woodland Park." It details the making of Golden Gate Park and Hall's tenure as its first superintendent from 1871 to 1876. Against the background of San Francisco's rise as instant city, his spirited account of the struggles with shifting sand dunes and powerful politicians was very helpful. The experience of his fifty-year career as an engineer offers new perspectives on engineering nature in a setting Olmsted had considered ill-suited for the transformation into a big park.

The annual publication of the San Francisco Board of Supervisors, *Municipal Reports* (1859–1917), contains the report of the Board of Park Commissioners. Beginning in 1871, the reports offer in particular a wealth of information on the plants and trees introduced in the park, and they document the engineering of nature in yet another area of park design. There are many reports about the building of the park in San Francisco newspapers, as well as in the *Overland Monthly*, the *Pacific Rural Press*, and the San Francisco *Real Estate Circular*, and they furnish running comments on the interaction between nature and culture.

The idea of San Francisco as instant city has been developed by me in *Instant Cities: Urbanization and the Rise of San Francisco and Denver* (New York, 1975). For the concept of metropolism see my "Metropolism and Urban Elites in the Far West," in Frederic Cople Jaher, ed., *The Age of Industrialism in America: Essays in Social Structure and Cultural Values* (New York, 1968), 158–87. The legal maneuvers over the so-called Outside Lands have been most recently described by Christian G. Fritz, in "San Francisco's First Federal Court: Ogden Hoffman and the Northern District of California, 1851–1891" (Ph.D. diss.) University of California, Berkeley, 1986), 290–342.

Guidebooks, promotional literature, reports about the dedication ceremonies, and collections of charters, rules, and regulations I found most useful for tracing the relationship of the park cemetery to nature. I gained additional perspective on changing attitudes by comparing the reflections of an organizer of Mount Auburn—Jacob Bigelow, *History of Mount Auburn Cemetery* (Boston, 1860)—with the earlier *Picturesque Pocket Companion, and Visitor's Guide, Through Mount Auburn: Illustrated with Upwards of Sixty Engravings on Wood* (Boston, 1839), and John Elkington, *The Monument Cemetery of Philadelphia (Late Pere Lachaise)* (Philadelphia, 1837).

The persistence as well as the modification of cultural ideals in the westward migration of the park cemetery across the country is mirrored extensively in pamphlets. Specifically useful were the following: *Cemetery of Spring Grove: Its Charters, Rules, and Regulations. Also an Address Delivered at the Consecration by the Hon. John M'Lean and a Catalogue of the Proprietors on the 1st of May 1849* (Cincinnati, 1849); and St. Louis Bellefontaine Cemetery Association, *Original Charter, Amendments to Charter, Together with the By-Laws and Rules and Regulations of the Bellefontaine Cemetery, and Suggestions to Lot Owners, Etc. Also Containing an Historical Sketch* (St. Louis, 1878). *The Cincinnati Cemetery of Spring Grove: Reports, Forms, etc.*, enl. edition (Cincinnati, 1862); and *Dedication of the Bellefontaine Cemetery: Address of Professor Post, and Other Proceedings on that Occasion; Also the Rules and Regu-*

lations, Suggestions to Lot Owners, and Charter of the Rural Cemetery Association (St. Louis, 1850), illustrate the cult of monuments infringing on the natural setting with words and pictures.

In addition to *Organization of the Mountain View Cemetery Association,* cited above in connection with the Olmsted material, the *By-Laws and Rules of Mountain View Cemetery Association with History and Appendix* (Oakland, 1889), are helpful because the pamphlet reprints the California Rural Cemetery Act of 1859. Infighting among the association members found its way into another pamphlet, *Concerning Mountain View Cemetery: Its Management under the Late Superintendent—Present Conditions of Its Affairs. Public Lectures of Dr. Sam'l Merritt, Containing a Full Discussion and an Intelligible Statement of Facts* (Oakland, 1871). Charles Howard Shinn observed some of the changes in the development of Mountain View Cemetery in "A California Cemetery," *Garden and Forest: A Journal of Horticulture, Landscape Art and Forestry* IV (May 6, 1891), 206.

Notes

Introduction

1. Petrarch to Father Dionigi da Borgo San Sepolcro, April 26, 1336, in Morris Bishop, ed. and trans., *Letters from Petrarch* (Bloomington, 1966), 45.

2. Hans Jacob Christoffel von Grimmelshausen, *Werke,* 2 vols. (Frankfurt, 1967), I:409–11; Peter Triefenback, *Der Lebenslauf des Simplicius Simplicissimus: Figur-Initiation-Satire* (Stuttgart, 1979), 179–80.

3. James Kendall Hosmer, ed., *Winthrop's Journal "History of New England": 1630–1649,* 2 vols. (New York, 1908), I:73–74.

4. Herman Melville, *Moby Dick: or The Whale* (Chicago, 1952), 116–17. The novel was first published in 1851.

5. William Howarth, ed., *Thoreau in the Mountains: Writings by Henry David Thoreau* (New York, 1982), 143, 149.

6. George Lawrence, trans., J. P Mayer and Max Lerner (eds.), *Democracy in America: By Alexis de Tocqueville* (New York, 1966), 526.

7. Howarth, ed., *Thoreau in the Mountains,* 144.

8. Roger M. Keesing, "Theories of Culture," *Annual Review of Anthropology,* III (1974), 73.

1: On Nature's Edge

1. Stephen Parmenius to Richard Hakluyt, August 6, 1583, in David B. Quinn and Neil M. Cheshire, eds. and trans., *The New Found Land of Stephen Parmenius* (Toronto, 1972), 171.

2. Ibid., 175.

3. "Edward Hayes's Narrative of Sir Humphrey Gilbert's voyage," in David B. Quinn, ed., *New American World: A Documentary History of North America to 1612*, 5 vols. (New York, 1979), IV:33; ibid., "The Voyage of the *Grace* of Bristol," 65.

4. Parmenius to Hakluyt, August 6, 1583, in Quinn and Cheshire, eds. and trans., *Parmenius*, 171.

5. Ibid., 3.

6. "Hayes's Narrative" in Quinn, *New American World* IV:41.

7. Thomas More, *Utopia* (London, 1910), 15 (the book was first printed either late in 1516 or early in 1517); David B. Quinn, *The Voyages and Colonising Enterprises of Sir Humphrey Gilbert*, 2 vols. (London, 1940), I:89.

8. Jessie L. Weston, *The Quest of the Holy Grail* (New York, 1964), 64, 70, 108, 115, 122, 135. The study was first published in 1913.

9. Paul Hulton, comp., *America 1585: The Complete Drawings of John White* (Chapel Hill, 1984); Quinn, *New American World* III, "The Roanoke Voyages," 265–339; Paul Hulton, comp., *The Works of Jacques Le Moyne de Morgues, a Huguenot Artist in France, Florida and England* (London, 1977); Paul Hulton and David B. Quinn, *The American Drawings of John White*, 2 vols. (London, 1964).

10. Peter Laslett, ed., *Two Treatises of Government. By John Locke* (New York, 1965), 343. They were first published in 1690.

11. Ibid.

12. Richard S. Patterson and Richardson Douglass, *The Eagle and the Shield: A History of the Great Seal of the United States* (Washington, 1976), 83–110.

13. Quoted from Jeremy Moyle, trans., *Nature in the New World: From Christopher Columbus to Gonzalo Fernández de Oviedo. By Antonelli Gerbi* (Pittsburgh, 1985), 182, n. 216.

14. Richard Hakluyt, *Voyages*, 4 vols. (London, 1598–1600), III: A4.

15. Donald Jackson, ed., *Letters of the Lewis and Clark Expedition with Related Documents, 1783–1854*, 2 vols. 2d enl. ed. (Urbana, 1978), I:13.

16. Charles I to Hernando Cortés, June 26, 1523, in Warren L. Cook, *Flood Tide of Empire: Spain and the Pacific Northwest, 1543–1819* (New Haven, 1973), 2.

17. Georg Friederici, *Der Charakter der Entdeckung und Eroberung Amerikas durch die Europaeer: Einleitung zur Geschichte der Besiedlung Amerikas durch die Voelker der alten Welt*, 3 vols. (Stuttgart, 1926–1936), II:378–81; Lawrence C. Wroth, *The Voyages of Giovanni da Verrazzano, 1524–1528* (New Haven, 1970), 14–16, 79, 82, 85–86, 87, 89.

18. Ibid., 387.

19. John Seelye, *Prophetic Waters: The River in Early American Life and Literature* (New York, 1977), 19–20.

20. Roald Amundsen, *The North West Passage*, 2 vols. (London, 1908);

Samuel Eliot Morison, *The European Discovery of America: The Northern Voyages,* A.D. 500–1600 (New York, 1971), 613–15.

21. George Best, A *True Discourse of the Late Voyages of Discoverie for the Finding of a Passage to Cathaya* (London, 1578), in Vilhjalmur Stefansson, ed., *The Three Voyages of Martin Frobisher,* 2 vols. (London, 1938), I:5.

22. George Bancroft, *History of the United States, from the Discovery of the American Continent,* 8 vols., 14th ed. (Boston, 1848–1860), I:82–83.

23. Best, *True Discourse,* in Stefansson, *Frobisher* I:129.

24. Philip L. Barbour, ed., *The Jamestown Voyages under the First Charter, 1606–1609,* 2 vols. (Cambridge, 1969), I:49. Hakluyt Society Publications, 2nd ser., cxxxvi–cxxxvii.

25. Lyon Gardiner Tyler, ed., *Narratives of Early Virginia: 1606–1625* (New York, 1907), 123–24.

26. John Lankford, ed., *Captain John Smith's America: Selections from His Writings* (New York, 1967), 23.

27. Eva G. R. Taylor, ed., *The Writings and Correspondence of the Two Richard Hakluyts,* 2 vols. (Cambridge, 1935), II:492, n 3; Hakluyt Society, 2nd ser., lxxvi–lxxvii; Ferrar Map, New York Public Library, inserted in Edward Williams, *Virgo Triumphans* (London, 1650).

28. Father Paul Le Jeune, "Relation of What Took Place in New France in the Year 1640, Part I," in Reuben Gold Thwaites, ed., *The Jesuit Relations and Allied Documents,* 73 vols. (Cleveland, 1897–99), XVIII:235–37. Although having only Father Barthelemy Vimont's name on the title page, Part I of the 1640 *Relation* (Paris, 1641) seems to have been written by Le Jeune. Ibid., 251.

29. Father Barthelemy Vimont, "Relation of Occurrences in New France, in the year 1642 and 1643," Thwaites, *Jesuit Relations,* XXIII, 279.

30. Ibid.

31. Elliott Coues, comp., *History of the Expedition under the Command of Lewis and Clark,* 4 vols. (New York, 1893), II:377.

32. Francis Parkman, *La Salle and the Discovery of the Great West* 12th rev. ed. (Boston 1887), 196–97; Robert S. Weddle, ed., *La Salle, the Mississippi, and the Gulf* (College Station, 1987), 3, 29–30.

33. Parkman, *La Salle,* 39.

34. William J. Eccles, *Frontenac: The Courtier Governor* (Toronto, 1959), 337–41.

35. Claude Charles Le Roy Bacqueville de la Potherie, *Histoire de L'Amérique Septentrionale,* 3 vols. (Paris, 1722), III:96–97; "Narrative of the most remarkable Occurrences in Canada. 1689, 1690 [De Monseignat Letter]," in E. B. O'Callaghan, ed., *Documents Relative to the Colonial History of the State of New-York; Procured in Holland, England, and France,* 15 vols. (Albany, 1853–1887), IX:478–81; Friedrich Sieburg, *Frankreichs rote Kinder* (Frankfurt am Main, 1931), 41–45.

36. John Gilmary Shea, trans., *History and General Description of New France: By Rev. P. F. X. de Charlevoix, S. J.*, 6 vols. (New York, 1900), IV:144–45. The original edition was published in Paris in 1743.

37. William L. Stone, *The Life and Times of Sir William Johnson, Bart.*, 2 vols. (Albany, 1865), I:189.

38. O'Callaghan, *Documents* X:574–75.

39. Reuben Gold Thwaites, ed., *Original Journals of the Lewis and Clark Expedition, 1804–1806*, 8 vols. (New York, 1904–1905), II:340.

40. Thwaites, *Lewis and Clark Journals* I:243; Robert B. Betts, *In Search of York: The Slave Who Went to the Pacific with Lewis and Clark* (Boulder, 1985), 22, 40.

41. Louise Phelps Kellogg, *The French Regime in Wisconsin and the Northwest* (Madison, 1925), 364–85.

42. Reuben Gold Thwaites, ed., *New Voyages to North-America: By the Baron de Lahontan*, 2 vols. (Chicago, 1905), I:54.

43. Ibid. II:540, 541.

44. Ernst Rettich, *Der nackte Philosoph* (Munich, 1976), 70–71.

45. Franklin T. McCann, *English Discovery of America to 1585* (New York, 1969), 82–89. The study was first published in 1951.

46. "Journal of Antoine Bonnefoy (1741–1742)," in Samuel Cole Williams, ed., *Early Travels in the Tennessee Country, 1540–1800* (Johnson City, 1928), 157; Verner W. Crane, S. V. "Priber, Christian," *Dictionary of American Biography* XV:210.

47. Samuel Cole Williams, ed., *Adair's History of the American Indians* (New York, 1973), 257. This edition was first published in 1930; the original appeared in London in 1775.

48. "Bonnefoy's Journal," Williams, *Early Travels*, 157.

49. Ibid., 157.

50. Cole, *Adair's History*, 256.

51. Rennard Strickland, "Christian Gotelieb Priber: Utopian Precursor of the Cherokee Government," *Chronicles of Oklahoma* XLVIII (Autumn, 1970), 274–79.

52. W. Raymond Wood, ed., *The Explorations of the La Vérendryes in the Northern Plains, 1738–43: By G. Hubert Smith* (Lincoln, 1987), 8–10.

53. Lawrence J. Burpee, ed., *Journals and Letters of Pierre Gaultier de Varennes de La Vérendrye and His Sons* (Toronto, 1927), 487.

54. George R. Stewart, "The Source of the Name 'Oregon,'" *American Speech* XIX (April, 1944), 115–17; *Names on the Land: A Historical Account of Place-Naming in the United States* (Boston, 1967), 153–55. A copy of Lahontan's map can be conveniently found in Justin Winsor, *Cartier to Frontenac: Geographical Discovery of the Interior of North America in Its Historical Relations, 1534–1700* (Boston, 1894), 352–53.

55. "Robert Rogers' Instructions to James Tute, dated at Michilimackinac, September 12, 1766," in John Parker, ed., *The Journals of Jonathan Carver and Related Documents, 1766–1770* (St. Paul, 1976), 193.

56. Burpee, *La Vérendrye*, 503.

57. Jonathan Carver to Abigail Robbins Carver, his wife, dated Michilimackinac, September 24, 1767, in John Thomas Lee, "A Bibliography of Carver's Travels," *Proceedings of the State Historical Society of Wisconsin* (Madison, 1910), 149.

58. "Journals of the Travels of Jonathan Carver," Parker, *Journals*, 73, 77, 121, 125, 188, 202.

59. Jonathan Carver, *Travels through the Interior Parts of North America: in the Years 1766, 1767, and 1768* (London, 1778), v, ix, 77, 542.

60. J. B. Tyrrell, ed., *A Journey from Prince of Wales's Fort, in Hudson's Bay, to the Northern Ocean in the Years 1769, 1770, 1771, and 1772. By Samuel Hearne* (Toronto, 1911), 295.

61. Desmond Clarke, *Arthur Dobbs, Esquire, 1689–1765: Surveyor-General of Ireland, Prospector and Governor of North Carolina* (Chapel Hill, 1957), 62–64.

62. Tyrrell, *Journey*, 179, 266.

63. Ibid.

64. Ibid., 178, 329.

65. Ibid., 119; E. E. Rich, *The History of the Hudson's Bay Company: 1670–1870*, 2 vols. (London, 1959), II:53–55.

66. An engraving of Samuel Hearne's drawing of the Prince of Wales's Fort has been reproduced in Tyrrell, *Journey*, facing p. 61, and in Lawrence J. Burpee, *The Search for the Western Sea: The Story of the Exploration in North-Western America* (New York, 1908), facing p. 264.

67. Cyclone Covey, trans., *Cabeza de Vaca's Adventures in the Unknown Interior of North America* (New York, 1961), 120, 128. The first Spanish edition appeared in 1542.

68. T. H. McDonald, ed., *Exploring the Northwest Territory: Sir Alexander Mackenzie's Journal of a Voyage by Bark Canoe from Lake Athabaska to the Pacific Ocean in the Summer of 1789* (Norman, 1966), 117, 120. The subtitle should refer to the Arctic Ocean instead of the Pacific Ocean. In 1965, the editor, his wife, and his seventeen-year-old son, in a seventeen-foot canoe, retraced Mackenzie's voyage to the Arctic, with his manuscript as guide.

69. Milton Milo Quaife, ed., *Alexander Mackenzie's Voyage to the Pacific Ocean in 1793* (Chicago, 1931), 311; Alexander Mackenzie's *Voyages from Montreal, on the River St. Laurence, through the Continent of North America, to the Frozen and Pacific Oceans: In the Years 1789 and 1793* was first published in London in 1801.

70. Francisco Antonio Mourelle, *Voyage of the Sonora in the Second Bucareli*

Expedition to Explore the Northwest Coast . . . 1775 (San Francisco, 1920), 86–88.

2: On Culture's Edge

1. Thwaites, *Lewis and Clark Journals* II:149–50.

2. "Life of Salvator Rosa," *The Port Folio* VIII (Philadelphia, n. s., September, 1812), 284.

3. Thwaites, *Lewis and Clark Journals* II:149–50.

4. Ibid. I:125.

5. Ibid. II:150.

6. Ibid., 155.

7. Ibid., 153–54.

8. Ibid., 154.

9. Ibid., 171.

10. David McKeehan, "Preface," in Patrick Gass, *A Journal of the Voyages and Travels of a Corps of Discovery, Under the Command of Capt. Lewis and Capt. Clarke of the Army of the United States* (Pittsburgh, 1807), viii.

11. John G. Jacob, *The Life and Times of Patrick Gass, Now Sole Survivor of the Overland Expedition to the Pacific, under Lewis and Clarke* (Wellsburg, 1859), 93–94.

12. Jackson, *Letters of the Lewis and Clark Expedition* I:vii.

13. Hermann Hagedorn, ed., *The Works of Theodore Roosevelt*, 24 vols. (New York, 1923–26) XII:362.

14. John Ordway to Stephen Ordway, April 8, 1804, *Oregon Historical Quarterly* XXIII (September, 1922): 268.

15. Gass, *Journal*, 169–70; Thwaites, *Lewis and Clark Journals* III:246–47.

16. Lawson-Peebles, *Landscape and Written Expression*, 199.

17. Thwaites, *Lewis and Clark Journals* I:75.

18. William Peden, ed., *Notes on the State of Virginia: By Thomas Jefferson* (Chapel Hill, 1955), 24–25, 263–64.

19. Elizabeth McKinsey, *Niagara Falls: Icon of the American Sublime* (Cambridge, Mass., 1985), 88; Jeremy Elwell Adamson, "Nature's Grandest Scene in Art," in Corcoran Gallery of Art, *Niagara: Two Centuries of Changing Attitudes, 1697–1901* (Washington, D.C., 1985), 11–14.

20. "The Foresters; A Poem: Descriptive of a Pedestrian Journey to the Falls of Niagara, In the Autumn of 1804. By the Author of American Ornithology," *The Port Folio* III (n. s., March, 1810), 183.

21. Ibid., 186.

22. Clark Hunter, ed., *The Life and Letters of Alexander Wilson* (Philadelphia, 1983), 228, 255.

23. Stebbins, Troyen, and Fairbrother, *A New World*, 205–6.

24. Ibid., 37, 194–95.

25. Charles Francis Adams, ed., *The Works of John Adams,* 10 vols. (Boston, 1852–65), III:395.

26. Robert R. Hubach, comp., *Early Midwestern Travel Narratives: An Annotated Bibliography, 1634–1850* (Detroit, 1961), 32, 117.

27. Milo Milton Quaife, ed., *The Journals of Captain Meriwether Lewis and Sergeant John Ordway: Kept on the Expedition of Western Exploration, 1803–1806* (Madison, 1916), 222 (State Historical Society of Wisconsin Collections, XXII).

28. Thwaites, *Lewis and Clark Journals* II:100, 101, 104.

29. My general comments about Thomas Jefferson and Meriwether Lewis have benefited from Donald Jackson, *Thomas Jefferson & the Stony Mountains: Exploring the West from Monticello* (Urbana, 1981), 117–24, and Paul Russell Cutright, *Lewis and Clark: Pioneering Naturalists* (Urbana, 1969), 14–22.

30. Thwaites, *Lewis and Clark Journals* I:121–23; Coues, *History of the Expedition* I, 85–87.

31. Thwaites, *Lewis and Clark Journals* II:182–83.

32. Ibid. I:284.

33. Ibid., 284–85.

34. Ibid.

35. Ibid. II:82.

36. Ibid. I:112.

37. Ibid. II:368.

38. Ibid., 358.

39. Ibid., 336.

40. Ernest Staples Osgood, ed., *The Field Notes of Captain William Clark, 1803–1805* (New Haven, 1964), 19–21.

41. Thwaites, *Lewis and Clark Journals* II:332, 335.

42. Cutright, *Lewis and Clark,* 180.

43. Thwaites, *Lewis and Clark Journals* II:335.

44. "The Original Journal of Private Joseph Whitehouse," ibid. VII:137.

45. Ibid. III:40.

46. Ibid. V:224.

47. Ibid. II:358.

48. Ibid., 355.

49. Ibid. III:43.

50. Ibid. III:278.

51. Lankford, *Captain John Smith's America,* 18.

52. Thwaites, *Lewis and Clark Journals* III:120.

53. Ibid., 197.

54. Ibid. V:26.

55. Ibid., 117.

56. Ibid. IV:298.

57. Ibid. II:371–72.

58. James P. Ronda, *Lewis and Clark among the Indians* (Lincoln, 1984), 107.

59. Thwaites, *Lewis and Clark Journals* II:371–72.

60. Ibid. I:225.

61. Ibid. V:98.

62. Ibid., 117.

63. Gass, *Journal,* 223.

64. Thwaites, *Lewis and Clark Journals* V:132.

65. Father Nicolas Point, *Wilderness Kingdom* (New York, 1967), 166; Cutright, *Lewis and Clark,* 301.

66. Thwaites, *Lewis and Clark Journals* V:137.

67. Ibid., 140–42.

68. Ibid., 98.

69. Tracy I. Storer and Lloyd P. Trevis, Jr., *California Grizzly* (Lincoln, 1978), 14.

70. Cutright, *Lewis and Clark,* 141–42.

71. Thomas Smith to Robert Stevens, January 16, 1708, "A Letter by the Second Landgrave Smith," *in South Carolina Historical and Genealogical Magazine* XXXII (January 1931): 62; Frank J. Klingberg, ed., *The Carolina Chronicle of Dr. Francis Le Jau, 1706–1717* (Berkeley, 1956), 72–73.

72. Louis B. Wright, ed., *The Prose Works of William Byrd of Westover: Narratives of a Colonial Virginian* (Cambridge, Mass., 1966), 135–36.

73. Thwaites, *Lewis and Clark Journals* I:351.

74. Ibid., 372, 373–74.

75. Ibid. II:4.

76. Ibid.

77. Ibid., 24, 25.

78. Alexander Wilson, "Particulars of the Death of Capt. Lewis," *The Port Folio* VII (n. s., January 1812): 38.

79. William Clark to Jonathan Clark, October 28, 1809, in Jackson, *Letters of the Lewis and Clark Expedition* II:575. For a good summary of the much-discussed question of murder or suicide, turn to ibid., 747–49. See also a recent addition to the literature: Howard I. Kushner, "The Suicide of Meriwether Lewis: A Psychoanalytical Inquiry," *William and Mary Quarterly* XXXVIII (3rd ser., July 1981): 464–81.

80. Thwaites, *Lewis and Clark Journals* I:345, 346.

81. Ibid. III:232–33.

82. Ibid. V:203.

83. Ibid., 204.

84. Ibid. I:125, 127, 128, 138, 145.

85. Ibid. II:218.
86. Ibid., 182.
87. Ibid., 218.
88. Gass, *Journal,* 107.
89. Thwaites, *Lewis and Clark Journals* II: 218.
90. Gass, *Journal,* 107.
91. Thwaites, *Lewis and Clark Journals* II:169.
92. Ibid., 172.
93. Ibid., 126.
94. Ibid., 203.
95. Ibid., 209.
96. Ibid.
97. Ibid., 212.
98. Ibid., 217.
99. Ibid., 218.
100. Quaife, *Sergeant Ordway's Journal,* 244.
101. Thwaites, *Lewis and Clark Journals* II:220.
102. Jackson, *Letters of the Lewis and Clark Expedition* I: 12.
103. Thwaites, *Lewis and Clark Journals* III:233, 244.
104. Jackson, *Letters of the Lewis and Clark Expedition* I: 46–47, 109.
105. Thwaites, *Lewis and Clark Journals* II:382.
106. Ibid., 69.
107. Quaife, *Sergeant Ordway's Journal,* 287.
108. Thwaites, *Lewis and Clark Journals* III:72.
109. Ibid., 69.
110. Ibid., 68.
111. Ibid., 72.
112. Gass, *Journal,* 137.
113. Quaife, *Sergeant Ordway's Journal,* 287.
114. "Whitehouse's Journal," Thwaites, *Lewis and Clark Journals* VII:157.
115. Thwaites, *Lewis and Clark Journals* III:73, 74.
116. Ibid., 72.
117. Ibid., 83.
118. Ibid. V:165.
119. Ibid., 164.
120. Ibid. III:69, n. 2.
121. Ibid. V:164–65.
122. Ibid., 167.
123. Gass, *Journal,* 232.
124. Thwaites, *Lewis and Clark Journals* V:175, n. 1.
125. Ibid. III:207, n. 1.
126. Quaife, *Sergeant Ordway's Journal,* 311–12.

127. Thwaites, *Lewis and Clark Journals* III:229.
128. Quaife, *Sergeant Ordway's Journal,* 311–12.
129. Jackson, *Letters of the Lewis and Clark Expedition* II:474, n. 13.
130. Ibid., 594.
131. Thwaites, *Lewis and Clark Journals* I:xlvi.

3: Engineering Nature—Engineering Culture

1. George Lawrence, trans., J. P. Mayer and Max Lerner, eds., *Democracy in America: By Alexis de Tocqueville* (New York, 1966), 453.

2. William Cullen Bryant, "Inscription for the Entrance to a Wood," in George McMichael, ed., *Anthology of American Literature,* 4th ed., 2 vols. (New York, 1989) I:933.

3. Richard A. Etlin, *The Architecture of Death: The Transformation of the Cemetery in Eighteenth-Century Paris* (Cambridge, Mass., 1984), 164–228.

4. David Jacques, *Georgian Gardens: The Reign of Nature* (Portland, 1984), 11–18.

5. "Appendix E. Mr. Van Brugg's Proposal about Building ye New Churches," in Kerry Downes, *Vanbrugh* (London, 1977), 257–58.

6. Etlin, *Architecture of Death,* 344.

7. "Virginia in 1677," *Virginia Magazine of History and Biography* XXII (April 1914): 146–47.

8. "Burk's Garden Grave," *The Port Folio* II (n.s., July 1809):77.

9. Jacob Bigelow, *History of Mount Auburn Cemetery* (Boston, 1860), gives an insider's view of the early history.

10. Charles Sumner to Joseph Story, May 14, 1838, in Edward L. Pierce, ed., *Memoir and Letters of Charles Sumner,* 2 vols. (Boston, 1893), I:294.

11. "Der Friedhof auf Mount Auburn bei Boston," *Meyer's Universum, oder Abbildung und Beschreibung des Sehenswerthesten und Merkwuerdigsten der Natur und Kunst auf der ganzen Erde,* 3rd ed. (Hildburghausen/New York, 1853) XV:220.

12. *The Picturesque Pocket Companion, and Visitor's Guide, Through Mount Auburn: Illustrated with Upwards of Sixty Engravings on Wood* (Boston, 1839), 3.

13. John Elkington, *The Monument Cemetery of Philadelphia (Late Pere Lachaise)* (Philadelphia, 1837), 14, 25, 26.

14. Oakes I. Ames, "Mount Auburn's Sixscore Years," *Cambridge Historical Society Publications* XXXIV (1951–52): 78.

15. Bigelow, *Mount Auburn,* 119.

16. Quoted from Frederick A. Sharf, "The Garden Cemetery and American Culture: Mount Auburn," *The Art Quarterly* XXIV (Spring, 1961):84.

17. Goethe, *Wahlverwandtschaften* II:1.

18. John Francis Marion, *Famous and Curious Cemeteries: A Pictorial, Historical, and Anecdotal View of American and European Cemeteries and the Famous and Infamous People Who are Buried There* (New York, 1977), 61.

19. Constance M. Greiff, *John Notman, Architect: 1810–1865* (Philadelphia, 1979), 14, 53–60; Keith N. Morgan, "The Emergence of the American Landscape Professional: John Notman and the Design of Rural Cemeteries," *Journal of Garden History* IV (July–September 1984): 270–81.

20. Nicholas B. Wainwright, ed., *A Philadelphia Perspective: The Diary of Sidney George Fisher Covering the Years 1834–1871* (Philadelphia, 1967), 10.

21. Nehemiah Cleaveland, *Green-Wood Cemetery: A History of the Institution* (New York, 1866), 14, quoted in Donald Simon, "Green-Wood Cemetery and the American Park Movement," Irwin Yellowitz, ed., *Essays in the History of New York City: A Memorial, to Sidney Pomerantz* (Port Washington, 1978), 71.

22. Julian Cramer, "Greenwood Cemetery. Near New-York," *The Knickerbocker* XXI (January 1843):8.

23. Quoted in Frederick Law Olmsted, "The Beginnings of a Park for New York," Frederick Law Olmsted, Jr., and Theodora Kimball, eds., *Frederick Law Olmsted: Landscape Architect, 1822–1903*, 2 vols. (New York, 1922) II:22.

24. Ibid.

25. *Baltimore Sun*, July 15, 1839, in R. Kent Lancaster, "Green Mount: The Introduction of the Rural Cemetery into Baltimore," *Maryland Historical Magazine* LXXIV (March 1979):64–65.

26. Lancaster, "Green Mount," *Maryland Historical Magazine*, LXXIV (March 1979): 67–68; 78, n. 14; 79, n. 17.

27. *Cemetery of Spring Grove: Its Charter, Rules, and Regulations. Also an Address Delivered at the Consecration by the Hon. John M'Lean and a Catalogue of the Proprietors on the 1st of May 1849* (Cincinnati, 1849), 20, 29.

28. *The Cincinnati Cemetery of Spring Grove. Reports, Forms, etc.*, enl. ed. (Cincinnati, 1862), 6–7; Greiff, *Notman*, 28, 29.

29. "Certificate of Ownership. The proprietors of the Cemetery of Spring Grove . . . " in *Cemetery of Spring Grove* (Cincinnati, 1849).

30. F. G. Cary, "Spring Grove Cemetery," *The Cincinnatus* II (October 1, 1857): 470–71. The lithograph faces page 433.

31. Quoted from the St. Louis Bellefontaine Cemetery Association, *Original Charter, Amendments to Charter, Together with the By-Laws and Rules and Regulations of the Bellefontaine Cemetery, and Suggestions to Lot Owners, Etc. Also, Containing an Historical Sketch* (St. Louis, 1878), 30–31. I am indebted to the Missouri Historical Society, particularly Carol S. Verbe, for materials on the Bellefontaine Cemetery.

32. T. A. Post, *Truman Marcellus Post, D.D., A Biography: Personal and Literary*, 2nd ed. (Boston, 1891), 181–82.

33. William Hyde and Howard L. Conrad, eds., *Encyclopedia of the History*

of St. Louis: A Compendium of History and Biography for Ready Reference, 4 vols. (New York, 1899) I:337.

34. St. Louis *Intelligencer,* May 16, 1850, in *Dedication of the Bellefontaine Cemetery: Address of Professor Post, and Other Proceedings on that Occasion; Also, the Rules and Regulations, Suggestions to Lot Owners, and Charter of the Rural Cemetery Association* (St. Louis, 1850), 7.

35. "The Park and the Work Done Upon It," San Francisco *Real Estate Circular* XII (August, 1873): 4.

36. Henry Ward Beecher, *Star Papers; or, Experiences of Art and Nature* (New York, 1855), 263–70.

37. Quoted from Frederick Law Olmsted, "Origins of the Municipal Park Movement," Olmsted, Jr., and Kimball, eds., *Olmsted* II: 12.

38. Edith Wharton, *A Backward Glance* (New York, 1934), 55.

39. Clarence C. Cook, *A Description of the New York Central Park* (New York, 1869), 15.

40. William Cullen Bryant, "A New Park," New York *Evening Post,* July 3, 1844, in Allan Nevins, *The "Evening Post": A Century of Journalism* (New York, 1922), 193–94; and in Henry Hope Reed and Sophia Duckworth, *Central Park: A History and a Guide* (New York, 1967), 3.

41. Frederick Law Olmsted to Charles Loring Brace, December 1, 1853, in Charles E. Beveridge and Charles Capen McLaughlin, eds., *Slavery and the South,* 1852–1857 (Baltimore, 1981), 232–36 (Volume II of *The Papers of Frederick Law Olmsted* [Baltimore 1977–], Charles Capen McLaughlin, editor in chief).

42. Olmsted, "Municipal Park Movement," in Olmsted and Kimball, *Olmsted* II:14.

43. Henry Whitney Bellows, "Cities and Parks: With Special Reference to the New York Central Park," *Atlantic Monthly* VII (April 1861): 418, 421.

44. Ibid., 421.

45. The comments on the relationship between nature and democracy are derived from Henry W. Bellows, *Oration at the Funeral of William Cullen Bryant* (New York, 1878), 1–2.

46. Bellows, "Cities and Parks," *Atlantic Monthly* VII (April 1861):422.

47. "The Central Park," *Harper's Weekly,* October 1, 1859, p. 626.

48. "Growth and Grandeur of New-York," *New York Tribune,* November 26, 1862.

49. Bellows, "Cities and Parks," *Atlantic Monthly* VII (April 1861): 420–21.

50. Gunther Barth, "Demopiety: Speculations on Urban Beauty, Western Scenery, and the American Discovery of the Cityscape," *Pacific Historical Review* LII (August, 1983): 249–66.

51. C. Hartley Grattan, ed., *Recollections of the Last Ten Years. By Timothy Flint* (New York, 1932), 39, 40. The book first appeared in 1826.

52. After I had been working for a while with the concepts of demopiety and geopiety, I came across John Kirtland Wright's magistral discussion of geopiety: "Notes on Early American Geopiety," *Human Nature in Geography: Fourteen Papers, 1925–1965* (Cambridge, Mass., 1966), 250–85, which greatly helped my understanding of the phenomenon.

53. Thomas Cole, "Essay on American Scenery," *American Monthly Magazine* I (n.s., January 1836): 7.

54. Samuel Bowles, *Across the Continent: A Summer's Journey to the Rocky Mountains, the Mormons, and the Pacific States, with Speaker Colfax* (Springfield, 1865), 223.

55. For a succinct assessment of Frederick Law Olmsted's work at Central Park, I have relied on Charles A. Beveridge's Introduction, in Beveridge and David E. Schuyler, eds., *Creating Central Park: 1857–1861* (Baltimore, 1983), 1–48 (Volume III, *The Papers of Frederick Law Olmsted*).

56. Frederick Law Olmsted to Calvert Vaux, November 26, 1863, in Beveridge and Schuyler, *Creating Central Park,* 13.

57. Ibid., 42, n. 35.

58. Calvert Vaux to Henry W. Bellows, February 25, 1864, Beveridge and Schuyler, *Creating Central Park,* 13.

59. Frederick Law Olmsted, "Statistical Report of the Landscape Architect, 31st December, 1873, Forming Part of Appendix L of the Third General Report of the Department," New York City, Department of Public Parks, *Third Annual Report* (New York, 1875), 46–47; ibid., 17.

60. "The Winning Design by Olmsted and Vaux," Olmsted and Kimball, *Olmsted* II:46.

61. Frederick Law Olmsted, "A Review of Recent Changes, and Changes Which Have Been Projected, in the Plans of the Central Park," in Olmsted and Kimball, *Olmsted* II:248; Geoffrey Blodgett, "Frederick Law Olmsted: Landscape Architecture as Conservative Reform," *Journal of American History* LXII (March 1976): 877, 878.

62. Frederick Law Olmsted, "Rusticus in Urbe," San Francisco *Evening Bulletin,* August 4, 1865.

63. John H. Rauch, *Public Parks: Their Effects upon the Moral, Physical and Sanitary Conditions of the Inhabitants of Large Cities; with Special Reference to the City of Chicago* (Chicago, 1869), 31.

64. *Organization of the Mountain View Cemetery Association, Oakland, California: Officers of the Corporation, Rules, Regulations, and By-Laws, Including a Preface to the Plan by Frederick Law Olmsted. Services at the Consecration of the Ground, Etc. Etc.* (San Francisco, 1865), 23, 31, 32.

65. Ibid., 22.

66. Ibid., "Report of Mr. Olmsted," 47.

67. Ibid., 49.

68. Ibid., 48.

69. Ibid., 48, 49.

70. Ibid., 49.

71. For an example of the theological literature, see Horace Bushnell, *Christian Nurture* (New Haven, 1947). The book was first published in 1847.

72. *Concerning Mountain View Cemetery: Its Management under the Late Superintendent—Present Conditions of Its Affairs. Public Lectures of Dr. Sam'l Merritt, Containing a Full Discussion and an Intelligible Statement of Facts* (Oakland, 1871).

73. *By-Laws and Rules of Mountain View Cemetery Association with History and Appendix* (Oakland, 1889), 30.

74. Charles Howard Shinn, "A California Cemetery," *Garden and Forest: A Journal of Horticulture, Landscape Art, and Forestry* IV (May 6, 1891): 206.

75. B. E. Lloyd, *Lights and Shades in San Francisco* (San Francisco, 1876), 355.

76. For a discussion of San Francisco as instant city, see my *Instant Cities: Urbanization and the Rise of San Francisco and Denver* (New York, 1975).

77. "Report of Don Pedro de Alberni," July 1, 1796, in John W. Dwinelle, *The Colonial History of the City of San Francisco* (San Francisco, 1863), Addenda no. IX.

78. Olmsted, Vaux & Co., *Preliminary Report in Regard to a Plan of Public Pleasure Grounds for the City of San Francisco* (New York, 1866), 17.

79. D. L. Phillips, *Letters from California: Its Mountains, Valleys, Plains, Lakes, Rivers, Climate, and Productions. Also Its Railroads, Cities, Towns and People, as Seen in 1876* (Springfield, 1877), 17.

80. San Francisco *Evening Post,* August 22, 1879.

81. Christian G. Fritz, "San Francisco's First Federal Court: Ogden Hoffman and the Northern District of California, 1851–1891" (Ph.D. diss., University of California, Berkeley, 1986), 290–342, has most recently discussed the legal details.

82. F. Bret Harte, "San Francisco, by the Poets. Number Two. South Park—After Gray," *Californian,* September 24, 1864, p. 9; Gunther Barth, "Metropolism and Urban Elites in the Far West," in Frederic Cople Jaher, ed., *The Age of Industrialism in America: Essays in Social Structure and Cultural Values* (New York, 1968), 159, 162.

83. San Francisco Board of Supervisors, *Municipal Reports* (San Francisco, 1866), 33.

84. Olmsted, Vaux & Co., *Report for San Francisco;* Roper, *FLO,* 304–5.

85. Richard M. Gibson, "Golden Gate Park," *Overland Monthly* XXXVII (March 1901): 741.

86. An Act to Provide for the Improvement of Public Parks in the City of San Francisco, April 4, 1870.

87. San Francisco *Daily Alta California,* April 4, 1855.

88. Gibson, "Golden Gate Park," *Overland Monthly XXXVII* (March 1901): 751.

89. Raymond H. Clary, *The Making of Golden Gate Park: The Early Years, 1865–1906* (San Francisco, 1980), 3–4, 5.

90. *Pacific Rural Press,* August 6, 1881, p. 85.

91. William Hammond Hall, "The Romance of a Woodland Park: Golden Gate Park, 1870–1890," p. 206. William Hammond Hall Collection, Bancroft Library, University of California, Berkeley.

92. Ibid., 223.

93. San Francisco *Evening Bulletin,* August 24, 1874.

94. San Francisco *Chronicle,* May 14, 1876.

95. "Proposed Plan for the Improvement of the Site of the University of California at Berkeley, Designed at the Request of the Board of Regents by Wm. Hammond Hall, C. E., 1873," Hall Collection, Bancroft Library.

96. *Pacific Rural Press,* August 6, 1881, p. 85.

97. Hall, "Golden Gate Park," 466.

98. "Communication from Hon. Fred. Law Olmsted," in "Report of the Board of Park Commissioners," San Francisco Board of Supervisors, *Municipal Reports for the Fiscal Year 1888–1889, Ending June 30, 1889* (San Francisco, 1889), 809–11.

99. Friedrich Ratzel, *Staedte- und Kulturbilder aus Nordamerika* (Leipzig, 1876), 1, 4. I have used my translation, but the book is now also available in English: Stewart A. Stehlin, trans. and ed., *Sketches of Urban and Cultural Life in North America by Friedrich Ratzel* (New Brunswick, 1988).

Index